THE STORY OF

CRICKET

IN AUSTRALIA

Apart from *The Story of Cricket in Australia*, which is also available on video, Jack Egan has produced the television documentaries and accompanying books *The Bradman Era* and *Tennis: The Greats*.

His recent publications include *Extra Cover*, a book of interviews with past and present cricketers.

In 1990 he produced the television documentary *Bradman*, which featured the first extensive television interview with Australia's greatest cricketer.

For Tom Wills and Johnny Mullagh

THE STORY OF
CRICKET
IN AUSTRALIA

JACK EGAN

an
ABC
BOOK

Acknowledgments

Many people have helped me in the publication of the book and production of the film *Cricket in Australia*. To them I express my sincere thanks. First, the players of various eras for agreeing to be interviewed, checking drafts and answering questions: Ian Chappell, Bill O'Reilly, Ray Lindwall, Betty Archdale, Hunter Hendry and Geoff Marsh.

For help with illustrations and film: Susan Hall of Lotus Productions, Graham Parks and Bill Grey of Cinesound Movietone Productions, Rob Hamilton of the ABC, Cliff Winning and Brian Hughes of the NSW Cricket Association, Rex Harcourt of the Melbourne Cricket Ground Museum, Tony Skelton of the PBL Marketing and Helen Tully of the National Film and Sound Archive. And of course for their ideas and encouragement along the way: my friend David Moeller, Richard Smart and Michael Hast of Macmillan Australia, Walter Norris of the ABC and the cricket historian Richard Cashman.

I have quoted extensively from a number of books and used many others for general reference. The cricket books most often referred to were *Seventy-one Not Out* by Billy Caffyn, *With Bat and Ball* by George Giffen, *An Australian Cricketer on Tour* by Frank Laver, *They Made Cricket* by G. D. Martineau, *Australian Cricket: A History* by A. G. Moyes, *Australian Cricket: The Game and The Players* by Jack Pollard, *Test Cricket: England v Australia* by Ralph Barker and Irving Rosenwater, *England versus Australia: A Pictorial History* by David Frith, *The Paddock That Grew* by Keith Dunstan, *True to the Blue* by Philip Derriman, *Ancestor Treasure Hunt: The Wills Family* by R. V. Pockley, *Cricket Walkabout* by D. J. Mulvaney, and *Back to the Mark* by Dennis Lillee and Ian Brayshaw. The list would not be complete without mentioning the writings of Jack Fingleton, Ray Robinson and Neville Cardus. I also made frequent use of *The Land They Found* by Ronald Laidlaw, *The Australian People* by Donald Horne and *A Short History of Australia* by Manning Clark.

Where illustrations do not carry credits it is because the owner of rights could not be traced. Any person having a valid claim should contact the publisher.

Jack Egan, Sydney

Published by ABC Books for the
AUSTRALIAN BROADCASTING CORPORATION
GPO Box 9994 Sydney NSW 2001

Copyright © Jack Egan 1996

*First published 1987 by The Macmillan Company of Australia Pty Ltd
in association with the Australian Broadcasting Corporation
Second edition published 1991
This third edition published 1996*

National Library of Australia
Cataloguing-in-Publication entry
Egan, Jack, 1941– .
    The story of cricket in Australia.

    3rd ed.
    Includes index.
    ISBN 0 7333 0535 0.

    1. Cricket – Australia – History. I. Title.

798.3580994

*Cover designed by Janice Bowles
Cover photograph by Patrick Eagar
Set in 11/12 pt Plantin
by Midland Typesetters, Maryborough, Victoria
Colour separations by First Media, Adelaide
Printed and bound in Australia by
Southwood Press, Marrickville, NSW*

5 4 3 2 1

Contents

Author's note

The English cricket writer Neville Cardus said, 'A game is exactly what is made of it by the character of the people playing it'. I set out to tell the story of cricket in Australia through the people who have played the game and to show how our cricket and cricketers have reflected the changing times and character of the place.

J.E.

The first English team versus Eighteen of Melbourne at the Melbourne Cricket Ground in January 1862. The tour was a commercial venture organised by Felix Spiers and Christopher Pond. The players were paid £150 for the tour and received a bonus of 100 sovereigns each. Spiers and Pond made a profit of £11,000 from the tour. **Public Library of Victoria.**

CHAPTER 1

There's nothing new in cricket

I don't enjoy ringing people up and asking for interviews. I feel as if I am imposing on their time and I'm constantly surprised when they co-operate willingly. I had met Ian Chappell briefly a couple of times, but in view of his reputation for blunt talk and his obviously busy schedule, I was more nervous than usual when I rang him. He was out, expected in the office at about 10 o'clock. I left a message. At 10 o'clock he called back and we discussed the project. Would there be a problem arising from his contract with Channel 9? If there was, Chappell said, it would be very quickly sorted out; he had been captain of the Australian cricket team long before he was employed by Channel 9. I made it clear that he would be paid for his involvement. He wasn't sure that was appropriate. We could talk about it later.

Chappell works from a sparse, modern office in the Channel 9 'sports cottage' in a suburban street in the Sydney suburb of Willoughby. There are two or three posters and a couple of reference books on cricket statistics — his cricket library is kept at home. When I raised again the subject of his fee for helping with the project, he was embarrassed enough to blush. We sorted it out and got on with the interview.

Chappell's grandfather, Vic Richardson, captained the Australian cricket team during the 1930s and later became a radio broadcaster. Chappell followed in Richardson's footsteps, and became the most controversial character in modern Australian cricket. His involvement with the World Series Cricket revolution was pivotal. His stature in the game gave it an authority which was essential for its success. Because of this, and because

1

he has always said what he thinks, he has been called 'money-hungry', 'a traitor', and many things besides.

'Vic never tried to influence me,' Chappell said. 'I think he felt that it was up to me whether I played cricket or not. And when it became obvious that I loved the game, he didn't try to influence the way I played. But I can remember three things he told me. "If you can't be a good cricketer, at least you can look like one." That was about cricket gear and dress, of course, and I'm not sure how I measured up to Vic's standards there. Then when I became vice-captain of the Australian team he said to me: "If you ever get to captain Australia, don't do it like a Victorian." I think he was referring to Jack Ryder there, and perhaps also to my mate Bill Lawry. The other thing he told me was "There's nothing new in cricket".'

First-class cricket in Australia was born in commercialism and controversy. The first match between New South Wales and Victoria was played on the Melbourne Cricket Club's ground, now known as the Melbourne Cricket Ground, in March 1856. Although the New South Wales team had declined a challenge to play for £500, the Melbourne *Argus* reported that 'bets of 2 to 1 against New South Wales were freely offered' and 'takers were by no means scarce'. One of the New South Wales players, in a letter published in the *Sydney Mail* during the 1880s, described how the match was almost abandoned before it had begun: 'A misunderstanding occurred, and I remember Mr Driver coming to myself and two others of the players and saying that the umpires had tossed and we had lost the toss, and our opponents had decided on sending us to the wickets. I remonstrated with him (being our secretary), and said there is an old law of cricket which says "that parties leaving home have the option of going in first or not", and I for one declined to play. But our opponents argued that the rule referred to had become obsolete, and that it was customary for the umpires to toss; but as several of our players, including myself, decided to leave the ground and not play unless we were allowed the privilege, which we maintained as visitors we had a right to, our opponents gave way and we sent them in first.' Victoria made 63, New South Wales replied with 76. The Victorians, in the second innings, could only manage 28, but they took 7 wickets before the visitors scored the 16 runs needed for victory.

Sponsorship and profit-sharing by players were part of cricket more than 100 years before television rights were an issue and Kerry Packer became part of the game's history. The first English team to come to Australia was sponsored by a firm of caterers. Spiers and Pond of Melbourne, who called themselves 'refreshment contractors', paid the members of George Parr's 1862 team £150 each, met all their expenses, and made a profit of £11,000 from the tour.

The first Australian team went to England in 1868. It was captained by Charles Lawrence, who had come to Australia with the first English touring team in 1862 and stayed to become Australia's first paid coach. He led a team of 13 Aborigines from the Edenhope district of Victoria. The tour, funded by Lawrence and others including the manager, William Hayman, and George Smith, a former Lord Mayor of Sydney, was opposed by the Aboriginal Protection Board on the grounds that the Aborigines were being exploited.

Argument, complaint, drinking and questioning umpires' decisions were not exclusive to the 'sons of convicts'. The game's most famous player, W. G. Grace of Gloucestershire and England, led a touring side to the colonies in 1873–74. In Ballarat, according to the local paper, 'the sun shone infernally, the eleven scored tremendously, we fielded abominably, and all drank excessively'. In his memoirs, Grace complained at length about travel arrangements, perhaps with some justification. He described the track from Ballarat to Stawell, where the next game was to be played, as 'quite undeserving of the name of a road'. Outside the town, the English team were met by a welcoming party, including two brass bands. 'The horses in one of the waggonnettes at once took fright and overturned the vehicle,' he wrote. 'Luckily, though the trap was smashed to atoms, no one was injured.' He described the match against Twenty-two from Stawell, played on a dust-heap and won by the locals, as 'a ludicrous farce'. After the game Grace warned his team about drinking while play was in progress. George Giffen, who later captained Australia, saw Grace's team in Adelaide, playing against Twenty-two of South Australia, and wrote later that, when Grace was caught on the boundary, 'The champion questioned whether he had been caught within the playing space, but the umpire decided against him'.

The list goes on. In 1879, at the Sydney Cricket Ground during a full-scale riot over an umpiring decision, English captain Lord Harris was hit with a stick and some of his team had their clothes torn by the crowd. In 1912 Australia's six best players, including the saint-like Victor Trumper, were omitted from the Australian team to tour England because of a dispute over tour management. Bodyline threatened the established relationship between England and Australia in 1933.

In 1952, members of the Australian Cricket Board were made to look foolish in court, in a case arising from Sid Barnes's exclusion from the Australian team. The controversy over throwing which plagued Australian cricket during the 1960s was an echo of events 100 years earlier; both Tom Wills, captain of Victoria during the 1850s and 1860s, and Dave Gregory, Australia's first Test captain, were no-balled for throwing in first-class matches. 'It is most incomprehensible how the Sydney umpire would no-ball Wills and yet allow Dave Gregory's most palpable throwing,' said a contemporary report in *The Australasian.*

When, in 1877, John Conway proposed the idea of sending a representative team to play in England, there was little public enthusiasm for the venture, and less support from the colonial cricket associations. The men who backed the idea were those who knew the game; the men who played it. And so, on to the World Series Cricket revolution in 1977, when the game which had been hijacked by administrators in 1905 was re-captured by commercial interests, to the immense benefit of the players.

These incidents are the exception, not the rule, but they are not just isolated events; they reflect the ways in which people deal with each other, and they are part of the fabric and history of the game. The attitudes they represent are, in some ways, still the same. In other ways they are quite different.

CHAPTER 2

A gentleman of Broadcourt

Edward Wills, the son of Edward Wills, gentleman, of Broadcourt, Long Acre, in the county of Middlesex, was born in 1778. He married Sarah Harding in 1795, and in 1796 their first child, also named Sarah, was born. In January 1797, in company with two other men, Wills was arrested for highway robbery, and on 20 March, at Kingston-on-Thames, they were charged with assault and with stealing a watch and £2.19.4. They were found guilty and sentenced 'to be hanged by the neck until dead'.

Wills's father organised an appeal against the sentence, with petitions from a clergyman, his son's employer, and John Martin, who was the victim of the assault. It was heard at Whitehall on 27 March 1797. The sentence was reduced to transportation: 'Having been humbly recommended as fit objects of the Royal Mercy His Majesty has now been graciously pleased to extend His Royal mercy on condition of their being transported for the term of their natural lives to the Eastern Coast of New South Wales.'

Wills spent the next 19 months in the hulk *Stanisklaus*, moored in the Thames. On 18 October 1798, 56 convicts from the *Stanisklaus* were taken on board the *Hillsborough*, for the voyage to New South Wales. William Noah, a convict on board the *Hillsborough*, wrote in his diary of the voyage that the men from the *Stanisklaus* were 'deplorable and ragged, and I hardly knew them from vermin'. They were ironed 'two together' with 'double irons of the weight of eleven pounds'. There were 300 convicts on the *Hillsborough*, and six women, including Wills's wife Sarah and their two-year-old daughter.

Noah's diary tells how during a gale one of the seamen helped distressed convicts to 'cut their irons' so they were not shackled together. When the captain discovered this, the convicts were flogged, some receiving two dozen lashes, some five dozen. They were shackled again, and handcuffed, and some had an iron collar place around their necks. Johnson, the seaman who had assisted the convicts, was 'left to the mercy of his shipmates, when every seaman but one gave him a lash apiece'. In heavy seas the ship took on water, which 'poured down the hatchways, drenching the convicts' deck and bedding. Fifty-one days out from Portsmouth, 33 convicts were dead. The fleet arrived in Sydney after a voyage of nine months. During that time 95 convicts had died. Six more died within a few days of arrival. Governor Hunter wrote that most of the survivors 'must for a time be placed in the hospitals', and described them as 'a cargo of the most miserable and wretched convicts I ever beheld'.

Edward Wills received a conditional pardon in 1803. He died in 1811, leaving an estate of £15,000. His grandson, Thomas Wentworth Spencer Wills, went to Rugby School in England and became the leading figure in Australian cricket during its most important formative years, the 1850s and 1860s.

The first mention of cricket in Australia is in the *Sydney Gazette* of 8 January 1804: 'The late intense weather has been very favourable to the amateurs of cricket who have scarce lost a day for the last month. The frequent immoderate heat might have been considered inimical to the amusement, but was productive of the very opposite consequences.'

The game which developed into what we now call cricket was played in England during the seventeenth century and became more formalised in the early part of the eighteenth century. One of the first accounts of a cricket match was published in 1706, in Latin verse. Kent played London, at Islington, as early as 1719. In 1727 articles were drawn up between the Duke of Richmond and Mr A. Brodrick of Surrey for two 12-a-side matches, to be played in Surrey and Sussex respectively. It may have been recognisable, but it would certainly have been different; clause 14 provided that 'The Batt Men for every One They count are to touch the Umpire's Stick'.

The Duke of Richmond is credited with giving the game patronage and early direction, and cricket was 'taken up by society'. Frederick, Prince of Wales, popularised the game in the 1730s and 1740s, playing challenge matches for stakes as high as £1000, which he frequently lost. Broadhalfpenny Down, near the little Hampshire village of Hambledon, where the Hambledon Club was founded and financed by Charles Powlett, became 'the cradle of cricket' in the middle of the century. During the 1770s the main fixture on the cricket calendar was Hambledon versus England. Hambledon's leading player was John Small, a shoemaker by trade, a stealer of singles, and a prolific run-maker. His trade led him naturally to the making of cricket balls. As a batsman, he adopted the 'new upright style of play', which made the curved cricket bats of the time awkward to use. Small turned his talents to the making of 'straight' bats, with shoulders, which were commonly used after 1775.

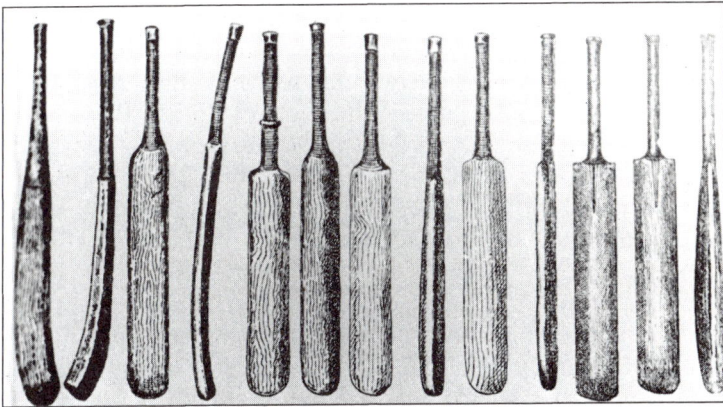

BBC.

The Marylebone Cricket Club was formed in 1787, on a ground in London provided by Thomas Lord. The MCC moved to a new ground, near St John's Wood, in 1811, but had to relinquish it to make way for the Regent's Canal. Thomas Lord obtained a field close by, and the MCC moved to the present site of Lord's, 'the home of cricket', in 1814.

Early cricket was a game for the wealthy, some of whom had 'gardeners, grooms and gamekeepers kept to play cricket', employed partly for their cricketing skills, the game's first professionals. But Georgian England was not a pleasant society for the less well-off. England was changing from an agricultural

7

to an urban nation. The cities were crowded with the poverty-stricken and poorly educated, many of whom had no alternative but to live off their wits as pickpockets or petty thieves. The simplest crimes were punishable by death; men and women were hanged in public. The more fortunate were lashed, branded, locked in the stocks, or sold to contractors for transportation to America, to be auctioned to American settlers. Prisons were used mainly to hold people waiting to be tried.

In 1776, the American colonies rebelled against the British, and refused to take any more convicts. As the War of Independence dragged on, British prisons became increasingly overcrowded. Convicts were housed for a time in derelict ships known as 'hulks', but these were soon riddled with disease. The situation became unmanageable.

Captain James Cook landed on the east coast of Australia in 1770 and named it New South Wales. He anchored for a week in a large bay which he first named Stingray Harbour, but after going ashore he wrote in his diary of Saturday 5 May 1770, 'The great quantity of plants which Mr Banks and Dr Solander collected induced me to give it the name of Botany Bay'.

Cook's diary also recorded his impression of the Australian Aborigines: 'Their skins were so uniformly covered with dirt, that it was very difficult to ascertain their true colour: we made several attempts, by wetting our fingers and rubbing it, to remove the incrustations, but with very little effect . . . Their features are far from being disagreeable, their noses are not flat, nor are their lips thick; their teeth are white and even, and their hair naturally long and black . . . Upon such ornaments as they had, they set so great a value, that they would never part with the least article for anything we could offer; which was the more extraordinary as our beads and ribbons were ornaments of the very same kind, but of a more regular form and more showy materials. They had indeed no idea of traffic, nor could we communicate any to them: they received the things that we gave them; but never appeared to understand our signs when we required a return. The same indifference which prevented them from buying what we had, prevented them also from attempting to steal: if they had coveted more, they would have been less honest; for when we refused to give them a turtle, they were enraged, and attempted to take it by force, and we had nothing else on which they seemed to set the least value.'

Fifteen years later, Joseph Banks had become a man of influence in England and an authority on the Pacific Ocean. He had at first proposed that New South Wales should become a colony of free settlers, but later he argued that it was a suitable place for a penal colony. Lord Thomas Sydney, Secretary to the Home Office, announced in August 1786 that convicts were to be transported to Botany Bay and gave Captain Arthur Phillip his instructions. The first fleet sailed from Portsmouth on Sunday 13 May 1787. By 20 January 1788 the fleet had arrived in Botany Bay which, despite Joseph Banks's recommendation, Phillip found unsuitable for settlement. Within a few days they found the entrance to Sydney Harbour, which had been charted but not entered by Cook. 'We got into Port Jackson early in the afternoon,' Phillip wrote, 'and had the satisfaction of finding the finest harbour in the world, in which a thousand sail of the line may ride in the most perfect security.'

By 26 January the fleet had moved to the new harbour, and the colonists went ashore and raised the Union Jack on a point which Phillip named Sydney Cove. On the first evening the new settlers were drenched by a thunderstorm. The European population of the colony was some 20 officials and 210 marines, with 27 of their wives and 19 of their children. There were 548 male and 188 female convicts and 14 convict children, along with 44 sheep, 28 pigs, nine horses, six cattle, three goats, and various poultry. Twenty-three convicts had died on the voyage to Australia. The Aboriginal population at that time was estimated at more than 500,000.

The second fleet arrived in 1790, having set out with 1000 convicts, a quarter of whom died on the voyage. This fleet brought with it the first detachment of the New South Wales Corps, later known as the Rum Corps, to replace the marines. A third fleet arrived in 1791 with 1800 surviving convicts. Although the colonists were mainly still huddled in the vicinity of Sydney Cove, by 1790 James Ruse, the first convict to be granted land, was working his holding 'Experiment Farm', at Parramatta, 25 kilometres to the west. John Macarthur's first holding was next door to Ruse. By 1795 Macarthur was working 160 hectares, growing wheat, corn, maize, vegetables and fruit trees and breeding horses, sheep and cattle. In 1805, he took up a grant of 2000 hectares at the Cow Pastures, now known as Camden, 60 kilometres to the south-west of Sydney, where he concentrated on breeding sheep.

If cricket was played in the colony before the summer of 1803–04, there is no record of it. Opportunities and facilities would certainly have been limited. In *Australian Cricket — A History*, A. G. Moyes says 'The accepted view is that the officers of the *Calcutta* were the first to play in any organised way'. Jack Pollard, in *Australian Cricket — The Game and the Players*, says the game referred to in the *Sydney Gazette* of January 1804 may have been between 'civilians who found time for recreation' and men from the *Calcutta*, which landed in Sydney in December 1803.

Cricket had become a more popular recreation by 1810. The government order under which Governor Lachlan Macquarie named Sydney's Hyde Park in October 1810 referred to the area as having previously been known as 'The Racecourse', 'The Exercising Ground' and 'The Cricket Ground'. The game had the governor's approval; in August 1821 the storekeeper of His Majesty's Lumberyard delivered to the Reverend Thomas Reddall's Academy at Macquarie Fields 12 cricket bats and six cricket balls, along with four spades, six hoes and two rakes. These were a gift from the Crown to the school, where Macquarie's son Lachlan was a student. A memo written by the governor directs that 'The above articles are to be considered as belonging to Lachlan as long as he remains at the Reverend Mr Reddall's school, and afterwards to be left for the use of the School'.

Macquarie arrived in December 1809, and found 'the colony barely emerging from infantile imbecility, and suffering from various privations and disabilities; the country impenetrable beyond forty miles from Sydney; agriculture in a yet languishing state; commerce in its early dawn; revenue unknown; threatened with famine; distracted by factions; the public buildings in a state of dilapidation and mouldering to decay'.

Arthur Phillip had returned to England weak and in ill health in 1792. During the next three years the colony was governed by the commanding officer of the Rum Corps. His fellow-officers wasted no time in exploiting the situation: cornering the market in essential supplies and selling them at inflated prices, obtaining grants of land and illegally buying up the small farms held by freed convicts, diverting convicts from public works and using them for their own benefit, and importing rum for sale at profits of up to 1000 per cent.

Although some of the freed convicts had been able to improve

State Library of NSW.

their situation, for the most part the lot of the poorer people was little better than it had been in England. Many lived close to starvation. Successive governors — Hunter, King and Bligh — had tried to curb the power of the Rum Corps, but were defied. Rum was the currency, and drunkenness was an epidemic. Events came to a head when in January 1807 a petition was drawn up calling upon Governor Bligh to resign. When he refused, the officer commanding the military led 300 troops to Government House and arrested him. He remained a prisoner in his own residence for 12 months.

Macquarie was a Scot and a soldier. His own regiment, the 73rd Highlanders, took over from the New South Wales Corps, which was recalled to England in disgrace. Macquarie's senior aide was Captain Henry Colden Antill, who later married Eliza Wills, the second daughter of the convict Edward Wills.

Macquarie went about the task of reforming and developing the colony with a sense of high moral purpose. He promoted attendance at church, encouraged convicts to marry, closed a number of public houses and reduced the hours of others, built schools and found teachers for them, signed a contract for the building of a proper hospital, and organised regular street-cleaning gangs. It was during Macquarie's time that the continent came to be known as 'Australia'. Although James Cook had called it New South Wales, it had been known to Europeans since the beginning of the sixteenth century, and was referred to in British scientific and naval circles as Terra Australis, Latin for South Land. As the eastern and southern coastlines were charted, and naval men became familiar with the continent on the frequent voyages after 1788, they began to call it Australia. By 1817, Macquarie was using the word in dispatches.

The children of the first settlers were called 'currency lads' and 'currency lasses' to distinguish them from the British-born, known as 'Sterlings'. By the 1820s they were calling themselves Australians. The children of the convicts were mostly un-educated and often quick-tempered, but in a society which was continually short of labour, they could earn a living and thus their self-respect as soon as they could work. Many were able to break the bonds of poverty and lack of opportunity which had made 'criminals' of their parents. They were described as 'moral, law-abiding, industrious and surprisingly sober'. In this new climate they grew up 'tall, slim, tough and active'.

Two cricket clubs were formed in 1826. The regiments of the colony founded the Military Cricket Club, and the Australian Cricket Club was formed by the native-born youths of the colony. The Sydney Cricket Club, which played 'in a Government paddock on the site of the turnpike', near the present site of Central Station, was founded in 1829.

The first recorded match was played on 'the Racecourse' in Hyde Park in 1830, between the Military club and the 'native-born youths' of the Australian club. Hours of play were 11 a.m. to 5 p.m., and the stakes were £20 a side. The local youths must have collapsed early in the day; the *Sydney Gazette* reported that 'at two o'clock it was thought the natives had no chance'. But they recovered during the afternoon, winning the match 76 and 136 to 101 and 87. 'A prettier day's play was certainly never witnessed in the colony,' said the *Gazette*. 'At four o'clock it is estimated that there were upwards of 200 spectators on the ground.' The 'natives' won the return match on 3 March by 95 and 75 to 82 and 52. The military wore tall black hats on the field, while the Australian-born players adopted 'cabbage tree hats' made of straw.

The Australian club emerged as the driving force in the colony's cricket in the 1840s. The club's meetings were held in

William Tunks's hotel, on the corner of Bathurst and Castlereagh Streets. Tunks himself was a member, as was Harry Hilliard, who later played for New South Wales in the first intercolonial match against Victoria. They practised in a graveyard near where St Andrew's Cathedral now stands in George Street, and from which they were occasionally removed by the police. After the game both sides usually adjourned to a pub on the corner of Elizabeth and Park Streets, which also served as a pavilion during the game and was owned by a cricketer named Mountford Clarkson.

The Australian Cricket Club was probably the first Sydney club to play in country towns. They defeated a team from Maitland in Sydney on 19 May 1845. A month later they travelled to Maitland, 150 kilometres north of Sydney where, according to the *Maitland Mercury*, 'the ground was in first rate order, and the weather fine and bracing'. The Sydney men, who had a couple of hard-hitting left-handers in the side, insisted that the venue be changed to 'a place near the verge of a declivity, down which the left-handed hits of Hatfield and Clarkson sent the ball at a fearful rate'. After the Sydney men had won by an innings and 13 runs, they were challenged to a single wicket game of four from each club, played for £5 a side. During this game, the *Mercury* reported, 'Hatfield had struck a ball to a great height and distance, and Wright ran to catch it. Just before the ball dropped on him his foot slipped on a small stump and the instep was badly sprained; the ball struck him on the upper lip, cutting it to the bone, and knocking him down. He was obliged then to be removed and his lip rubbed and his foot dressed. After walking up and down for some time he was so far recovered as to be able to limp along by himself. When his turn came to go in he was perfectly willing, but asked if another man might run for him. This the Australians would not grant, as the Maitland men had kept them very close to a hasty bargain previously. Wright therefore ran and hopped the distance for his six notches, amidst the cheers of the lookers on'.

Clearly the Australian club players were a competitive and well-organised group. The *Mercury* said of them, 'There was no confusion or waste of running, but the instant the ball had left the bat, there was someone ready to lay hold of it, and it was thrown in instantaneously . . . Ritchie, as backstop, was particularly efficient, scarcely a ball passing him through the innings'. In contrast, the *Mercury* refers to 'the inferior fielding of the Maitland men in the early part of the innings, arising from their want of practice together. They appeared to us to be not only slower and less certain than their competitors but to be very confused and irregular, leaving openings for various runs of four and five, and even a six'. This last shot by Clarkson, down the hill. Clarkson, Still and Hatfield were apparently big hitters, while Ritchie was a deflector: the *Mercury* describes him as 'making most of his runs by a skilful turn given to the ball as it passed him, rather than by hitting at it'.

The following year, in a fixture against neighbouring villages played at Morpeth, the *Mercury* was again on the job, reporting that the ground 'was found to answer the purpose except that the grass was too high for the bowlers. Mr Dee of Morpeth insisted, on the authority of a book of rules which he produced, that the stumps must be 22 inches high' and 'Mr Honeysett was compelled to use the straight, instead of the usual round-arm bowling'.

Maitland, on the Hunter River, became an important coal mining and timber centre. Charles Macartney, one of our greatest cricketers, was born there in 1886.

CHAPTER 3

Toffs versus Pig and Whistles

In 1798 the naval surgeon George Bass and his friend Matthew Flinders, in the 25-tonne Australian-made sloop *Norfolk*, sailed around Tasmania, confirming that it was an island and opening a new route for shipping through Bass Strait. By 1803 Flinders had sailed around the continent and charted the coastline.

During the 13 years of Macquarie's governorship the colony of New South Wales began to expand into the vast inland. William Wentworth, whose parents had been transported to Norfolk Island, was born in a small stone cottage on the island in 1790. He went to school in England and returned to live on the mainland. In 1813, with two free settlers, Gregory Blaxland and William Lawson, he found a route over the Blue Mountains, the dividing range between the coast and the temperate pastoral areas which were to be the first source of the colony's wealth. Men like John Oxley, Thomas Mitchell and Charles Sturt soon investigated the land to the west of the range. They were puzzled by the rivers which flowed westwards into an increasingly dry continent.

Tasmania
At the start of the new century the British, and the members of their new colony in New South Wales, were becoming concerned at the French exploration off the south coast of Australia. In 1802 the Frenchman Nicholas Baudin surveyed the Tasmanian coast; when his expedition called at Sydney for fresh supplies, it emerged that the French were thinking of settling Tasmania. Governor King sent a small party under Lieutenant John Bowen to settle the Derwent River, where they

arrived in September 1803. A month later Lieutenant-Colonel David Collins landed in Port Phillip Bay, south of modern Melbourne, under orders from the British Government to establish a penal colony in Bass Strait. Collins did not consider the area suitable, so in 1804 he joined Bowen's party at Risdon Cove on the Derwent and later moved the settlement across the river to Sullivan's Cove, under Mount Wellington. He named it Hobart Town, after Lord Hobart, the Colonial Secretary. By the 1830s the European population of the island was 70,000. The Aboriginal population had been systematically decimated and reduced to an estimated 300.

Hobart 1832. **State Library of NSW.**

References to Tasmanian cricket date back to 1825, the year the colony gained its independence from New South Wales, but there is no detailed mention of matches before 1832, when the Hobart Town Club, later known as the Derwent Club, was formed. In 1835 a game was played against the crew of HMS *Hyacinth*, and in 1839 there was a match between teams led by J. Marshall and J. Fisher, the nephew of the Governor, Sir John Franklin. Each player received a sovereign and Marshall received a silver cup as captain of the winning team. By the mid-1840s the club had a permanent ground and had been joined by a number other cricket clubs in the town including the

Garrison, Sorell, Clarence Plains, Richmond, New Norfolk and Green Ponds.

Victoria

Melbourne remained unsettled for a time after Collins's departure. A small military and convict settlement was established on Westernport Bay in 1806, but was abandoned two years later, again on the grounds that the area was not suitable. In 1824 explorers Hamilton Hume and W. H. Hovell saw the country around Port Phillip Bay and predicted a great future for the area. In 1827 John Batman from Tasmania realised the area's potential and requested a grant of grazing land at Westernport Bay, but was refused. The Henty family established a settlement in 1834. Batman followed them across the Tasman the following year. He settled the present site of the city of Melbourne after 'purchasing' an area of about 240,000 hectares from the local Aborigines, for a consideration of assorted knives, axes, scissors, blankets, mirrors, handkerchiefs, red shirts and other clothing, and 50 bags of flour.

Melbourne 1841. **State Library of NSW.**

It was not until 1836, when Thomas Mitchell, Surveyor-General of New South Wales, travelled to the Port Phillip area and returned singing its praises, that settlers from southern New

South Wales began to move into the area. Port Phillip was proclaimed a 'district open to settlement' and Captain William Lonsdale was appointed resident magistrate. Governor Bourke visited the settlement and named it after the British Prime Minister. Other names canvassed included Batmania, Doutta Galla, after the local Aboriginal tribe, and El Dorado. As free settlers, men of enterprise and capital arrived from New South Wales, England and Scotland, the colony developed very quickly. By 1840 more than 10,000 people were living in the Port Phillip District, and it was proclaimed a separate colony in 1850.

By 1838 the Melbourne Cricket Club, which was to play such a vital role in the game's future, had been formed from 'gentleman civilians of the district of Port Phillip'. The club was founded in November 1838 and played its first match, against the Military, during the same month. Played where the Royal Mint now stands in William Street, this was the first game recorded in the settlement. The *Port Phillip Gazette* reported: 'Yes, it was pleasurable to witness those whose enterprising minds had turned this, but short time since wilderness, into a busy emporium of traffic, relinquishing for a time their occupations and writings . . . It was a heartening sight to witness from an adjacent hill the ground as it was laid out. Camps pitched, banners tastefully arranged, and all the enlivening smiles of beauty that would have graced a far-famed tournament of other time, formed a scene which we trust often again to witness. At 12 o'clock precisely a signal called the players to their post, when the game commenced, the Military taking first innings. We have not the particulars of the game before us, and can therefore but briefly notice those who particularly distinguished themselves. After a duration of some hours, the match concluded by a triumph on the part of the civilians. Mr Powlett's and Mr D. G. McArthur's bowling, and Mr Russell's batting, attracted universal applause. On the whole the game was played with an esprit de corps, a judgment, and an activity that a first-rate club in England might not have been ashamed to boast.'

In 1839 the Melbourne Union Cricket Club was formed, with membership drawn mainly from the retail trade, and in that year two games were played between 'Gentlemen of the District' and 'Tradesmen of the Town'. Several games were played between 'Married' and 'Single' sides, the series being won by the bachelors, largely through the efforts of F. A. Powlett, a founding member of the Melbourne Cricket Club and its first president. Powlett, who is credited with the first century scored in the settlement, was a descendant of Charles Powlett, the founder of England's 'cradle of cricket', the Hambledon Club.

The Brighton Cricket Club was formed in 1842 and the Williamstown club was probably started at about this time, although its official existence dates from 1852. Founding members of the club at 'Williams Town' included several knights and a Mr Richard Seddon, who later became Prime Minister of New Zealand. In the club's early days every member was required to do half an hour's rolling of the wicket each week. The club's records disclose a request to a Mr Lyons to 'discontinue placing his cows on the Williamstown Cricket Ground'.

There are records of a game between Melbourne and Geelong in 1845, and a series of games between the same clubs in 1847. In 1848 the Melbourne club, with 147 members, moved to what had previously been a wheatfield on the south bank of the Yarra, in what is now South Melbourne. There, on 18 November 1848, eleven 'New Hollanders' (New South Wales still included the settlement at Port Phillip) defeated eleven natives of Europe by one run, 59 and 42 against 25 and 75. The construction of Australia's first railway line, from Melbourne to Sandridge (now Port Melbourne) forced the club to move again. In July 1853 they selected an area in Yarra Park called the 'Richmond Paddock' and erected an iron fence around it. The first game on what is now the Melbourne Cricket Ground was played on 4 November 1854.

Western Australia
Fear of the French also led to the British colonisation of Western Australia. In December 1826, on the orders of Earl Bathurst, the Colonial Secretary, a small settlement was established at Albany on the south coast. Life proved very difficult at this remote outpost, a month by ship from Sydney.

The Swan River, discovered by the Dutchman Willem de Vlamingh in 1697 and named for its black swans, was explored by Captain James Stirling in 1827. Stirling was impressed by its potential and sailed home to England dreaming of a colony under his command. The British told Stirling that they would approve the new colony only if businessmen could be found to finance its establishment. With some difficulty, Stirling achieved this, the main backer being Thomas Peel, brother of the then British Prime Minister, who invested £50,000.

Perth 1842. **State Library of NSW.**

The Swan River Colony was founded in 1829, when a party of soldiers, settlers and officials, with Stirling as Lieutenant-Governor, landed on the present site of the city of Perth. They wanted to establish a 'squirearchy' of gentlemen farmers without convicts, but were not aware that to the east lay one of the world's largest arid zones. Without cheap labour the colony developed painfully slowly. Some of the early settlers returned to Britain, others moved to the eastern colonies. Governor Stirling wrote: 'People came out expecting to find the Garden of Eden, and some were astonished at finding hard work an indispensable preliminary to meat and drink.' Twenty years after foundation there were only a few thousand settlers.

In 1850 the British Government gave in to the colonists' petitions for convict labour. By 1868, when transportation to Western Australia ceased, the population had grown to 25,000 and wool-growing had become an established and profitable industry. The success of the colony was confirmed in 1884 with the discovery of gold. Western Australia was granted self-government in 1890.

Despite the Swan River colony's slow start and development, the early days of cricket are well documented. On 5 April 1835 a local newspaper carried the following advertisement: 'The mechanics engaged in building the Commissariat store challenge those employed in erecting the Government House to play them one or more games of cricket on any terms which may be agreed upon.' The challenge was accepted by advertisement a few days later, but no record of the game has been found. On 13 April the *Perth Gazette and Western Australian Journal* said: 'This manly exercise has been started with some spirit within the last fortnight in Perth, and we understand a club is likely also to be formed at Guildford. The Perth club consists at present of about 22 members. They meet each Saturday afternoon at the Flats. The ground is not well adapted for the purpose, but it is expected that His Excellency the Governor will grant a suitable piece of ground adjacent to the town . . . The revival of the sports of our native country in a distant land, forms a link of connection which it should be our pride, and it will be found our interest, to encourage. The Perth Club does not number very many efficient hands. There are, however, some gentlemen amongst whom are two men of Kent who play an excellent game both in batting and bowling.'

The first game with full scores reported was played in May 1846 between the Perth Cricket Club and the Tradesmen of Perth: 'We have seldom seen any of our public amusements so well attended. The day was cool, but the ground horribly dusty and a brisk breeze having set in from the north-west, the clouds of dust were stifling . . . Throughout the innings the bowling was admirable, chiefly being of the "slow school", but not less dangerous than the rapid play of some modern artists. As the scores show, the incautious or hasty player had no chance, but so wary were the strikers in most cases that sometimes three overs were called without a notch.' The Tradesmen scored 38 and 26, against the Perth club's 45 and 5 wickets for 21. The *Gazette* observed that 'In general the batting was not good. There was a visible want of practice in most of the men on both sides, but there was occasionally some exquisite play'.

A return match a few days later was also won by the Perth club, by 26 runs. These amusements must have attracted criticism from some quarters. The *Gazette* of 23 May 1846 takes the critics to task: 'All we have to observe on this point is that we pity the narrow-minded individuals who entertain such opinions, and sincerely hope their hours of seclusion from what they term the vanities of the world, may be as innocently spent as in the instance of our present remarks. There was no rioting, drunkenness, or unseemly conduct evinced either on this or previous occasions; a number of persons met together to enjoy a manly sport, in which one and all participated.'

By 1850 cricket was more frequent and widespread. York issued a challenge to any eleven in the colony for a match on the day of the York races, for a sum of not more than £40. A 'Married' versus 'Single' match was played at Bunbury in March 1850, and in November 1852 Perth defeated Fremantle by three wickets. A week later Fremantle had its revenge, by the same margin, in a game covered by the *Independent Journal of Politics and News:* 'The ground, which is on the shores of the estuary, a short distance from the town, is not at all adapted for the purpose of Cricket, being sandy and scrubby, with a bank close to the wickets on the upper side . . . The field presented a most lively appearance, and tents were erected for the accommodation of the spectators. Great credit is due to the Fremantle folks for the handsome manner in which they treated their visitors, keeping them well supplied with champagne and refreshments of various kinds.'

South Australia

Captain Charles Sturt set out down the Murrumbidgee River in 1829 in a whaleboat with six men, to solve the puzzle of the inland rivers. He emerged where the Murray River flows into the sea and brought news back to Sydney of fertile land near the city we now call Adelaide.

At this time in England, Robert Gouger and Edward Gibbon Wakefield (a resident of Newgate prison, convicted for kidnapping a young heiress) were formulating their 'theory of systematic colonization'. They proposed the sale of government land at a relatively high price, which would prevent it being dispersed too quickly and would provide funds to pay the passage of selected labourers. The theory was that the immigrants would provide labour until they had saved enough money to purchase land. In 1833 Robert Gouger formed the South Australian Association and persuaded the Colonial Office to form a colony based on his theories.

The first colonists arrived in 1836, landing first on Kangaroo Island, south of the Murray River, where they found whalers and squatters already in residence. By the end of the year some 550 immigrants had arrived on the mainland. In 1837 they settled the present site of Adelaide, named after the wife of King

Site of Adelaide 1836. State Library of NSW.

William IV. Captain John Hindmarsh of the Royal Navy was the first governor of the new, independent colony, charged by the Colonial Office with creating a model of liberty and rationality, and with leading the Aborigines into voluntary and peaceful acceptance of the Christian religion.

The early days of cricket in South Australia provide a clue to what was to happen to these high-minded ideals; within a few years the game was flourishing, promoted by the owners of the many public houses in the new settlement. By 1838 the population of the colony was 5000. In November that year advertisements in local newspapers proclaimed meetings at the London Tavern for the purpose of forming a cricket club and advising that two members of the club were seeking a challenge match of single wicket cricket for £10 or £20.

On 19 October 1839, John Bristow, owner of the Great Tom of Lincoln at Thebarton, advertised in the *South Australian Gazette and Register*: 'A grand match will be played on Monday, October 28, on the Thebarton Cricket Ground between Eleven Gentlemen of the Victoria Independent Club, and Eleven Gentlemen of Adelaide, for twenty-two guineas a side. Wickets to be pitched at 10 o'clock. Refreshments will be provided, and everything done that can add to the pleasure of the public.'

The Adelaide Cricket Club was apparently formed in the early 1840s. Members of the club were known as 'the Toffs'. C. P. Moody, in his book *South Australian Cricket*, tells the story of a Mr Colman of Strathalbyn, who rode his horse 48 miles to play for the club, played all day, then saddled his horse and rode home again. The game was based around the pubs until the arrival in 1846 of John Cocker, who claimed to have opened the innings for Kent and was an accomplished under-arm bowler. He owned a pub, the Kentish Arms in North Adelaide, and wasted no time in forming a second cricket club, which he named Kent and Sussex. Cocker, it was said 'would play cricket all day no matter how hot it was, on the level ground in front of his hotel. If he could not get men to play with him, he would go out with the lads, and many a boy he taught to play cricket. Nothing delighted him more than to be bowled by one of his protégés. Then in the evening he would entertain us with his fiddle in the parlour of his hotel, and many's the pleasant evening we have spent there listening to his music and his yarns about Alfred Mynn, Fuller Pilch, and the other identities he played with in Old England'. A sailor named Wilkins, from the 'old country' and not impressed by the local standard, issued a challenge for a single wicket match, each man to do his own fielding. Cocker took him up and, having won the toss, made 109 in front of a crowd of several hundred people before giving his wicket away. Wilkins could only manage 7 in two innings. He did not take up his option for a return match.

Cocker's Kent and Sussex Club had a fierce rivalry with 'the Toffs' of the Adelaide club. North Adelaide teams were called 'Pig and Whistles', after the pub where they met. When they changed their meeting place to a church hall, they became known as 'the Holy Boys'. In the early 1850s the Union Cricket Club was formed, named after the hotel where it held its inaugural meeting, and in 1854 the Union Club beat a Rest of the Colony XI, including Cocker and Tom Botten, South Australia's first round-arm bowler, by 96 and 134 to 44 and 59. The Union Club apparently languished 'for lack of opposition' and within a year was easily beaten by the Adelaide club, with Cocker and Botten playing for Adelaide on this occasion. The South Australian club became the driving force of South Australian cricket in the 1860s.

Queensland

When the penal settlement for incorrigible convicts at Port Macquarie, north of Sydney, became difficult to administer, Governor Brisbane, who succeeded Macquarie, decided to look for suitable sites further to the north. John Oxley, who was by now surveyor-general, sailed up the coast in the *Mermaid* and recommended a site at Red Cliff Point in Moreton Bay. This site was settled briefly in September 1824, but after Oxley had explored the Brisbane River further the party moved to the area later known as North Quay.

Lieutenant Henry Miller, who was in charge of the outpost, had instructions from Brisbane to 'use every effort to prevent the introduction of spirituous liquors . . . all letters or parcels coming to the settlement for convicts are to be delivered to yourself, and you are hereby required to give them over to the person to whom they are addressed after having opened and read them in his presence . . . the ration to be issued to each convict is to consist of four pounds of salt meat and flour . . . the hours of morning labour will be from daylight till eight, when one hour and a half will be given for cleanliness and breakfast. Work will be resumed from half past nine until twelve. Two hours will then be allowed for dinner, and labour will afterwards continue from two o'clock until sunset. On Sunday mornings the convicts are to bathe, and when perfectly clean are to be mustered for Divine Service, which is to be performed by yourself . . . No other dress will be allowed to be worn at the settlement than that which is furnished by the Government. The yearly allowance to every convict is to be two shirts, two frocks, two pairs of shoes and two pairs of trousers, and the number affixed in the register before mentioned to the name of every convict is to be marked upon each article . . . the occasional augmentation of labour with solitary confinement upon bread and water will be far more effectual in the correction of offences than corporal punishment'.

By the middle of the 1830s, fewer convicts were being transported to Australia and the gaol at Port Arthur in Tasmania had been developed to handle incorrigible cases. In 1839 the remaining convicts in Brisbane were sent back to Sydney. The 'Northern District of the Colony of New South Wales', as Brisbane was called, became a free settlement. Land could be purchased for 12 shillings an acre. The colony was named Queen's Land and separated from New South Wales in 1855. Sir George Bowen, the first governor, arrived in 1859, by which time the population of the colony was 25,000.

The first reference to cricket in Queensland appears in the *Moreton Bay Courier* of 27 June 1846: 'As a finale to the

Brisbane 1851. **State Library of NSW.**

amusement of Race Week, a challenge from eleven of the working men of Brisbane to play an equal number of gentlemen for five pounds ten shillings a side was accepted by the latter, and the match came off on the terrace leading to the government gardens. The gentlemen were successful, beating their opponents easily. The stakes were generously handed over by the losing party. Arrangements were made for another match to come off in the next year's Race Week'.

The game must have been in a fairly crude stage at this time. In August 1847 the *Courier*, under the heading 'Hints for Cricketers', advised its readers that 'The stumps must be three in number; twenty seven inches out of the ground; the bails eight inches in length; the stumps of equal and sufficient thickness to prevent the ball passing through'. At about this time a club must have been established in Brisbane; in October 1848 the *Courier* reported that a club with 20 members had been established in Ipswich, now a suburb of Brisbane, which intended to challenge the Brisbane club.

By 1850 cricket had come to the country. The *Courier* of 14 May 1850 reported that after the races at Drayton, now a suburb of Toowoomba, a match 'was got up on the afternoon of the two following days between eleven squatters and eleven Draytonians'. The Squatters XI, 40 and 48, defeated the Draytonians, who could only manage 24 and 21. As a result the Ipswich Cricket Club challenged the Squatters to a match played at Ipswich on 14 June, and won by the home side 66 and 68 against 69 and 59.

CHAPTER 4

A breach of hospitality

The Australian Colonies Government Act, which gave the settlement at Port Phillip its freedom from New South Wales, passed through the British House of Commons on 1 August 1850. When the news reached Melbourne on 11 November, the mayor declared a three-day public holiday and the city celebrated for a week. Balloons proclaimed the news from the sky. There were processions, fireworks, a 21-gun salute, special services of thanksgiving, and free beer. The Melbourne Cricket Club celebrated by proposing a game of cricket—Port Phillip versus Van Diemen's Land—and the club adopted its red, white and blue colours for the match. Practice was set down for Tuesdays, Thursdays and Saturdays, with any member who missed more than one day a week without a satisfactory explanation in writing to be fined one guinea. Thirteen players from Port Phillip paid £5 a head for the crossing on the *Shamrock* and the first intercolonial game was played in Launceston on 11 and 12 February 1851.

The match and accompanying festivities were well covered by the newspapers of the time: 'No sooner had the *Shamrock* discharged her passengers at Launceston than the whole town was in a buzz, each and every person trying to outdo his neighbour in every kind attention which the most genuine hospitality could suggest. Everybody invited everybody, and the difficulty was to partake of all that was offered. From the time of landing to the time of embarking, the same spirit continued—dinners, balls, musical parties, picnics, and every description of entertainment was got up to give a hearty welcome to the strangers from Port Phillip.'

The Tasmanian captain was the wicket-keeper J. Marshall, known as 'the father of Tasmanian cricket' and a member of the Derwent club. The Melbourne side was captained by W. Philpott. F. A. Powlett, probably Melbourne's best player, was unable to make the trip as he had sprained an ankle at practice. The *Launceston Examiner* said: 'Several booths were erected on the ground and a large number of persons assembled to witness the game.'

A Melbourne paper reported that 'little was known of the style of play of the Tasmanians except that it was rumoured that their bowling was peculiarly slow and of an entirely different character from that of Port Phillip, which is, for the most part, swift. Nothing could be learned of their batting, but it was conceived that the swift round-arm bowling would prove too much for those who had been accustomed to underhand bowling. On proceeding to the cricket ground, which is prettily situated on the old racecourse, it was evident that every attention had been paid to the convenience and comfort of the players and visitors, but scarcely enough to the state of the ground itself which was of the roughest description; indeed so bad as to render it pretty certain that swift round-arm bowling would be entirely thrown away on it. The Tasmanians expressed themselves as sorry at being obliged to offer such a bad ground, which they accounted for by having commenced to make it only twelve months since; further the extraordinary dryness of the season had been very much against it being got in good order. It was with considerable difficulty that the umpires could select a piece of ground for the occasion. This being done, and the toss won by the Van Diemen's Land men, the Port Phillip men were put in and at 11 o'clock the game commenced'.

Victoria made 82. The Tasmanians replied with 104, top-score being Du Croz, who made 27 before his stumps 'were lowered by a ripper from Antill', who took seven wickets. Victoria made 57 in their second innings, leaving the home side 36 runs to win. They had lost 6 for 15 by close of play on the first day.

'Upwards of 80 sat down to dine' that evening. 'The toasts and song continued until the small hours, and the visitors showed how much they appreciated the unlimited kindness and hospitality of their hosts by continuing among the last . . . however they all mustered on the ground at 11 o'clock, and all pronounced themselves up to the mark.'

Antill's hands 'refused to hold' a catch from Tabart from the second ball of the day, and the game slipped away from the Victorians. When Tasmania hit the winning run, 'not the slightest breath of applause escaped from the multitude, numbering over 1500, but a marked silence ensued as though they had committed a breach of hospitality to their guests'.

The Victorians took their unexpected defeat in the right spirit and their departure was as emotional as their arrival: 'The two elevens, with their friends, walked arm in arm to the steamer, the band playing before them. On their arrival at the wharf, God Save the Queen was played, and Mr Philpott, in a few brief remarks, thanked the assembled multitude for their unbounded kindness, and especially for the last pleasing demonstration at parting. The Victorians assembled on the deck of the *Shamrock* echoed the feelings of Mr Philpott with a thrice renewed explosion of cheers—a compliment loudly reciprocated on the shore.'

CHAPTER 5

A public favourite

Edward Wills received a conditional pardon from Governor King in 1803 and was probably assigned to his wife Sarah, who had 'arrived free'. He was granted a 'free pardon' by Governor Macquarie in 1810. By this time, with his wife's help, he had become a successful merchant; he owned a general store near Sydney Cove, a half share in a 40-foot sloop which was used in the seal-skin trade, a pub in George Street and a small farm at Prospect, west of Sydney.

He died in 1811, aged 33, leaving an estate of £15,000 and four surviving children. One daughter was married to William Redfern, an ex-convict who was to become Assistant Surgeon of the colony. Another girl, Eliza, later married Henry Colden Antill, aide to Governor Macquarie. Sarah must have had a head for business; she carried on and expanded Wills's various interests. Five months after her husband's death, she had their sixth child, named Horatio Spencer Howe Wills.

Horatio Wills ran away to sea when he was 15 and was given up for dead when the ship he was thought to have been on was reported wrecked. Two years later, in 1828, he returned to the colony. In 1829 he became editor of the *Sydney Gazette* and in 1832 he started a rival newspaper, the *Currency Lad*. He married Elizabeth McGuire of Parramatta in 1833. In 1836 they took up land at Molonglo, near Canberra. Meanwhile, his eldest brother was prospering on the land at Port Phillip. In April 1840 Horatio Wills and his wife, with their first child, Thomas Wentworth Spencer Wills, their servants, 5000 sheep and 500 cattle, set out for Victoria and settled at Ararat, which he named 'because like the ark, I rested there'.

Local graziers were soon having trouble with the Aborigines. Wills wrote to Charles La Trobe, the Superintendent of the District, in 1842, describing the loss of horses and several hundred cattle, and pointing out 'the injury inflicted upon the grazing interests of the colony by the present method of granting Black Reserves. The finest Stations are usually selected and it destroys the confidence of the sheep-farmers'. Later the Wills family became friendly with the local tribes. Young Tom 'learnt to speak their language and sing their songs'. Horatio had built his holding up to 120,000 acres, running 28,000 sheep and 3000 cattle by 1851, when he sold it and moved to Geelong.

Tom Wills. **Melbourne Cricket Ground Museum.**

Young Tom went away to Rugby School in England. In 1853 Horatio wrote to his son, aged 18: 'You continue to write with a scrawl that would make a writing master eat his nails . . . You must shortly commence your studies for a profession — Law is the most honourable, the merchant also has a fair time of it. If you have the brains, take the Law. Come out here 5 or 6 years hence a barrister. Remember that everything you do is for yourself, and that if you do not succeed in life and obtain the reputation of a clever, gentlemanly fellow, no one will be to blame but yourself.' Tom Wills was in the school's First XI from 1852 to 1854 and captained both cricket and football in 1855. He also played for Kent and the MCC. He was enrolled at Cambridge in 1856 and had one game for the university. Then, against his father's advice, he decided to return to Victoria, where he very soon made a name for himself as a cricketer. James Lillywhite said of him, 'He carries a three-pound bat and hits terrific', but it was as a fastish round-arm bowler that he dominated the intercolonial matches from 1857 to 1860. He was described as 'the best all-round man in Australia, and a public favourite of the most pronounced type . . . he was wonderfully quick in detecting the weak points of batsmen, and always had absolute command of his field. As a captain he was considered one of the most astute tacticians that ever led a team to victory, being the most fertile in resource, and ever ready for the moves of the enemy'.

The techniques and tactics which Wills had learned in England helped bring Australian cricket up-to-date. His personality and performances caught the imagination of the public and did much to popularise the game. *The Australasian* said: 'He was, in fact, the Grace of Australia'.

As secretary of the Melbourne Cricket Club in the 1857–58 season, Wills was concerned that many cricketers were inactive during the winter and were therefore not fit when the cricket season started. He wrote to *Bell's Life* suggesting that a football competition be started to keep players fit. With a number of friends, including his cousin Henry Colden Antill Harrison, he helped to draw up a set of rules for a game suitable for Australian conditions. The grounds in Australia were considered too hard for the tackling game which Wills had learned at Rugby. The game they started came to be known as Australian Rules.

CHAPTER 6

Gold Gold Gold

Gold had been discovered in the Bathurst area west of the Blue Mountains as early as 1823. The early finds were not greeted with much enthusiasm by the authorities, who were afraid that a stampede for gold would be hard to control. Governor Sir George Gipps is said to have told one of the early discoverers, 'Put it away, Mr Clarke, or we shall all have our throats cut'.

Edward Hargraves worked the Californian goldfields in 1849, was reminded of the country west of the Blue Mountains, and concluded that there must be significant quantities of gold in Australia. When he came back to Sydney in 1851 and told his friends of his theory, he was 'ridiculed as a madman'. Undaunted, he went to Bathurst and searched the land along the Macquarie River until he found the country he had dreamed of in California. When panning proved his theory correct, he said to his companion: 'Here it is. This is a memorable day in the history of New South Wales. I shall be a baronet, and you will be knighted, and my old horse will be stuffed, put into a glass case, and sent to the British Museum.' The discovery was announced in the *Sydney Morning Herald* of 15 May 1851.

Within a few months thousands of people had rushed to the area. Sofala, 150 kilometres west of Sydney, became the first major centre, with 4000 miners in that small town alone. The Victorian government offered a reward of £200 to anyone who found gold and it was claimed immediately. After discoveries at Ballarat and Bendigo, 'the towns of Melbourne and Geelong were almost emptied of men. Cottages were deserted; businesses were deserted; ships in Port Phillip Bay were deserted. Even some masters of ships, accepting the loss of the crew as inevitable, teamed up with their men and set off for the diggings'.

News of the goldfields spread quickly around the world. Free men flocked to the goldfields in Australia in tens of thousands; English, Scots and Irish, Americans from the goldfields in California, and Chinese. By 1860 the population of Australia had increased from 400,000 to more than a million. The old orders of society — officials, squatters, landholders and convicts — were outnumbered by the immigrants, most of whom stayed after the gold rush was over to stake their claims as Australian citizens. They provided an enormous source of labour and created an instant demand for housing, goods and services.

Among the thousands on the Victorian goldfields during the 1850s were a number of graduates of Oxford and Cambridge Universities. As a result of a debate about the respective standards of cricket at the universities, a six-a-side challenge match took place on the goldfields in 1853, between 'Dark Blues' and 'Light Blues'. The match was reported in Boyle and Scott's 1880–81 Cricket Annual, the reporter being one of the participants: 'Stumps were easily made, but it took some time to form bats out of ironbark. The next thing was a ball, and after the whole of the diggings had been searched, and we were about to give the matter up in despair, a man was found with a good-sized india-rubber ball in his possession. A special holiday was then declared for the match.'

Dark Blues made only 43 and heavy betting was reported during the lunch interval. The account of the game also notes that the score sheet 'consisted of the inside cover of a novel', but it is clear that the game was played in a competitive spirit, with strict adherence to the laws of the game and with some degree of skill in the field. The Light Blues reached 15 without losing a wicket when, according to the reporter, 'I tried underhand lobs, and the first was hit for five, and then a wicket fell, and indeed two more at the same score. An old Cantab by as correct play as could be shown on the peculiar pitch increased the score to 35'.

The score had reached 40 — three runs to get, one wicket to fall — when 'one of their batsmen made a good hit. They ran one and the fielder fumbled the ball. "Go again" yelled the crowd, which they did, and the fielder, recovering the ball, took a shot at the wicket and knocked a stump out of the ground. He was carried from the field in triumph'. By the diggers who had backed the Dark Blues, no doubt.

CHAPTER 7

Sydney grubbers

By the early 1850s a number of clubs had been established in Sydney. Apart from the Australian, there were Marylebone, Parramatta and the Albert club, formed in 1852, which became the leading Sydney club during the 1860s.

Richard Driver. **NSW Cricket Association.**

In November 1855 the Melbourne Cricket Club put an advertisement in the *Argus* inviting challenges from other cricket clubs in Victoria. The response was disappointing, so in January 1856 the club approached a group of Sydney players with a view to arranging a game, for a stake of £500. The challenge came to the attention of William Tunks, one of Sydney's early entrepreneurs. Tunks, who began his working life as a carpenter, became Mayor of North Sydney and later a Member of the New South Wales Legislative Assembly. He owned a pub and later had contracts for supplying blue metal to the Sydney Council and erecting telegraph lines throughout New South Wales. Tunks placed advertisements in the Sydney papers calling a meeting in the Currency Lass Hotel, Pitt Street, at 8 p.m. on 29 January, 'to take into consideration a challenge received from the cricketers of Melbourne'. The meeting was run by Richard Driver, a young solicitor who was to be the main force in New South Wales cricket for 25 years. (Today, the main entrance to the Sydney Cricket Ground is on Driver Avenue, named in his honour.) Driver told the meeting that a challenge had been issued from Melbourne to an eleven from New South Wales for a match in Melbourne and a return game in Sydney, for £500 a match. The meeting agreed to accept the challenge and a committee was formed to arrange the first fixture. When the committee met a week later, they decided not to play for money; the stakes were large and it was thought that Melbourne would be the stronger team. Driver wrote to the Melbourne match committee: 'Cricketers here wish it to be understood that their object in accepting the challenge is a desire to promote and encourage the game itself, and not from any pecuniary motive.'

The game was played on the Melbourne Cricket Club's ground — the Richmond Paddock — on 26 and 27 March 1856. There was very little grass on the ground and the boundary was made up of iron hurdles. According to the Melbourne *Argus*: 'The weather was good and there was a great congregation of all classes of society on the ground. The fairer portion of creation were well represented, as were the plainer. An excellent German band was in attendance and efficiently supplied the place of the regimental orchestra which ought to have been there . . . The homely appearance of the Sydneyites had, since their arrival, created a prejudice against them which was augmented by the glimpse of their play which the Melbourne public had on the occasion of their practising. The preliminary "weighing" did not favour them, and prior to the bell being run for the occupation of the field, bets of 2 to 1 against New South Wales were freely offered. To be candid, takers were by no means scarce, though the popularity of the Melbournites never decreased below that quotation. At 10.30 the umpires tossed and the choice fell to the Victorians. A disagreement unfortunately ensued on the ground that the visitors were entitled to the choice. They insisted and won the point, although the rule, as we interpret it, is decidedly in favour of the Melbourne people, the custom referred to by the other side being obsolete.'

This, the first match between the colonies, was the game which was almost abandoned before it had begun. Several of the New South Wales XI, including Richard Driver, refused to play until the umpire's decision was changed. So the colonial sporting event of the century was delayed while the Melbourne team in their 'correct attire', probably heavy cream flannels, argued the rules with the Sydney men, whose 'homely appearance' was due to their outfits of white drill trousers, guernseys and caps. Some of the Sydney men went barefooted, others wore socks without boots. Sydney society was very much looked down upon by the free settlers of Melbourne.

The pavilion of the Melbourne Cricket Ground during the first match between New South Wales and Victoria, played in March 1856. State Library of NSW.

Eventually, the New South Wales captain, George Gilbert, a cousin of Dr W. G. (William Gilbert) Grace, opened the bowling. The Victorian opening batsman D. M. Sargeant took two from the first ball, and went on to make seven before 'a trimmer from McKone lowered his stumps'. The next batsman was Coulstack, who after scoring four runs, according to the *Argus*, 'caught the ball on his bat, and in a rather unaccountable manner as far as the spectators were concerned, was declared leg-before-wicket'. Victorian wickets fell steadily. Mather was run out for 16, trying for a fifth run. After Morres was bowled by Gilbert, the odds changed to even money. Hotham 'received a ball from McKone which rattled among his bails'. The same bowler was too good for Lowe, whose 'stumps became unsettled to such an extent that the air of the pavilion was considered best for him'. McKone bowled under-arm, grubbers apparently, as one report described his bowling as having a subterranean touch'. Melbourne made 63, McKone 5 wickets for 25 from 68 balls, Gilbert 4 for 24. New South Wales replied with 76, McKone and Driver both contributing 18.

On the second day Melbourne could manage only 28. A New South Wales victory seemed assured, but the Sydney men suffered a terrible collapse. Seven wickets were lost before they scored the 16 runs needed for victory. Gilbert top scored with seven. The Melbourne *Herald* attributed the loss to the 'irregular bowling of the Sydneyites', adding obtusely that 'no cricketer who witnessed this game can deny that the match would in all probability have resulted differently had the bowling on the Sydney side been equal to that of their rivals'. Gilbert and some of the Melbourne players bowled round-arm, but apparently the Melbourne bowling was 'regular', or predictable, while the Melbourne batsmen were somewhat nonplussed by the variations in line, length and flight of the Sydney bowlers.

The press also covered the financial aspects of the game. Takings for the first day were £60.5.0. The NSW team's costs, including the sea passage, were £181, £173 of which was recovered from a collection taken up among Sydney cricketers. News of the victory was carried home by the New South Wales team on board the steamer *City of Sydney*.

The return match was to be played the following year in Sydney, where the main ground was still in Hyde Park. The *Sydney Morning Herald* described it as a 'piece of rough and uneven ground, as bare as a well-travelled road in parts, with alternate hillocks of earth and pebbles, long grass, and ridges, holes and drains innumerable' and 'a low gambling ground for quoit players' where 'people destroy the ground and obstruct the play with impunity'. A better ground was needed and William Tunks persuaded the Governor, Sir William Denison, to let the cricketers have part of the Domain. Tunks also organised the funding and preparation of the new ground and the first game was played there on 6 December 1856, between Sydney club players. The second match between New South Wales and Victoria was played in the Domain on 14 and 15 January 1857.

The teams were much the same as for the first encounter; new players included Captain Ward, who ran the Sydney Mint, and Tom Wills for Victoria. Both were round-arm bowlers. Ward had a 'slim, erect, military figure' and a 'jerky little delivery as he advanced to the wicket with a little hop and run'. New South Wales won by a comfortable margin, 80 and 86 to 63 and 38. Ward took 2 for 23 and 5 for 15, Wills 6 for 26 and 4 for 40. The crowd on the second day was said to be 15,000.

The Victorian captain, W. J. Hammersley, wrote some years later: 'It was the queerest match I had ever taken part in, as some of the Sydney men played without shoes, in their stocking-feet, and one or two even discarded those necessary articles and were in their bare feet! However, Victoria got licked by 60 runs, I think. I know I was in an hour for about 10 runs in the second innings, and then one of Ozzie Lewis's grubbers got by, and there was a rattle. I remember we had a grand dinner somewhere, at which Sir W. Denison was present and lots of officers in gaudy uniforms. There were about 250 at the banquet; and if Sydney did beat us she did it handsomely, and what with dinners and picnics, eating oysters down the harbour, yachting, and other little games, we Victorians were a very limp lot when we returned home.'

As Philip Derriman says in *True to the Blue*, there must have been some regret among the New South Wales players that they had not accepted the stakes offered by the Victorians, for if they had, they would have been £1000 the richer. Perhaps, though, it was as well for them: in 1858, despite a hat-trick by Gilbert, the first in Australian first-class cricket, Victoria won by 171 runs. They also won the next four intercolonial games, due mainly to the captaincy and all-round ability of Tom Wills. In the 1858 match he made 49 not out and took 5 for 25 in the first innings. In 1859 he took 11 wickets for 90 runs for the match, and in 1860 his match figures were 9 for 39.

By modern standards, the cricketers of the 1850s would have appeared an eccentric lot. McKone, with his 'subterranean' bowling, was said to be ahead of his time as a batsman, because he played forward all the time. Captain Ward, apart from his 'jerky little delivery', also turned his backside toward the bowler when batting and peered at him over his left shoulder. Harry Hilliard bowled 'Sydney grubbers' — low under-arm deliveries which pitched short, spun and sometimes bounced a number of times before reaching the batsman. In later years there was Dickson, who 'stood behind his bat and walked around it as the ball was coming', the short-sighted John Kinloch, who wore a monocle while playing, and the big-hitter Tom Lewis, who on one occasion could not reach a ball down the leg side, so threw his bat at it. The umpire at square leg, according to the report, 'received the full force of the bat in the stomach'.

W. J. Hammersley, the Victorian captain, gained a Blue at Cambridge in 1847 and came to Australia during the 1850s. Later, under the name 'Longstop', he wrote for *The Australasian*. Clearly he thought the New South Welshmen unsophisticated, an attitude he shared with most of the Victorian population. In a letter to the Melbourne *Argus*, George Marshall, the Victorian wicket-keeper, described an incident in the New South Wales versus Victoria match in 1863: 'The ball went through to the longstop and was returned to me. Jones, in attempting to regain his equilibrium, drew one foot over the crease and I put down the wicket, and threw up the ball. While the ball was in the air, the Sydney umpire called "over", and on my appealing to our umpire, Jones was given out. The consequence was that a scene ensued which I am happy to say is never witnessed out of Sydney. The mob refused to let Jones retire, or Thompson come in, although the Sydney captain, Lawrence, ordered it, and we were all compelled to leave the ground. Wills received a severe blow in the face by a stone thrown by a cowardly vagabond, and Huddlestone and Hope were both struck by heavy sticks from behind. I was bullied and threatened not only at the ground but even at my hotel, where deputations waited on me with the avowed purpose of assaulting me.' Marshall refused to take any further part in the game. With one of his team-mates, he caught the next ship back to Melbourne, leaving the Victorian side two men short.

It worked both ways, of course; according to *The Australasian*, the attitude in New South Wales was: 'There's a Victorian cricketer, 'eave arf a brick 'im.' As late as 1890 the *Bulletin* was sneering at the 'plump, raw, beefy, smooth' and greatest insult of all, 'quite Hinglish' faces of the Victorian

Eleven. Bickering over umpiring, terms of play and, later, the selection of Australian teams continued for the rest of the century and beyond.

In April 1859, an advertisement in the *Sydney Morning Herald* invited secretaries of cricket clubs in Sydney to meet 'for the purpose of forming an Association'. As Philip Derriman suggests, this may have been a reaction to the defeat by Victoria a few months earlier. The April meeting called another meeting for 3 June, of which there is no record, but at a meeting of club representatives held to plan the next match against Victoria on 2 November, it was decided that the management of intercolonial matches should be by a 'Cricketing Association'. William Tunks and Richard Driver were appointed joint secretaries.

Tunks and Driver called a meeting of cricketers for 4 p.m. on 13 December 1859, on the cricket ground in the Domain. Some 25 people turned up, but Tunks and Driver were not among them. The *Sydney Morning Herald* reported that 'owing to the non-appearance of either of the secretaries (at which much disapprobation was expressed) the business did not commence till some time afterwards'.

John Kinloch, the man with the monocle, who was secretary of the University club, eventually stood in for the absent convenors and submitted a number of rules for the association, which were accepted after some amendments. The meeting retained Tunks and Driver as joint secretaries, and directed them to call a further meeting. In September of the following year a more comprehensive set of rules was published in the *Sydney Morning Herald*. In November 1860 office-bearers were elected. The Governor, Sir William Denison, agreed to be patron.

CHAPTER 8

The Eleven of England

Among the 700,000 people who came out to Australia during the 1850s following the discovery of gold were two Englishmen named Felix Spiers and Christopher Pond. They did not make their fortunes on the goldfields, but like many others they stayed and prospered in the boom times which followed. Felix Spiers owned the Cafe de Paris, a fashionable restaurant in Bourke Street, Melbourne, when he met Christopher Pond. They went into business together as 'refreshment contractors' and won the contract to provide food and drink on the Melbourne to Ballarat railway. Looking for ways to publicise their business, and make money, they hit upon the idea of promoting a speaking tour by Charles Dickens. But the great writer did not accept their invitation, so in 1861 they decided to promote a tour of the colonies by a cricket team from England. Mr W. B. Mallam was sent to England with 'instructions to procure the best eleven he could obtain', and contract them for the tour of Australia.

William Caffyn, the Surrey all-rounder, was one of the best cricketers in England at the time. In his book *Seventy-one Not Out*, Caffyn tells how Mallam, after seeking advice from Mr Burrup, the honorary secretary of the Surrey club, went to a dinner held at the Hen and Chickens Hotel in Birmingham, during a North versus South of England game. There he 'unfolded his views to the two elevens present', the cream of English cricket. Spiers and Pond offered to pay each player £150 and all travelling expenses, first-class.

Caffyn said, 'George Parr and the Northern players did not seem to relish the scheme at all, thinking that the sum of money offered was quite inadequate; and as it would have been impossible for anything like a representative team to have been formed without including some of the great players of the North, the affair was considered to be as good as off'. But Mallam persisted. After further meetings with Mr Burrup and the players, he 'succeeded in inducing' H. H. Stephenson, W. Mortlock, G. Griffith, Tom Sewell, Charles Lawrence and Caffyn, all members of the Surrey Eleven, to make the trip. To this nucleus was added W. Mudie of Surrey, Tom Hearne of Middlesex, 'Tiny' Wells of Sussex, Roger Iddison and E. Stephenson of Yorkshire and George Bennett of Kent.

The first English team 'taken just previous to their departure for Australia, October 1861'. W. B. Mallam, who arranged the tour for Spiers and Pond, is at the centre wearing a tall hat. The players, from left: W. Mortlock, W. Mudie, George Bennett, Charles Lawrence, H. H. Stephenson, Billy Caffyn, G. Griffith, Tom Hearne, Roger Iddison, Tom Sewell, E. Stephenson. NSW Cricket Association.

'The team was a good one,' Caffyn wrote, 'but was not of course anything like representative.' The captain, Heathfield Harman Stephenson, was a leading player and a respected figure in English cricket. A batsman, wicket-keeper and round-arm fast bowler with 'a pronounced break-back', he was also a good public speaker and a 'wise counsellor' to those interested in the arts and advancement of the game. 'Tiny' Wells, who took his wife on the tour, sailed before the remaining eleven. The rest of the team assembled in London, where a banquet was given at the London Bridge Hotel. 'Success to the English cricketers was enthusiastically drunk', and a song composed for the occasion was sung:

> 'Success to the Eleven of England!
> The toast is three times and once more.
> May they all meet success o'er the briny,
> And safely return to our shore!'

The team was photographed in the stableyard of the Anglesea Hotel the following morning, before leaving for Liverpool to board the *Great Britain* for the voyage. 'The team sang "The Anchor's Weighed", and I gave them "Cheer, Boys, Cheer" on the cornet as the vessel moved off,' wrote Caffyn.

'There were great demonstrations on our arriving at Melbourne, flags being hoisted on most of the ships in the harbour, and a crowd of over 10,000 people gathered to welcome us as we came ashore. Previous to our leaving the *Great Britain* Messrs Spiers and Pond came aboard and presented us with an address of welcome. As soon as we got on terra firma we were driven off in a coach-and-four to the cafe of Messrs Spiers and Pond in Bourke Street, a great crowd of people following us. We were photographed on the coach before alighting. We all wore white pot-hots with a blue ribbon.'

The first game was played on New Year's Day 1862, against Eighteen of Melbourne. According to press reports, the biggest crowd ever seen in Melbourne, estimated at between 15,000 and 25,000 in a city of 125,000, assembled for the game. Every road to the Melbourne Cricket Ground was blocked with carriages and buggies. A grandstand more than 200 metres long, with room for 6000 spectators, had just been built. Underneath the stand was an area reserved for publicans, who advertised that they would have 500 cases of beer available. On the outskirts of the ground there were roundabouts, shooting galleries, Aunt Sallies and other amusements and stalls. Total attendance at the match was 45,000. The minimum entrance fee was two shillings and sixpence.

'We lost the toss,' wrote Caffyn, 'and H. H. Stephenson led us into the field. We had been supplied with very light white hats of the helmet shape. Each of us had a coloured sash and a ribbon round his hat—one man's colour being blue, another green, another crimson, and so on. These colours were printed against each of our names on the score-card, so that anyone provided with one of these could at once identify every member of our

The England XI v Eighteen of Melbourne at the Melbourne Cricket Ground, January 1862. **State Library of NSW.**

team. My own colour was dark blue. The National Anthem was played as we entered the field, amidst the silence of the vast concourse of spectators. When the band stopped playing a tremendous burst of cheering rent the air. The weather was so hot as to fetch the skin off some of our faces.'

The game lasted four days. The Victorian Eighteen scored 118 in the first innings. Stephenson's team replied with 305, then bowled the Victorians out for 92. Caffyn, who top-scored for the Englishmen with 79, wrote: 'There had been a sweepstakes got up over the match, the first prize being, I believe, quite £100. I remember the gentlemen who drew me gave me a £10 note for making the highest score and thus winning him the prize.'

The next fixture was at Beechworth, 'a journey of about 200 miles by coach. This conveyance was drawn by five horses — three in front and a pair behind them. A very shaky and fatiguing journey this was, and glad indeed were we all when it was over'. This game was won by an innings and almost 200 runs. Then, following a draw against Twenty-two from Melbourne, and a nine-wicket win over Twenty-two from Geelong, the tourists travelled to Sydney by sea. A crowd of 15,000 was at the quay. There was a public breakfast and a dinner the same evening at the Victorian Club. An 'enormous and fashionable' crowd, including the Governor Sir John Young and Lady Young attended on each of the four days of the game against Twenty-two from New South Wales. The English team won by 48 runs and a grand banquet at the Exchange followed the game.

Then to Bathurst, where a band met the tourists four miles out of town and a violent storm caused the game to end in a draw. Back in Sydney the Englishmen were beaten by 12 wickets by a combined Twenty-two from Victoria and New South Wales. Perhaps the pace was too much for them: Caffyn said: 'Scarcely a day passed without our being entertained to champagne breakfasts, luncheons, and dinners. A performance at the Victorian theatre was given for our benefit, the house being simply packed. Between the pieces H. H. Stephenson read out a farewell address. After various speeches had been made we adjourned to Tattersall's, where parting bumpers were drained. A large body of people then escorted us to the Circular Quay to see us start on our voyage to Tasmania. Rockets and blue-lights were fired as we went out to sea.'

More of the same in Tasmania, where they won by four wickets, then back to Melbourne for a 'Surrey versus The World' game, the six Surrey players in Stephenson's team being joined by five from Surrey living in Melbourne. The World won by five wickets. Then to Ballarat, Sandhurst and Castlemaine before a final visit to Melbourne to play Twenty-two from Victoria. After the game, which was drawn, the team planted 12 elm-trees on the outskirts of the ground.

The tour was a success from every point of view. The Melbourne Cricket Club gave each Englishmen a bonus of 100 sovereigns. Spiers and Pond, who outlayed some £7000 but made a profit of £11,000 on the tour, divided half the receipts of the final game among the English players and offered them £1200 to stay for another month in Australia. They could not accept the offer, as many had commitments in England. They played 13 matches, all except one versus 18 or 22, as well as two scratch games. Two games were lost—both against 22 opponents—and five were drawn. Back in England, Roger Iddison was asked his opinion of the Australian cricketers: 'Well, I don't think much of their play, but they're a wonderful lot of drinking men.'

The all-rounder Charles Lawrence, who took 46 wickets on the tour at an average of 5.28, was offered a job by the Albert club in Sydney and stayed on as Australia's first professional coach.

Two years later, in 1864, the Melbourne Cricket Club asked George Parr from Nottinghamshire, who had declined the first tour because £150 was 'inadequate', to organise and lead a second team. Caffyn described Parr, who was known as 'The Lion of the North', as 'a queer-tempered man, but one of the easiest to get on with if one knew his peculiarities; but one had to make up one's mind never to take offence at his remarks'. Parr was 'rather over medium height with round shoulders and powerful arms. He stooped slightly and limped somewhat in his walk, seeming to have a fagged and tired appearance'. He had 'a florid complexion, large blue eyes, auburn hair, and thick chestnut-coloured moustache and whiskers'. Apart from being one of the best batsmen in England, Parr extended the techniques of the game. Although 'he played thoroughly sound cricket', he 'played a different game to anyone who preceded him, using his feet and going out to drive straight balls far more than anyone else'. He also 'hit more balls to leg than anyone else'—it was as a 'leg-hitter' that he was best known. One of the game's more durable stories is said to have originated with George Parr: in a match against Cambridge, it is said, he picked up a good length ball on middle stump and lofted it sweetly over midwicket and out of the ground. Such shots were not regarded as 'proper form' in those days and the bowler, furious at this breach of etiquette, glared down the wicket and demanded, 'Do you know where that pitched?' 'In the hedge, I think,' was Parr's reply.

The Domain, Sydney, in March 1864. George Parr's English team playing Twenty-two of New South Wales. **State Library of NSW.**

From Caffyn's description, Parr initiated the sweep: 'His method was to reach out with the left leg straight down the wicket, bending the knee, and to sweep the ball round in a sort of half-circle behind the wicket.'

Caffyn was the only member of the second team who had been on the first tour to Australia. Parr's team also included Dr E. M. Grace, a brother of WG, Bob Carpenter, the 'champion back-player', and a brilliant batsman from Surrey with the quaint name of Julius Caesar. The main bowlers were Cris Tinley, who bowled lobs, and two fast men, John Jackson, known as 'Demon', and George 'Tear 'em' Tarrant. Jackson was quick and not above unsettling a batsman with the occasional bean-ball. Tarrant was express. His uninhibited style and terrific pace impressed a spectator at one of the Sydney games, an 11-year-old schoolboy named Frederick Robert Spofforth. Spofforth said later, 'He was the fastest bowler I ever saw. I tried to copy him. My one aim was to bowl as fast as possible'.

The second tour was as successful as the first. Parr's team was undefeated in a dozen games in Australia and four in New Zealand. According to Billy Caffyn, 'We each cleared about £250 from the trip, after paying all expenses. Ten of the English team set sail in the *Bombay* on the 26th of April. Dr Grace stayed behind for some little time in order to visit friends. I myself also remained, having accepted an engagement with the Melbourne Club, and I did not again see my native land till seven years later'.

It was to be almost 10 years before another team came from England.

CHAPTER 9

Culture shock

During the 1860s seemingly limitless tracts of pastoral land had been discovered. Much of this country was used for grazing by settlers who had become wealthy since their arrival in the colonies, or had brought their wealth from England. The white society produced its own outcast-heroes, the bushrangers, from among those who failed to measure up to its standard of success. They did not all come from the convict class; some of them were the sons of free settlers or of the early officials of the colony. Later they were joined by selectors who had failed to make a go of it on the land. In February 1868, Henry Colden Antill II, a son of Governor Macquarie's aide and Eliza Wills, the daughter of Edward Wills, was convicted of 'robbery being armed' and sentenced to 15 years' hard labour on the roads, the first year in irons. Four years later, on the petition of his elder brother, he was released from Darlinghurst Gaol, 'sentence remitted to exile'. He lived in New Zealand for six years, was allowed to return to Australia in 1874, and died in 1919, within a month of his 93rd birthday.

The legend created for Australia's bushrangers is that they were native youths with a grievance against society. We can only wonder at the sense of grievance felt by the real natives, the Aborigines. As their culture had no concept of ownership of land, the fact that the land they lived on now belonged to the King of England probably meant nothing to them. But as the white population moved inland and settled permanently on the most fruitful areas, the Aborigines were increasingly dispossessed.

Horatio Wills became a member of the Victorian Legislative Council, and in 1856 was elected to the first Legislative Assembly of Victoria. In 1859 he toured Europe, visiting three of his children at school in Bonn, Germany. When he returned he decided to go back to the land and bought a property, 'Cullin-la-ringo', 300 kilometres west of Rockhampton in Queensland. With a party of 25 men, women and children, including his son Tom, he set off from Sydney in February 1861 with 10,000 sheep, and set up camp at 'Cullin-la-Ringo' on 6 October. On 17 October local Aborigines attacked the camp, killing 19 people. One man, John Moore, escaped to raise the alarm; Tom Wills and four others who were away from the camp at the time escaped the massacre. A week later a party of police and local civilians tracked down the suspected tribe and trapped them in a gorge. Some 60 or 70 blacks were shot before the police ran out of ammunition.

Tom remained at 'Cullin-la-ringo' trying to establish and develop the property for a couple of years after the massacre, but by 1864 he was back in Victoria, playing against George Parr's English team.

Many Aborigines lived semi-tribal lives on the large sheep and cattle stations run by the squatters. The women worked as housemaids and nannies, the men as stockmen. The system was paternalistic, but usually worked to the apparent satisfaction of both camps. Just as the Aborigines were natural stockmen, many of them—lithe, fleet of foot and sure of eye—were natural athletes. There are frequent reports of Aborigines playing cricket in country areas. In the Edenhope district in the south-west of Victoria, a number of Aborigines played 'station cricket' with local teams. In the early 1860s William Hayman, who had a holding in the area, thought so highly of their skills that he had the idea of organising and sponsoring a game for them in Melbourne. Hayman knew Tom Wills and arranged for him to coach the Aboriginal team.

On Boxing Day 1866, led by Wills, they played the Melbourne Cricket Club. The leading players were Johnny Mullagh and Cuzens, both all-rounders, and Bullocky, a batsman and wicket-keeper. Others who played in this game were Dick-a-dick, Peter, Jellico, Officer, Tarpot, Paddy and Sundown. The match was well advertised and a crowd of 10,000, who 'cheered everything they did', was reported, but most of them did not do themselves justice in this strange atmosphere. Batting first, they made only 39, Bullocky (14) and Mullagh (16) being the only players to reach double figures. The Melbourne club replied with 100, Cuzens taking 6 for 24. The Aborigines made 87 in their second innings, Mullagh 33, Wills not out 25. The MCC lost one wicket in getting the 27 runs required.

Aboriginal team at the Melbourne Cricket Club in 1867. From left, standing: King Cole, Tarpot, Tom Wills, Johnny Mullagh, Dick-a-Dick. Seated: Jellico, Peter, Red Cap, Harry Rose, Bullocky, Cuzens. This was the nucleus of the team that went to England in 1868. Melbourne Cricket Ground Museum.

The Melbourne *Herald* reported that 'they were thoroughly acquainted with various points of the game' and 'the fielding was very fair'. Mullagh and Cuzens were picked in the Victorian team to play Sixteen from Tasmania a few weeks later. When Mullagh became ill and could not play, Bullocky was picked in his place.

Hayman and Wills were then persuaded by Captain W. Edward Brougham Gurnett to sign a contract for a year-long tour of Australia and England by the Aboriginal team. More players were recruited and the team went on tour in Victoria led by Charles Lawrence, the Englishman who had toured with Stephenson's 1862 team and remained in Australia to coach at the Albert club in Sydney. After several games in the country they returned to Melbourne where they won a game against a County of Bourke XI.

Some suspicions concerning Edward Gurnett surfaced before the team left for Sydney. Some of his cheques had been dishonoured and he had to make special arrangements with his creditors before the team could leave Victoria. In Sydney they were beaten by 132 runs by the Albert club, in a match which was a financial disaster. A proposed game in Brisbane fell through because of Gurnett's excessive demands for financial guarantees. The team was not paid and they returned to Melbourne destitute and sick. Watty died from 'diseased lungs', probably associated with alcohol, on the way home. Jellico and Paddy died from pneumonia soon after they got back to Victoria. Another member of the original team, Sugar, died before the match in Melbourne on Boxing Day 1866. The *Hamilton Spectator* said, 'It is evident that Hayman and his blacks entrusted themselves to hands which were not quite trustworthy'. In October 1867 a Dr Molloy from Balmoral in Sydney wrote to the Aboriginal Protection Board opposing the proposed tour of England, on the grounds that the climate in England could seriously affect their health. The board also felt that the blacks were being exploited, and many of the public shared this view.

Despite these setbacks, Charles Lawrence believed that the tour to England would prove a good investment. He persuaded the authorities that it would be properly managed, he found investors, including a former Lord Mayor of Sydney, Alderman George Smith, and the team came to Sydney early in 1868 for a couple of matches before the journey to England. They played very well against a strong side at the Albert club, losing by only 15 runs and then, on 4 February, they defeated a Navy and Army team which included Billy Caffyn and Edward Gregory, who later became a Test player. In this game Cuzens took 8 for 23 and made 86 before being run out. They left Sydney on 8 February 1868 on the wool clipper *Parramatta* for the three-month trip to England.

Led by Charles Lawrence and managed by William Hayman, the team consisted of Bullocky, Cuzens, Dick-a-dick, Charley Dumas, Jim Crow, King Cole, Mosquito, Johnny Mullagh, Peter, Red Cap, Sundown, Tiger and Twopenny. Tarpot, who was selected, became ill at the last moment and had to be taken off the ship before it sailed. In an extraordinary feat of endurance, in what must have been very strange climatic and social conditions, they played 47 games in a little over four months between May and October. They won 14, lost 14, and 19 were drawn.

Some of the fears of the Aboriginal Protection Board were

justified; King Cole died of tuberculosis in June, and in August Sundown and Jim Crow, who became too ill to play, were sent home. Reports of the financial arrangements vary, the most authoritative, from the cricket historian Arthur Haygarth, being that they played for £200 a match or, alternatively, for the match proceeds, out of which they paid £20 to the host club. Haygarth also says the tour was 'very lucrative'. As crowds were sometimes more than 5000, this may be true, but other reports say that expenses were so high that there was very little profit. Certainly there is no sign that the players were paid, let alone able to put aside any money from the tour. By today's standards, no doubt they were exploited.

In other ways the tour was a success. Given the substantial problems, it must have been well organised and well managed. Originally only 10 games were scheduled, but their popularity was such that 37 additional fixtures were arranged, including one against the MCC, which had at first declined the fixture. They were praised in the English press for their 'gentle and by no means unintellectual appearance', and 'manly, dignified and pleasantly confident gait and bearing'. In general they were treated well. They were barred from the luncheon tent at York, but were very well looked after by the Surrey club, home of several players who had been to Australia with the English teams of 1862 and 1864. A Surrey player, W. Shepherd, played several games with the Aboriginal team after their numbers had been reduced through sickness.

Their boomerang and spear-throwing exhibitions after games or during intervals were very popular with the crowds, as were other athletic feats. Dick-a-dick had an extraordinary ability to run backwards at speed; he was timed at 14 seconds over 100 yards. Johnny Mullagh was able to clear up to 5 feet 7 inches (170 centimetres) at the high jump. W. G. Grace, then a tall, gangling young man of 20, joined them for an exhibition of throwing the cricket ball at one game, where he recorded successive throws of 116, 117 and 118 yards. Lieutenant-Colonel Bathurst, the Earl of Coventry, and Viscount Downe played for the MCC against them at Lord's, where the Aborigines led on the first innings. Johnny Mullagh made 75 out of a total of 185, in reply to the MCC's 164. Faced with 100 to win in the second innings, the visitors collapsed for 45.

The team was carried by Mullagh, Lawrence and Cuzens. Mullagh played in 45 games, made 1670 runs at an average of 24 and took 257 wickets at an average of 10. Lawrence played 40 games for 1192 runs at 22 and also took 257 wickets at an average of 12. In 46 games Cuzens made 1367 runs at 18. He also took 114 wickets at 11.

Johnny Mullagh.

They left England in October 1868 on the *Dunbar Castle*, arriving home in February 1969. After a couple of games together they dispersed and within a few years several of them had died. Cuzens played in a trial match for the Victorian XI in 1870, but failed and was not picked to play for the State. He died of dysentery in 1871. Twopenny had one game for New South Wales without success and later worked as a stationhand at Molonglo, near Canberra, where he died of alcoholism in 1883. Johnny Mullagh went home to the country, where he played in the local competition for a dozen years or so. He is remembered there for a unique shot against fast bowling; dropping on one knee with his bat over his shoulder, he would deflect the ball over the wicket-keeper's head. A decade after the tour to England, Mullagh had his only game for Victoria, against Lord Harris's 1879 English team. He scored a stylish 36 in the second innings, after which a collection of £50 was raised by the crowd.

Johnny Mullagh lived most of his later life in a camp in the bush, alone but apparently quite contented, in his native Edenhope district, where he died in 1891 aged about 50.

In the schoolyard at Edenhope, on the banks of Lake Wallace, a two metre high slab of granite stands as a memorial to the first Australian cricket team to tour England. The memorial was unveiled by Victor Richardson in 1951. It bears the names of the players, the record of the tour and the words:

IN THIS VICINITY
THE ABORIGINAL CRICKET TEAM
FIRST AUSTRALIAN CRICKET TEAM
TO TOUR ENGLAND
TRAINED PRIOR TO ITS DEPARTURE IN 1868

Tom Wills was not involved in the tour to England. He played and coached in Melbourne in the 1867–68 season and for some years afterwards. It is said that he began to drink heavily after the massacre at 'Cullin-la-ringo', but continued to play cricket during the 1870s. In 1878, with Charles Lawrence, he helped sponsor the first white team to tour England.

Wills committed suicide at Heidelberg in Victoria on 2 May 1880. The *Argus* reported that he 'possessed himself of a pair of scissors and, despite the exertions of his wife who endeavoured to prevent him, stabbed himself three times in the left breast, in the region of the heart'. At an inquest into his death, a jury found that he had 'committed suicide while of unsound mind from excessive drinking'.

Apart from Eddie Gilbert, an express bowler who took 87 wickets for Queensland in the 1930s and had the rare distinction of bowling Bradman for a duck, Alex Henry and Ian King from Queensland and Jack Marsh from New South Wales are the only Aborigines to have played first-class cricket.

CHAPTER 10

The Australian dream

The 1860s and 1870s were years of development and improvement in social conditions. Businessmen and tradesmen prospered as a result of the population explosion which followed the discovery of gold. The clothing, brewing and printing industries flourished. There was a boom in the building trades; the demand for timber and bricks and men who knew how to use them created more wealth and employment. Although there was still much poverty, many working class people found good jobs and rows of homes were built around the cities to house the developing middle class.

In the country the excesses of the squatters were brought under some sort of control as the colonies legislated to answer the cry to 'unlock the land'. Settlers were allowed to take up small areas, generally only a few hundred acres. Because the areas were so small and the price was relatively high, usually about £1 an acre, most of the new selectors lived in relative poverty and many failed. They had no help from the squatters, who resented the alienation of the land they had struggled to open up. Only the best of the newcomers survived to prosper and to play the squatters at their own game of using 'dummies' to secure large areas.

Transport and communications began to improve. In 1853 an American named G. F. Train imported a coach with springs which greatly improved transport between Sydney and Melbourne. Cobb & Co began running their stagecoaches between Melbourne and Bendigo in 1854 and later developed a network of routes throughout the eastern colonies. Railways began operating in Melbourne in 1854 and in Sydney the following year. By 1862 the Victorian government had built railways from Melbourne to Bendigo and Ballarat. Sydney and Melbourne were linked by rail in 1883. Four years later the line between Victoria and South Australia was completed and the following year New South Wales was linked with Queensland.

By 1870 the eastern colonies were all linked by electric telegraph. The link from Perth to Adelaide was completed in 1877. In 1878 the first telephone exchange began operating in Melbourne and within 10 years the telephone was in use in Sydney, Brisbane, Adelaide, Hobart and Perth. Paddle steamers were found to be an efficient way of transporting wool and supplies on the inland rivers. The opening of the Suez Canal in 1869 and the increasing use of steam instead of sail reduced the travelling time to Europe to less than two months. The first shipments of frozen meat and dairy products were sent to Britain in 1879.

By 1861 half the population had been born in the United Kingdom. Ten years later 60 per cent were native born. Western Australia asked for convicts to provide a labour force in 1848, but transportation to the eastern colonies finished in 1852, mainly as a result of the actions of the Anti-Transportation League. Non-whites were prevented from immigrating to Australia on the grounds that jobs needed to be protected for Australians. In other ways, Australia became a less harsh, more democratic society. Unions based on trades grew during the late 1870s and fought for better pay and working conditions.

Australia in the early 1860s was 'cricket mad'. The English touring team was told in 1862 that there were 70 cricket clubs in Victoria alone. The *Australian and New Zealand Gazette* said 'One of the first requirements that a newly laid out township seems to feel in Australia is a racecourse and a cricket ground'. Australian cricket was beginning to achieve some loose organisation. The New South Wales Cricket Association had been formed in 1859 and during the 1860s more than 20 clubs were playing regular cricket in Sydney.

Grounds and equipment were still crude. F. R. Spofforth wrote: 'Everyone came to practice in his ordinary clothes, cricket boots were seldom worn, and flannels were unknown. There was no place of shelter to change in, and even in a match, more than half the players would turn out with no alteration to their costume. I remember that as boys we used to think a great deal of a man who appeared in flannels; it was a sure sign that big things were expected of him . . . Artisans and gentlemen played together in all the clubs, and if the ordinary boots got slippery, off they came; even socks were discarded by the artisans. Very few players had bats of their own: a stock of materials were kept in a huge canvas bag at the house of the secretary of the club or at some member's house near the ground.'

All important matches in Sydney were played on the ground in the Domain, but it became increasingly unsatisfactory. Batsmen disliked it because of the surrounding dark trees. The fielding surface was poor and frequently covered in cow-pats: 'They have become a perfect nuisance,' said *Bell's Life* in 1860, 'and one cannot walk even on the footpaths without falling in with the annoyance we allude to.' The Victorian players regarded the Domain as second-rate. 'Twenty runs on the Domain ground are equal to 30 or 35 on the Melbourne,' said the *Victorian Cricketers Guide* of 1861. The Domain was a public area. Those who did not like cricket resented its use for 'private' purposes and there were disputes about the cricket association's right to charge for admittance to the ground.

Several members of the Albert club bought a piece of land in Elizabeth Street, Redfern, and built a cricket ground there which was known as the Albert Ground. It was opened in 1864 and was for almost 15 years the main ground in Sydney. The association, reluctant to support the Alberts, continued to look for a ground of its own. The British soldiers had made a field for themselves behind Victoria Barracks and, when they left the Barracks in 1870, it was taken over by the NSW military, who made little use of it. In 1875, the association approached the Minister for Lands, asking that the Military and Civil Ground, as it was called, be leased to the association. The Minister, Thomas Garrett, whose son, also named Thomas, was one of the colony's leading cricketers, agreed. It was arranged that the ground should be controlled by three trustees, two to be appointed by the association, one by the government. The ground was levelled and re-turfed and the first match organised by the association was played there in October 1877. It was formally opened in February 1878, during the annual match against Victoria. Within a few years the Albert ground had been sold off for home sites.

The Melbourne Cricket Ground had been occupied by the Melbourne Cricket Club since November 1854. Although a

View of the Adelaide Oval in 1876. **South Australian Cricket Association.**

Victorian Cricket Association was formed in 1864, the Melbourne Cricket Club dominated cricket in Victoria for the rest of the century and was the single most powerful force in Australian cricket until 1905.

In Tasmania, North versus South matches began in 1850. A Southern Tasmanian Cricket Club was formed in 1858 and a Southern Tasmanian Cricket Association in 1866. Regular games were played against Victoria, although after a heavy loss in 1869 the Tasmanians said they would only continue to play if the fixtures were all-amateur games. The Northern Tasmanian Cricket Association was not formed until 1886.

Club cricket gained strength in Adelaide, too, and cricket was flourishing in country areas of South Australia, even if the gear was primitive; one piece bats, with no spring, were made of local timber and balls were 'knitted with string'. The South Australian club had secured a lease of six acres in an area known as the Park Lands in 1859. In the late 1860s, when there was talk of a match against Victoria, a local player named H. Yorke Sparks went to Melbourne to learn about ground preparation and administration. He then set about raising money to begin preparation of the pitch and to build a fence around what is now the Adelaide Oval. Battles with the city council over the lease, finances and admittance charges led to the formation of the South Australian Cricket Association in 1871. The association had to postpone a proposed match with Victoria in 1873 because 'locusts have eaten our grass twice'. In 1878 the Sussex professional Jesse Hide was engaged as coach and groundsman

59

at an annual salary of £200. He stayed for five years and is credited with improving the standard of play and wicket preparation.

By the early 1860s several clubs were active in Brisbane and there is mention of teams from Toowoomba, Dalby and Maryborough. A meeting was called in 1861 to form a cricket association and resulted in a body named the Brisbane Cricket Club, which was apparently not very active.

Even in those days Queensland seemed to have a rather tropical atmosphere. In 1864 the first match was played against New South Wales. The Brisbane season started in March and went through the winter; the game against New South Wales was played in June. A trial game against Ipswich was something of a disappointment for the organisers, as Sixteen of Ipswich made 56, then got the Brisbane side out for 4; top score was G. Cowlishaw (2), there were two byes, 10 ducks, including five run outs. T. B. Foden took 4 for 2 and earned a place in the Queensland team. Other trials were more satisfactory.

New South Wales, led by Charles Lawrence, made only 32 in the first innings (Foden 6 for 16 from 69 balls) but they won this match and a return match in Sydney the following year quite comfortably. Queensland did not play another intercolonial match for 10 years, but club cricket continued to flourish. The Queensland Cricket Association was formed in 1876. During the 1870s, major matches were played at Eagle Farm racecourse. Later the Exhibition Ground became the leading venue; the first Test played in Brisbane, against England in 1928, was played there. Some first-class matches were played on the ground at Woollongabba, known as the 'Gabba, after 1897, but it was not used for a Test match until 1931.

Western Australia, thousands of kilometres by sea from its nearest interstate rival, did not have a cricket association until 1885 and did not compete against the other States until 1893, when it played matches in South Australia and Victoria, losing to South Australia by 10 wickets and to Victoria by an innings and 243. In 1889 the association secured a 99-year lease over 28 acres of swampland which is now the site of the Western Australian Cricket Association ground.

CHAPTER 11

The Surrey pet

In New South Wales and Victoria, the interest raised by the visits of the English teams in 1862 and 1864 proved that money could be made out of the game and that it was worthwhile providing facilities for practising, playing and watching. The presence of professional coaches of the highest standard meant that the game could make real progress.

Billy Caffyn, known in England as 'the Surrey Pet', came to Australia with the 1862 team, returned in 1864, and stayed on as coach of the Melbourne Cricket Club. In his book *Seventy-one Not Out*, Caffyn said: 'The cricket out there during the ten years that had elapsed between the first visit of an English eleven and my leaving the country had made phenomenal improvement . . . It is a source of the greatest satisfaction to me to think that I have in some measure contributed to this successful state of things. I must, however, take this opportunity to speak of the good work done towards the development of Australian cricket by Charles Lawrence, who by his perseverance, energy and ability did a great deal towards the raising of the game to its present standard.'

Caffyn described his coaching methods and his thoughts on Australia and Australian cricketers in some detail: 'I did a good deal of bowling at the club members, and soon succeeded in improving the play of many of them. The system I worked on was never to try to make all bat alike. If a man was a hitter, I tried to make him hit with as great safety as possible; and if, on the other hand, another player was naturally a "stone-wall" batter, I encouraged him in this style of play. Of course I was careful not to induce either batsman to carry out his particular style of play

Billy Caffyn.

too far. After a time, at the suggestion of some of the members themselves, I would take the bat and give an exhibition of batting at the net. There were no side nets in those days, so we were obliged to have several fielders. I used to bat for an hour at a time with three bowlers at me, and found it very hard work under the intensely hot sun, especially when there was a hot wind blowing at the same time. A great crowd of people would stand and look on while I was batting, and they would cheer me lustily whenever I made a good hit. I never saw such painstaking cricketers as the Australians were in those days, and it was most interesting work teaching them when one could see the way they improved . . . Some of the younger players used, I could see, to try and copy my own style of batting to the letter, and I had to caution them against doing this in every particular. For instance, in playing back I never used to move my right foot, and all my pupils endeavoured to play back in the same way . . . I could soon perceive that some of them were able to be much more effective in their back play by stepping nearer the wicket in making the stroke; and whenever I found this to be the case I used to advise their adopting the custom . . . They were delightful pupils for one to have to teach, even as far back as the "sixties" — always willing to be shown a new stroke and quick to do their best to retrieve an error, never taking offence at having their faults pointed out, and never jealous of one another.'

Caffyn thought the bowlers at that time were 'undoubtedly in front of the batters. Even at that time there were some of them very tricky as regards pace and break, although most of them seemed not to have the confidence to attempt this "head work" when engaged in a match'.

His personal life was touched with sadness. 'I had been engaged to be married some time before I left England, and soon after I settled in Australia my wife who was to be came out to me there, and we were married at Melbourne. After I had been at Melbourne twelve months, I happened to hear of a good opening at Sydney for a hairdressing business, and believing that this might be the means of a livelihood for me after I should be past playing cricket, I induced the Melbourne Club to cancel my engagement with them in order that I might remove to Sydney. I felt leaving Melbourne very much indeed, as I had become to feel quite at home there, and had been so kindly treated by all with whom I had come in contact.

'I started business at my old trade of hairdressing in George Street, Sydney. This was the principal street of the city, and was nearly two miles long. My wife, like myself, had been brought up to the business, and was very clever at dressing ladies' hair, and between us we made a good deal of money. Unfortunately the climate of Australia never seemed to suit my wife, who was very delicate, and for a long period we never had the doctor out of the house.

'At Sydney I once more renewed my acquaintance with my old friend Charles Lawrence, who had now been engaged about three years with the Albert Club in that city, to whom he had been of invaluable assistance in improving the cricket. I became engaged with the Warwick at Sydney, at a less salary than I had been receiving at Melbourne, but a handsome one nevertheless. I coached the members of the Sydney Warwick Club in the same manner as I had taught the Melbourne players, giving an exhibition of batting at the net most days. Sometimes, however, we dispensed with the net and had the field set out as in a match, in order to improve the fielding of the members. This fact shows how keen the Australian cricketers of that day were to perfect themselves in every department of the game. The fielding of the

The leading players of the 1860s at the New South Wales v Victoria match in 1866. From left, standing: John Conway (organiser of the first tour to England), O'Mullane, Greaves, Rees, Fowler, Turner, Wilkie, Gibson, Tom Wills, Dave Gregory (Australia's first captain), Oliver, Charles Lawrence (Australia's first coach), Jones, Thompson, Curtis, Kellick, Hewitt, Martyn, the fast bowler Sam Cosstick and the coach Billy Caffyn. At front: Phillips and Kelly. State Library of NSW.

Australian team who visited England in 1878 was a matter of surprise and admiration to the English spectators, and I can assure my readers that their excellence in fielding had not been arrived at without a great deal of practice and perseverance.

'The best bat I ever saw or coached in Australia was undoubtedly Charles Bannerman, nor do I think his superior has yet appeared in that country. Messrs Spofforth and Murdoch — two mighty names indeed — came to the front after my time.

'I left Australia in May 1871. The cricket out there during the ten years that had elapsed between the first visit of an English eleven and my leaving the country had made phenomenal improvement, as was proved when a third team went out two years after my return to England. Four of my children were born in Australia — three boys and one girl. Two of the boys died there.'

CHAPTER 12

Grace under pressure

In 1873–74, 10 years after the tour by George Parr's team, the third England team, led by 'The Champion', W. G. Grace, toured Australia. From reports in *Bell's Life* and the *Australasian*, it seems negotiations for a third tour had been going on since 1866. A proposed tour in 1872 had been called off because Grace 'demanded' £1500 plus expenses. No doubt he was worth it. Australian cricketers were lucky to be able to see the man who was undoubtedly the best cricketer in the world and the most influential figure in the game's history.

Grace himself said of English cricket that the 1860s was its 'most criticial period'; action was taken to bring the laws of the game up-to-date; facilities at major grounds were improved; attention was paid to care of grounds and the preparation of pitches; over-arm bowling became the accepted style. Early in his career Grace bowled with a round-arm action, but when in 1864 over-arm was allowed under the Laws of Cricket, Grace changed his style. Cricket at that time became formalised and recognizable as the game we know today.

The impression we have of W. G. Grace is of a corpulent, heavily bearded old man, irascible and full of his own importance: 'They've come to see me bat, not you bowl,' he said to a youth who appealed for lbw against him. As with most public figures, the picture is probably a false one. As a young man he was described as 'tall, lean and loose-limbed, with a rather shy manner'. No doubt he was well aware of his place in the game, but those who knew him liked him and stressed his kindness and geniality. What we see now as sharp practice may have been partly the result of a quick and impish sense of humour.

In *They Made Cricket*, G. D. Martineau says 'Modern cricket, the infinite art, comprehensible to only a devoted minority, is really the work of "The Champion". If John Small "found out cricket" in the eighteenth century, W. G. Grace transformed it in the nineteenth. No other cricketer can do what he did; for it is no longer there to be done'. Grace was born in 1848 and made his first century in first-class cricket in 1866. In 1906, after he had scored 74 for the Gentlemen at the Oval, he came in and threw his bat on the table, saying, 'I shall not play any more'. In the intervening years he took 2876 first-class wickets and made 54,896 runs. As a batsman he had no 'pet stroke', but was master of them all. This, with his 'great coolness at the wickets', his consistency, his ability to avoid mistakes and his will to succeed were the secrets of an extraordinary career.

The English team of 1873–74, captained by Dr W. G. Grace. From left, standing: G. A. Bush, W. Oscroft, R. Humphries, J. Southerton, M. McIntyre, F. H. Boult, A. Greenwood, W. R. Gilbert. Seated: J. Lillywhite, W. G. Grace, H. Jupp, G. F. Grace. Melbourne Cricket Ground Museum.

The tour by Grace's team, which included his brother G. F. Grace and the fast bowler James Lillywhite, was organised by a syndicate of members from the Melbourne Cricket Club. For Dr Grace it was a honeymoon trip; his wife stayed with friends in the cities, while the doctor toured around the country with the team. They arrived on 13 December, after a voyage lasting 52 days, and played their first game against a Victorian Eighteen.

Victoria had three fast bowlers: Sam Cosstick, who came to Australia to look for gold and stayed to become curator and professional at the Melbourne Cricket Ground, bowled fast round-armers; Francis Allan, a tall left-hander, could swing the ball in the air and move it off the pitch; Harry Boyle concentrated on length and could move the ball away from the batsman off the pitch. Victoria made 266, (W. G. Grace 10 for 49) then dismissed Grace's men for 110 and 132. W. G. Grace was bowled by Boyle in the first innings and was 51 not out in the second.

Grace's team went next to Ballarat, where they again faced Allan and Cosstick. This time they fared rather better, making 440 in a drawn game, including 126 from W. G. Grace and 112 from his brother, despite temperatures of 'a hundred degrees in the shade'. According to his reminiscences, Grace had an unhappy time of it in the Australian bush. It must have seemed a far cry from his native Gloucestershire. The team's adventures in Ballarat and Stawell have already been described; their 'trap was smashed to atoms', Grace had to issue a warning about drinking during the game, and he described the match on a dust-heap at Stawell as 'a ludicrous farce'. The next game was at Warrnambool, 50 kilometres away, but rain turned the track into a quagmire and the journey took 19 hours, with the tourists drenched to the skin for most of the journey.

Then they went by boat to Melbourne and on to Sydney where they were beaten by Eighteen from NSW, 92 and 90 against 127 and 9 wickets for 57. The New South Wales team included Fred Spofforth and Dave Gregory. A match at Maitland was abandoned due to flooding, then their itinerary took them to Bathurst and back to Sydney where they had a good win against a Combined Fifteen from NSW and Victoria. This game was marred by an incident involving a NSW batsman who decided, after returning to the pavilion, that he was not out after all. He returned to the centre determined to continue his innings; Grace had to take his team off the field before the matter was sorted out. Back in Melbourne, after a couple of minor games they beat Fifteen of Victoria by seven wickets. After two games against Tasmania they set out in stormy weather for South Australia.

The South Australian Cricket Association had not been able

to agree terms with the Melbourne Cricket Club syndicate organising the tour. The syndicate was asking £800 for the fixture, but the association declined these terms, so the first match was held at Kadina, 150 kilometres north. After a rough sea passage and the coach trip to Kadina Grace wrote, 'We went out in search of the cricket ground; and a search it really proved. We came to an open space and asked to be directed to the cricket ground. "This is it," someone said, and we whistled in astonishment. There was scarcely a blade of grass to be seen, while the whole area was covered with small stones'. They won at Kadina and a game was organised at the last minute in Adelaide, Grace agreeing to play a three-day fixture for £110 and half the gate takings. 'This addition to the programme necessitated an all-night journey from Kadina which led to uncomfortable adventures. In the dark we lost the track and began driving about in the bush until at last, as we had taken several hours to cover 35 miles, we thought it wiser to wait until daylight before proceeding on our journey. We reached Adelaide in the afternoon stiff and tired, but the Twenty-two of South Australia did not take advantage of it as they lost their first eight wickets for ten runs and were out for 63.'

The English team won comfortably, although Grace failed; he was spectacularly caught on the boundary for three in the first innings—a catch which he disputed. George Giffen, 15 years old at the time, saw the match: 'The champion questioned whether he had been caught within the playing space, but the umpire decided against him. Verily there were hundreds among the spectators who, much as a victory for the 22 would have gratified them, wished that the umpire could have given his decision in W.G.'s favour . . . in the second innings the mighty batsman was bowled for 1, so that the spectators' cup of disappointment was filled to the brim . . . what struck me most forcibly about the play in that match was the pitiable helplessness of most of our batsmen against the tricky bowling of Southerton, who, in the first innings, captured 13 wickets for only 24 runs.'

Grace's team played 15 matches, won 10, lost three and had two draws. 'The Champion' topped the batting averages with 711 runs at 35.55 and James Lillywhite, who two years later brought out the team which played the first Test matches, topped the bowling with 172 wickets at an average of 2.29.

CHAPTER 13

Home-grown heroes

Due to the work of Lawrence and Caffyn, the foresight of the Melbourne Cricket Club and the Albert club in Sydney, and the example set by the various English touring teams, Australia by now had a number of very competent cricketers. Some were native-born, some were born in England. To a man, they represented the emerging middle class in Australia. Most of them started their working lives as office workers. Later, the Bannerman brothers gave their occupations as professional cricketers, and in fact most of them made their living from cricket during the next 10 years or so.

Charles and Alec Bannerman — New South Wales
Born in England in 1851, Charles Bannerman was a very correct right-handed bat. Billy Caffyn described him as 'the best bat I ever saw or coached in Australia'. Tom Garrett said, 'All his runs were made in front of the wicket. He never used the modern strokes of the late cut or the leg glance, but his drives were most powerful, and he was a fast scorer. In physique he was a pocket Hercules'. A dour, rather self-centred man, he was well aware of his stature in the game. After a mix up in running between the wickets during an Australia versus The Rest match, he found himself at the same end as his brother, Alec. 'You're better out than me,' he said and, stepping inside the crease, pushed his brother towards the other end. In 1877, Bannerman became the first batsman to take strike in a Test match. His 165 retired hurt in an Australian total of 245 won the game for Australia.

Banjo Patterson later said, 'There should be a statue to him on

Billy Murdoch, Fred Spofforth, Harry Boyle and Alec Bannerman.

Tom Horan, an Irishman, a cricketer and later a writer.

every cricket ground in Australia: but he never looked after his money and when the crowd had done with him I have seen him holding a bag for a kindly bookmaker at Randwick'. Drink and gambling got the better of Charles, it was said, but he lived past his 80th year. The New South Wales Cricket Association gave him a benefit match in 1922, which raised £490, and was the first game of cricket broadcast on radio in Australia.

His brother Alec (or Alick), born in Australia, probably in 1854, was known as 'Barndoor' Bannerman because of his stone-walling tactics, although George Giffen said, 'He was something more than a mere stonewaller, for when a really good opportunity occurred he could hit very hard'. Giffen wrote: 'He was always very keen and hard-working; in fact his keenness often developed into downright seriousness.' He took a dim view of a young player who 'to beguile the tedium of waiting between overs, sang snatches of music hall ditties. Alec stood it for a while, then marched up to our merry friend, and, with the sternness of a judge sentencing a murderer to death, made this speech, "Do you know, my friend, you are playing cricket? If you want to play cricket, play it; and if you want to sing, go and sing. But for Heaven's sake don't sing comic songs in the slips".'

Thomas Horan—Victoria

The first of a long line of Irishmen to make a major contribution to Australian cricket, Horan was born in County Cork in 1854 and came to Australia as a child. He was forthright, with a strong personality, solidly built and powerful, with heavy mutton-chop whiskers. 'Perhaps in the matter of mere style he would suffer by comparison with some artists of the willow, but his defence was wonderfully strong . . . he could clump the ball when he chose, and as a leg-hitter Australia has not had his equal,' George Giffen said. Horan's services to the game did not end with his playing days; 'As "Felix" he regularly contributes charming cricket chatter, full of life and vigour, to the *Australasian*, and one can safely say that Horan's writings are doing much to cultivate a true, genuine interest in our beloved game'. Horan wrote on cricket for the *Australasian* for many years after his playing days and his writing has been a valuable source of reference for the game's historians.

David and Ned Gregory—New South Wales

Born near Sydney in 1845, the son of a schoolteacher, David Gregory was one of 13 children. Seven were boys, five of whom played for New South Wales. Tall, upright and heavily bearded, and known as 'Handsome Dave', Gregory's presence and astuteness led to his election as captain of the first Australian Test team. His batting was orthodox and sound and he was a useful bowler, although his action was considered doubtful. During a match in 1872 his brother Ned was no-balled twice in succession and turned on the umpire demanding to know why: 'For throwing.' 'I never threw a ball in my life,' said Ned, 'you've mistaken me for my brother Dave.' 'I beg your pardon,' said the umpire.

Ned, who also played in the first Test, was a stylish batsman and a magnificent fielder. He became curator of the Sydney Cricket Ground, laid out the field, and designed and built the first comprehensive cricket scoreboard there. Ned's son Syd also played Test cricket and their brother Charles was the father of Jack Gregory, who played for Australia in the 1920s.

John Blackham—Victoria

Born in Melbourne in 1854, and trained as a bank clerk, Blackham was dark with a neat, full beard. He stood up to the stumps against all types of bowling, wearing only light leather gloves. George Giffen wrote of him: 'During the whole of his

The Gregory brothers, Charles, Dave and Ned. Dave Gregory was Australia's first captain. NSW Cricket Association.

John Blackham, Australia's wicket-keeper from 1877 to 1894.

first-class career he was peerless as a wicket-keeper. One could not help admiring him as he stood behind the stumps at a critical period of a game. With eyes keen as a hawk, and regardless of knocks, he would take the fastest bowling with marvellous dexterity, and woe betide the batsman who even so much as lifted the heel of his back foot as he played forward and missed the ball. I have seen him do some marvellous things.' An unorthodox batsman, he was not 'a reliable run-getter', but could be counted on in a crisis. 'How he could demoralise the bowling!' Giffen said. 'Let him get a start and it was difficult to place a field for his strokes.' He captained the Australian team in England in 1893 and for the first Test in 1894–95, but then had to retire because of a finger injury.

Harry Boyle — Victoria

A round-arm, medium-pace bowler and a competent batsman, Boyle was christened Henry Frederick, but was known as Harry or 'Boyley'. Born in New South Wales in 1847, he lived most of his life in Victoria. George Giffen said he was 'as fine a length bowler as one could wish to have on one's side, with a little work from the leg and sometimes a deceptive flight, and he could stand being hit, although it was seldom, so unerring was his length, that he had to submit to punishment'. Boyle was also a 'free hitting' batsman and has the distinction of creating a new fielding position; he was the first man to stand close in on the leg side, at silly mid-on. He specialised in that position; 'Throughout his English tours he stood there unflinchingly,' according to Giffen, 'notwithstanding repeated threats from E. M. Grace and others that he would be killed'. After his Test days were over, he managed the 1890 team which toured England.

Harry Boyle.

F. R. Spofforth, known as 'The Demon'.

Frederick Spofforth — New South Wales

Born in the Sydney suburb of Balmain in 1853, Spofforth spent part of his childhood in New Zealand. He was Australia's first great bowler and because of his feats on the cricket field he became one of Australia's early national heroes. As an 11-year-old, he saw George Parr's team play in Sydney, and was hugely impressed with the fast bowler George Tarrant. 'At once my great ambition was to bowl fast like Tarrant,' Spofforth wrote 'who, I well remember, always sent the stumps flying whenever he bowled batsmen out.' Spofforth varied his pace according to the pitch and conditions. He could move the ball both ways off the pitch and was a master of the variations of length and flight and of the psychological ploys of cricket; the packed field, the scornful air, the dark look. Not for nothing was he known as 'The Demon'.

Giffen rated Boyle a better bowler on a batsmen's wicket, but where the pitch gave any help, he said that Spofforth could be unplayable. Spofforth was a bank clerk in his younger days, and after he retired from big cricket he lived in England, where he was a director of the Star Tea Company. When he died in 1926 he left an estate valued at £164,000, several million dollars at today's values.

William Murdoch — New South Wales

Billy Murdoch was born at Sandhurst in Victoria in 1843 but later lived in Sydney, where his brother Gilbert was Mayor of Balmain. Billy lived in Balmain and played for Sydney University as a batsman and wicket-keeper. Thick-set with, later in life, a well-fed look, an open face and a full moustache, Murdoch was intelligent and charming, with a whimsical sense of humour. The English Test player and scholar C. B. Fry said: 'Murdoch does not commit puns, of course, nor sputter epigrams: he is simply, genuinely, and unaffectedly amusing. It's the way, not the words.'

Caffyn wrote of Billy Murdoch: 'For neatness of style combined with sound correct cricket, Australia never produced a batsman to equal him.' Giffen wrote of his 'courage in trying circumstances. No matter how tight the hole we were in, Billy, with a smile of assurance and a cheering word, would go in himself and often master the bowling with his splendid defence'. Murdoch retired from Australian cricket for a period after 1885, and played in England, where he captained Sussex, played for the Gentlemen of England eight times and kept wicket for England in a Test in South Africa in 1891–92. He also became a firm friend of W. G. Grace. Murdoch returned to captain Australia in the 1890 series in England.

CHAPTER 14

England versus Australia

When James Lillywhite's team, made up entirely of professionals, arrived in Australia in December 1876, there was no thought of playing a Test match; there was no such thing as Test cricket. As often happens, the name came after the event. The itinerary consisted of State and regional matches, with no scheduled fixtures against a Combined XI. But when the tourists were beaten by Fifteens from New South Wales and Victoria, the locals began to think they could match the English side man-for-man. The Victorian Cricket Association, which promoted the tour, agreed, no doubt with an eye to the crowds such games would bring in.

The games were promoted as 'All England versus All Australia', which was not altogether true. The Australian team was selected from Victoria and New South Wales only and some of their best men did not play. Edwin Evans, a very good all-rounder, was unavailable. Spofforth, who had played all his first-class cricket with Murdoch behind the stumps, would not play because Murdoch had not been selected. Spofforth apparently believed that no other 'keeper was up to the task, but the selectors, who had picked John Blackham, could not be swayed and Spofforth dropped out. Francis Allan, the left-handed medium-pacer from Warrnambool, sent a telegram at the last minute saying he could not spare the time; the Warrnambool Fair was on, Allan said, and he wanted to meet his friends there. Melbourne *Punch* reckoned Allan was scared: 'And when the day came and everybody was expecting the great bowler to come and bowl like winking, behold, he never came.

And all that could be heard of that great bowler on that great day was a telegram and a beautiful white feather.'

England, without any of their amateurs, were of course not representative, and they were rather disadvantaged as they had arrived back in Melbourne from the New Zealand leg of their tour the previous day; some were still recovering from a rough voyage. They were without Pooley, their wicket-keeper, who had been detained by the police in New Zealand, charged with assault, of which he was later acquitted.

James Lillywhite bowling at the Melbourne Cricket Ground, probably during the match against Fifteen of Victoria during the 1876–77 season. **Illustrated Australian News.**

The game began at one o'clock on Thursday 15 March 1877 on a fine, sunny day before a crowd of 1000, which built up to about 3000 during the afternoon. David Gregory won the toss and Charles Bannerman and Nat Thompson opened the batting, facing the bowling of Alfred Shaw. At the close of play on the first day Bannerman was still there with 126 to his credit. Australia was 6 wickets down for 166. Bannerman went on to make 165, retired hurt with a split hand, in an Australian total of 245. England replied with 196, spin bowler William Midwinter taking 5 for 78 from 54 four-ball overs. By the Saturday, when Australia's second innings began, the crowd was more than 10,000. Bannerman was bowled for 4 in the second innings and Australia was bundled out for only 104, Horan top-score with 20; England needed 154 to win.

The slow left-hand bowler Thomas Kendall had the English-men in trouble from the start. He had both openers out early; Hill caught before a run had been scored, Greenwood when the score was 7. Further wickets fell at 20 and 22. Ulyett and Selby took the score to 62, but when Kendall bowled Ulyett, the English side collapsed. They were all out for 108, Kendall 7 wickets for 55 from 33.1 overs. Collections taken up from the crowd for Bannerman and Kendall brought in £87 and £23 respectively.

The match now known as the second Test was played over four days, again in Melbourne, beginning a couple of weeks later on 31 March. Murdoch was picked this time and Spofforth played, although Blackham kept wicket; his only dismissal during the match was a stumping off Spofforth. Batting first, Australia made 122 and England replied with 261. Australia had a chance to win after making 259 (Dave Gregory 43) in the second innings and when the first three English wickets had been lost with only nine runs scored, an Australian win seemed likely. But George Ulyett, who top-scored in the first innings with 52, won the game for England, hammering the Australian bowlers all over the paddock. He was out for 63 when England needed only a few runs to win. The margin was four wickets.

Games between representative English and Australian teams soon came to be called 'Test matches'. But it was not until 1894, when the cricket historian Charles Moody classified all the representative matches to that date and suggested the games which were worthy of the title, that these two games became generally recognised as the first Tests.

CHAPTER 15

A useless and
presumptuous adventure

John Conway was born at Fyansford in Victoria in 1842 and
learnt to play cricket at school in Melbourne. An all-rounder, in
1862 he took 4 wickets for 60 against H. H. Stephenson's touring
team. Conway captained the South Melbourne club for many
years, was active in the game's administration and is credited
with discovering the talents of Tom Horan and John Blackham.
In later years he wrote cricket columns for newspapers in both
Sydney and Melbourne.

Conway was an adviser to James Lillywhite during the
professional tour of 1876–77. It may be overstating his role to
say that he conceived the idea of sending the first representative
team to England—that idea must have been in many minds
after the Australian XI's victory over the English professional
side—but it was Conway who organised the tour.

There was little public enthusiasm for the tour and no support
from the NSW and Victorian Cricket Associations. It was
thought that the best of Australia was not yet ready to meet the
Englishmen on their own ground and the tour was described in
some quarters as 'a useless and presumptuous adventure'.
Those who were prepared to back the idea were those who knew
the game: James Lillywhite, Charles Lawrence, who had led the
Aboriginal team to England in 1868, and his friend Tom Wills.
The players of the day were keen to go and a company was
formed to finance the venture. Each of the players put in £50
and profits were shared between stockholders according to their
investment. Alec Bannerman, noted for his caution, was the
only player to receive a fixed fee for the tour.

The team gathered in Sydney on 3 November 1877 for a

preliminary fund-raising tour of Queensland, New South Wales, Victoria and New Zealand. Conway was manager, Dave Gregory captain and the rest of the team—Blackham, Horan, George Bailey from Tasmania, Alec and Charles Bannerman, Murdoch, Spofforth, Francis Allan, Garrett and Boyle—were close to the strongest combination Australia could muster. William Midwinter joined the team in England. They sailed on the *City of Sydney* on 29 March 1878; the first stop was San Francisco, then overland to New York and then on the *City of Berlin* to Liverpool, where they arrived on 13 May.

The Australian team in England, 1878. From left, standing: F. R. Spofforth, J. Conway (manager), F. E. Allan. Seated, centre: G. H. Bailey, T. Horan, T. W. Garrett, D. W. Gregory, A. C. Bannerman, H. F. Boyle. In front: C. Bannerman, W. L. Murdoch, J. M. Blackham. MCC.

Photographs of the team show them in whites, with stovepipe trousers, probably of flannel, but possibly of duck or moleskin. The wearing of ties on the field had apparently gone out of fashion, although some wore scarves tied at the throat. Others had shirts buttoned at the neck and sleeves buttoned at the wrist. The team's blazer was white with a narrow blue stripe. Cricket hats were odd-shaped affairs, like cut down sailors' hats, in the same colours as the blazer. Caps, when worn, also sat high on the head and had a narrow visor which would have done nothing to reduce the glare. Boots were heavy and dark, with sprigs; a photograph of the 1876–77 England team shows the wicket-keeper, J. Selby, seated at the front, with more than 20 sprigs embedded in his boots; an artist from the *Illustrated Australian News* drew Spofforth bowling at the Melbourne Cricket Ground in 1879, with three sprigs in the heels and three more in the soles of his boots. White boots came into fashion during the 1880s.

Spofforth wrote: 'No one but the very best cricketers owned pads or even bats . . . the team had an immense canvas bag with "Australian Eleven" in bold letters across it. We used to draw lots to decide who would look after it from match to match . . . the "Caravan", we called it . . . we carried it to England, and landed it safely at Nottingham, but in London it was lost, and no man knows its burying-place.'

They lost the first game of the tour, played at Nottingham in bad weather, by an innings. In the next game, against the MCC at Lord's, they played against some of the best cricketers in England. The Australians were not highly regarded; only a few hundred people saw the start of play. Spofforth wrote of the match: 'This has not been counted as a Test match, but it really was; for in those days cricket was almost solely managed by the Marylebone Club, and they had the call of any cricketer they wanted. It was a fine eleven, and when we arrived at Lord's, fresh from our first defeat at Nottingham, we were not very confident. Dr W. G. Grace and Mr A. N. Hornby started the batting, and our bowlers were Messrs Boyle and Allan. Now, although the latter got Grace caught at short leg, off a shocking bad stroke, he was changed and I was deputed to bowl. The fun then commenced, and the strong MCC team were out for 33 runs, I myself taking six wickets for 4 runs, and Boyle three for 14 runs. But more was to happen. Australia only made 41. MCC commenced again with "W.G." and A. N. Hornby. I began the bowling to "W.G.", and Mr Murdoch, behind the wickets, missed him off my first ball, much to my sorrow; but the next ball knocked his leg bail thirty yards, and I screamed out "Bowled".

'My third ball clean bowled A. J. Webbe, Boyle quickly disposed of C. Booth and A. W. Ridley, and A. N. Hornby had the misfortune to be "cut over" and had to retire. Mr Boyle then bowled Wild and Flowers, and G. G. Hearne and Mr Vernon fell to me. A. N. Hornby then resumed, but could only just stand, and Boyle bowled him. Boyle's analysis read six for 3 runs, and mine four for 16, total 19. We had 12 runs to get, and lost C. Bannerman in getting them. Thus four innings, including luncheon and intervals, occupied only five and a half hours. The news spread like wildfire, and created a sensation in London and throughout England, and our hotel was almost besieged.'

The *Home News* said of the Australians: 'Their fielding is the admiration of all. Left-handed Mr Allan is known as the "Bowler of a Century", Mr Boyle is described as the "Very Devil", but Mr Spofforth as the "Demon Bowler" carries off the palm. His delivery is quite appalling, the balls thunder in like cannon shot, and yet he has the guile, when seemingly about to bowl his fastest, to drop a slow which is generally fatal to the batsman.'

The success of the tour was assured. The next game against Yorkshire resulted in an easy victory for the tourists. Against Surrey, 30,000 came over the two days and the crowd broke down fences in the crush and spilled onto the field. There were setbacks, including a running battle with W. G. Grace, which came to a head over Midwinter playing with the Australians while he was under contract to Gloucestershire, Grace's county. Conway had previously objected to Grace receiving a fee of £60 for playing in an Amateur and Gentlemen team. Grace apparently decided to square the matter by holding Midwinter to his contract. He appeared at the Australians' fixture against Middlesex and persuaded Midwinter that he was obliged to turn out for Gloucestershire at the Oval against Surrey. Midwinter left immediately and did not play for the Australians again. Grace then engaged in a heated discussion and an exchange of bad language with the Australians. He left them with the remark: 'You haven't a ghost of a chance with Middlesex.'

He later apologised to Boyle and Gregory, but not to Conway, which did not suit the Australians, who 'resolved not to play at Gloucester'.

Altogether, the Australians played 41 games, including 17 first-class matches and a few games in Canada and the United States on the way home. They won 19, including the games against Middlesex by 98 runs and against Gloucestershire by 10 wickets, in front of a huge crowd. They lost seven and 15 were drawn. Financially, the tour was extremely successful; stockholders received a return of £750 for their £50 investment.

The English perspective was rather different: there were rumblings in English cricket circles about the sportsmanship of the Australians and resentment at their complaints about English umpires.

CHAPTER 16

Lords and larrikins

The legend of the Australian bushranger was born in the 1850s, when the 'new chums' headed for the goldfields were easy prey for the outcasts of society, most of whom were escaped convicts. By the 1870s a new breed of bushranger had emerged from the thousands of settlers who could not make a go of it on their tiny selections in a hard and alien country. They were hounded by the police, who were generally thought to be inefficient and unnecessarily brutal. There was a good deal of public sympathy for the likes of Ned Kelly and his gang, who shot and killed three policemen at Stringybark Creek on 26 October 1878, and went on a spree of bank robberies which Kelly justified on the grounds that he 'never harmed a woman nor robbed a poor man', and similar Robin Hood rhetoric. They robbed the National Bank at Benalla in December 1878 and struck again at Jerilderie on Saturday 8 February 1879. In June 1880 the police trapped the gang in the hotel at Glenrowan and set fire to the hotel, killing Dan Kelly, Stephen Hart and Joseph Byrne. Ned Kelly emerged in his homemade armour, shot it out with the police and survived to be hanged on 11 November 1880.

In the towns, the tougher element of the native-born Australians was seen by the British as 'fond of Cavendish, cricket, chuckpenny, and systematically insolent to servant girls, policemen and new chums . . . He can fight like an Irishman or a Bashi-Bazook; otherwise he is orientally indolent, and will swear with a quiet gusto if you push against him in the street, or request him politely to move on'. (Cavendish was a brand of tobacco; chuckpenny, presumably, was later known as 'two-up', and Bashi-Bazooks were Turkish mercenary soldiers.)

Like the bushrangers, the larrikins, in their bell-bottom trousers and fancy boots, were feared for the violence they threatened, and admired for their belligerence in the face of authority. To the native-born Australian, Jack was as good as his master.

Soon after the 1878 team arrived home from England, the fifth English team, led by Lord Harris, arrived in Australia. In February 1879 another incident damaged the reputation of Australian cricket. Lord Harris, who was asked by the Melbourne Cricket Club to bring out a team of amateurs, had a strong side, the only professionals being the bowlers George Ulyett and Tom Emmett. They lost the only Test of the series by 10 wickets, due mainly to the bowling of Spofforth, who took 13 wickets in the match, including the first hat-trick in Tests. But they had a number of good wins to their credit when they came to play New South Wales at the association ground, now called the Sydney Cricket Ground, on Friday 7 February 1879.

Lord Harris's team batted first, scoring 267 after an opening stand of 125 by Hornby and Lucas. For once, the bowling of Spofforth was mastered. By mid-afternoon on the second day, a Saturday (the same day as Ned Kelly and his gang robbed the bank in Jerilderie), New South Wales were all out for 177,

Spofforth bowling to C. A. Absolom at the Melbourne Cricket Ground during the Test against Lord Harris's XI in January 1879. Illustrated Australian News.

Murdoch having batted through the innings for 82 not out. New South Wales then had to follow on and when the score was 18 Murdoch was given out — run out — by George Coulthard, a Victorian player who was accompanying the English team as umpire.

Betting on cricket matches was common in those days and New South Wales had been heavily backed early in the match. When Murdoch was given out there was a loud demonstration from a section of the crowd. The *Sydney Morning Herald* said the 'hooting and groaning proceeded first of all from about a dozen persons in the pavilion, some of whom were known to be pecuniarily interested in the result of the match. One well-known betting man himself acted as fugelman, and the crowd outside, encouraged by this bad example, worked themselves into a state of violent excitement, and presently broke through all bounds of decency and fair play'.

With the crowd in uproar, no batsman came out to replace Murdoch. Lord Harris left the ground to find out what was going on, and was met by Dave Gregory, the New South Wales captain, who told him that he was going to lodge an objection to Coulthard's umpiring. Lord Harris, in a letter published some weeks later in the London *Daily Telegraph*, said: 'I asked Gregory on what grounds the objection was raised and he at first said general incompetence, but afterwards admitted that the objection was raised on account of the decision in Murdoch's case. I implored Gregory as a friend, and for the sake of the New South Wales Cricket Association, which I warned him would be the sufferer by it, not to raise the objection, but he refused to take my view of the case.

'Looking back, I found that the ground had been rushed by the mob and our team had been surrounded. I at once returned to the wickets, and in defending Coulthard from being attacked, was struck by some larrikin with a stick. Hornby immediately seized this fellow and in taking him to the pavilion was struck in the face by a would-be deliverer of the larrikin, and had his shirt nearly torn off his back. He however conveyed his prisoner to the pavilion in triumph. For some thirty minutes or more I was surrounded by a howling mob, resisting the entreaties of partisans and friends to return to the pavilion until the field was cleared.'

According to Lord Harris's account, when the ground was finally cleared, Gregory still insisted that Coulthard be replaced, and when Lord Harris would not agree to this, Gregory said, 'Then the game is at an end'. The other umpire was Edmund Barton, who was active in New South Wales cricket and its administration and was later to become the first Prime Minister of Australia. Lord Harris asked Barton whether he could claim the match, and Barton said, 'I will give it to you in two minutes if the batsmen don't return'. Barton told Gregory of his decision, but before the batsmen appeared, the crowd invaded the ground again. A third invasion lasted until stumps. The match continued on the following day, but rain had fallen and New South Wales made only 49 in their second innings.

Was Murdoch out? Edmund Barton said he 'could see no trace of unfairness in the decision given by Coulthard'. On the other hand it is on record that Coulthard made mistakes; on the day before the riot he had turned down an appeal for caught behind against Lord Harris, a decision which the *Sydney Morning Herald* said was 'admittedly a mistake'. All umpires make mistakes, of course, but this would certainly have been fresh in the crowd's mind.

There seems no doubt that the crowd behaved appallingly and that the Englishmen had every reason to feel outraged, but it was said that members of Lord Harris's side did little to help matters and further inflamed the crowd by referring to them as 'sons of convicts'. A. N. Hornby may have been justified in seizing the person who hit Lord Harris with a stick, but this too would have incited the crowd. The controversy was renewed by Lord Harris's letter, written in Sydney a couple of days after the riot but not published in the London *Daily Telegraph* until 1 April and later printed in the Australian papers. He acknowledged that the members of the New South Wales Cricket Association 'did everything in their power to quell the disturbance', but he did not mention that the president and members of the association had made a point of expressing their sorrow and regret at the behaviour of the crowd. 'The disgraceful part of the business,' he said, 'is that other members of the Association, one a member of the Legislative Assembly, aided and abetted the bookmakers in their cry.'

The association certainly resented Lord Harris's inference. They wrote in reply to the *Daily Telegraph*: 'Certainly the conduct of Lord Harris did not tend to calm the general excitement. His Lordship elbowed his way out through the crowd in a manner so violent as to invite assault . . . Mr Hornby dragged a supposed offender of very diminutive stature through the mass of the pavilion, a hundred yards away, in triumph, with only a torn shirt as the penalty of his heroism.'

The association pressed charges against the men who had disrupted the game. Richard Driver appeared for the prosecution in court, where two men were charged with 'having participated in the disorder'. The *Sydney Morning Herald* reported that both 'expressed deep regret for what had occurred, and pleaded guilty' and 'the Bench fined them 40 shillings, and to pay 21 shillings professional costs and 5 shillings costs of the court'. Mr Driver told the court that 'the inmates of the Pavilion who had initiated the disturbance, including a well-known bookmaker of Victoria who was at the time ejected, had had their fees of membership returned to them, and they would never again be admitted to the ground'.

A second Test was cancelled because of the incident. Although Lord Harris's team finished the tour with a number of more pleasant matches in Victoria and were given a friendly farewell dinner by the Melbourne Cricket Club, the incident did nothing to help Australian cricket's damaged reputation in England.

CHAPTER 17

A national institution

The 1880 tour to England got off to an uncertain start. The tour was backed by the cricket associations, but up to the time the team arrived in England on 13 May, they had not been able to arrange any games in London. They had been told that they could not play the MCC because 'the list was full'.

The team was led by Murdoch and was similar in strength to the previous touring side. Charles Bannerman was unavailable through illness and the strength of the team was based around Murdoch, Alec Bannerman, Blackham, Spofforth and Boyle. Newcomers included Percy McDonnell, a Greek scholar and a right-handed batsman of great character, who was at his best on different wickets; George Bonnor, 6 foot 6 inches (198 cm) and 16 stone (101 kg), a big man and a big hitter; and George Palmer, who was married to Jack Blackham's sister. Palmer was an accurate medium-pace bowler and developed into a batsman of Test standard. They had some good wins in the North and the Midlands and an enjoyable trip to Ireland, but as they could not organise a fixture against a representative side they had actually started to advertise for matches when the Surrey club, through its secretary C. W. Alcock, came to their aid. With the help of two former adversaries, Lord Harris and Dr W. G. Grace, Alcock organised the game at the Oval which was to become the first Test played in England.

Australia was without Spofforth, who had broken a finger in a match at Scarborough. Although the English XI was not the strongest possible combination, it was a good side, with three Graces, W. G., E. M. and G. F., Lord Harris as captain, A. P. Lucas, W. Barnes, Frank Penn, A. G. Steel, the Honorable

Billy Murdoch, Australian captain from 1880 to 1884. A courageous and correct batsman, with a sound defence and a ready humour.

Alec Bannerman, who played 28 Tests between 1879 and 1893, mostly as an opening batsman.

Alfred Lyttelton, Alfred Shaw and F. Morley. The match seemed as good as lost when England batted first and made 420, W. G. Grace 152. Australia replied with only 149, and were 3 wickets for 14 when McDonnell joined Murdoch, who had made a duck in the first innings. This pair put on 83 before McDonnell was lbw to W. G. Grace, then Blackham and Bonnor helped Murdoch take the score to 170 for 6 at stumps on the second day, still 101 runs behind. The crowd on the first day was 21,000 and 20,000 came on the second day.

On the third day George Alexander, the tour manager and William Moule, playing in Spofforth's place, made 33 and 34 respectively while Murdoch carried his bat for 153 in a total of 327. This left the English team with 57 to win. Lord Harris changed the batting order. Boyle and Palmer soon had England on the run; G. F. Grace scored his second duck of the match, Lucas was caught by Blackham off Palmer for 2, Lyttelton was bowled by Palmer for 13, Boyle had Barnes caught by Moule for 5 and Palmer bowled G. F. Grace second ball for 0. At 5 wickets for 31 Australia, for the first time in the match, seemed to have a chance. But England's hero was still to come. 'The Champion', at the prime of his career, strode to the wicket. Australia's ace was missing; how Murdoch must have longed for the fire of 'the Demon' and cursed the ball from Ulyett which broke Spofforth's finger at Scarborough. Grace and Frank Penn saw England through to a five-wicket victory.

In 1881–82 Alfred Shaw, James Lillywhite and Arthur Shrewsbury organised a tour by a team of professionals, the first of three tours organised by this trio. Although, without W. G. Grace, they were certainly not the strongest team which England could muster, they played four games judged as representative; two against All-Australia and two against the Australian team picked to tour England in 1882. Shrewsbury was regarded as England's master professional, a batsman for all occasions; 'Give me Arthur,' W. G. Grace used to say whenever he was asked to name the great players. Another member of the touring side was William Midwinter, who had played for Australia in the first two Test matches and whom Grace had filched from the Australians during the 1878 tour. Newcomers in the Australian team included Hugh Massie, a hard-hitting right-handed batsman, and the Adelaide-born all-rounder George Giffen.

The first Test was drawn, the second and third, both played in Sydney, were won by Australia by five wickets and six wickets and the fourth was cut short by rain. Again, the tour was a financial success.

George Giffen played the first of his 31 Tests for Australia that summer. In his book *With Bat and Ball*, Giffen says he 'almost feared to ask for the necessary leave, but this was readily granted to me . . . Australian employers, Government and private alike, have been very good in allowing players leave of absence to participate in important cricket matches. Many of them are keen supporters of the game, and consider such applications in the light of patriotism; in fact, some public servants who once complained of the frequent absence of a prominent Victorian player, Harry Trott, were informed by the head of the Department that "Trott is a national institution"'.

Giffen took half an hour to make his first run in Tests, finished with 30, and went on to be picked for the 1882 tour. *With Bat and Ball* deals with the cricket, and also with the voyage and the events and characters of the tour; with 'Alec Bannerman and Tom Horan, who, professing vegetarian principles, sought to satisfy their appetites with apples'; with a shipboard concert where Billy Murdoch, having quickly used up his scripted jokes, was able to keep the company amused off-the-cuff; with George Bonnor, who 'on the day we landed in England, won 100 sovereigns from two or three of the passengers. It came about in this wise. In the course of conversation at our table Bonnor remarked that he could throw a cricket ball a distance of 120 yards. Some one doubted whether he could pitch it 115 yards. He offered to do so in one throw after landing, and a wager of 100 sovereigns was made about it'.

Even the members of the team doubted that Bonnor would win his bet after several weeks at sea. 'Bonnor, however, who was nothing if not confident in his own ability, was not to be baulked of his prize; and, after landing at Plymouth, with his first try threw 119 yards and some odd inches.' Bonnor could hit a lot further than he could throw, but if he heard himself referred to as 'nothing but a slogger', he would try to play 'the barndoor game', to the great frustration of the rest of the team, who knew that if he chose, and got going, he could pulverise the bowling and disorganise the field.

As in 1880, only one Test was played in England in 1882, but it was one of the greatest and certainly one of the most famous matches in the game's history. The Australians had started the tour well. They defeated Oxford University by 9 wickets, due to Massie's 206 in three hours. They scored 643 against Sussex, where Murdoch made 286 not out, Palmer took a hat-trick, and they won by an innings and 355 runs. They lost to Cambridge but then had a sequence of good wins leading up to the Test, which was played at the Oval against the best team in England.

The Australians' chances of winning were reduced when Palmer could not play. His replacement, 19-year-old Sam Jones, was mainly a batsman. It was bowlers Australia needed against England's great batting strength; A. N. Hornby, who had been one of the best bats in England for many years, batted at number 10 in the first innings. C. T. Studd, who had made a century against the Australians at Cambridge, was number 10 in the second innings.

Spofforth regarded it as the most exciting game he played in: 'Mr Murdoch won the toss, and sent in H. H. Massie and A. C. Bannerman, but we made a sorry show, being all out for 63, and were most disappointed. I might speak for myself, and say I was disgusted and thought we should have made at least 250; but when England went in they did very little better, only making 101. Australia's second innings started well enough, Massie and A. C. Bannerman putting on 66 before the former was bowled by A. G. Steel for 55. On returning to the pavilion Massie, disappointed, told me he was very sick, because he had no right to hit at the ball; but he said Steel was commencing to bowl well, and he thought another four would cause him to be taken off.

'The second wicket fell at 70, and with the exception of our captain, run out 29, no one did anything, and we were all out for 122, leaving England 85 to win.

'An unfortunate incident occurred in this match, namely, the running out of S. P. Jones, but so much has been written on the event that I merely mention it' (Jones was run out by W. G. Grace after he left his crease to repair some damage on the pitch) 'anyway it seemed to put fire into the Australians, and I do not suppose a team ever worked harder to win. W. G. Grace and A. N. Hornby commenced England's second innings. I bowled Hornby at 15, and Barlow at the same total, but then W. G. Grace, who had been missed by A. C. Bannerman, fielding very close in at silly mid-on, and Ulyett made a stand, and reached 51 before another wicket fell, Ulyett being caught at the wicket by Blackham. I had before asked Murdoch to let me change ends, as I was having no luck, and Boyle then got "W.G." caught by Bannerman.

'Then came the most exciting cricket I ever witnessed. Four wickets were down, and only 32 runs were required; but I must confess I never thought they would be got. A. Lyttelton and A. P. Lucas then came together, and at one time Boyle bowled no less than nine overs for one run, and I ten overs for two runs. Then we agreed to let Lyttelton get a run, so as to change ends. Bannerman was to allow one to pass at mid-off, which he did, and Lyttleton faced me, when I bowled him. This was the real turning-point, as Lucas, getting opposite me again, turned the first ball onto his wicket, and six wickets were down for 63, and we all felt we were on top.

'With seven more runs added I bowled M. Read, and Boyle got Barnes caught. A. G. Steel then came in. I pitched a ball about four inches outside his off stump, he started to play forward to it, before he had touched the ball I was off in the direction of silly mid-on, and Steel quietly played the ball right into my hands. C. T. Studd and Peate then came together, and Boyle bowled Peate for two, and Australia had won by 7 runs.'

Giffen wrote: 'That great crowd was like a man stunned. But they soon forgot their sorrow to applaud us, and we had cheer after cheer from those healthy British lungs. A small coterie of Australians, who sat in the pavilion, were wild with joy; and I remember Mrs Beal, the mother of our manager, running down the steps, and I being the first who came along, although I had contributed as little as anybody toward the victory, found her arms around my neck, and a motherly kiss implanted upon my brow.'

Punch congratulated the Australians with a poem:

> *'Well done, Cornstalks! Whipt us*
> *Fair and square,*
> *Was it luck that tripped us?*
> *Was it scare?*
> *Kangaroo Land's "Demon", or our own*
> *Want of "devil", coolness, nerve, backbone?'*

It was after this match that the London *Sporting Times* published the famous In Memoriam notice: 'In Affectionate Remembrance of English Cricket' closing with the line, 'The Body will be cremated and the Ashes taken to Australia'. In fact there were no Ashes at that time. They came into being during England's 1882–83 tour in Australia; after England had won the third Test, which put them 2–1 up in the series, a group of Melbourne women, friends of the English players, burnt a ball, sealed the ashes in an urn and made a velvet bag to keep the urn in. This was given to Ivo Bligh, the English captain, who bequeathed the Ashes to Lord's when he died in 1927.

After the win in 1882, the first win against the best of England's players, the Australian team, and especially Spofforth, became national heroes. When the team arrived back in Melbourne they were given a torchlight procession through the city. Crowds packed the footpaths, windows, even the roofs, as five bands and 300 firemen with flares accompanied them down to the Melbourne Cricket Ground where the Electric Light Company gave a special display, the bands played 'See the Conquering Hero Comes' and each player was presented with a gold medal. Fireworks spelt out 'Welcome Home', 'Success to Cricket', and finally, at 10 o'clock, 'Good Night'. Cricket was established as Australia's most popular sport, both for players and spectators.

The Australians in England in 1882. From left, standing: Tom Garrett, George Bonnor, Harry Boyle, Hugh Massie, George Palmer, C. W. Beal (manager), John Blackham. Sitting: George Giffen, Fred Spofforth, Tom Horan, Percy McDonnell, Billy Murdoch, Alec Bannerman.

Extraordinary claims have been made for the game, not least by the English. Bill Mandle, in an article for the Australian Historical Society titled 'Cricket and Australian Nationalism', said: 'Some examples of the English variety of chauvinism may serve to demonstrate the weight placed upon cricket as an indicator of national strength and moral worth. The *Quarterly Review* of October 1857 favourably compared the games-playing English public schoolboy with "the pale-faced student of Germany or the over-taught pupil of French polytechnique". The Englishman had nothing to fear from them, games had given him "pluck, blood and bottom".' In the 1870s Charles Box wrote: 'The effete inhabitants of cloudless Italy, Spain and Portugal would sooner face a solid square of British infantry than an approaching ball from the sinewy arm of a first class bowler'. During the First World War E. W. Hornung extended the genre in verse:

'Cricket! 'Tis Sanskrit to the super-Hun . . .
Playing a game's beyond him and his hordes
Theirs but to play the snake or wolf or vulture;
Better one sporting lesson learnt at Lord's than all their Kultur.'

As Bill Mandle said, 'Australian writing on cricket never went to such lengths, but Australians undoubtedly shared in a culture that was ready to see in sport, and especially in cricket, wide-ranging implications'. Cricket was especially important because it was played against England, 'and there was for many always a feeling that Australians were in Australia either because they were not wanted in England, or could not make a success of life there'. Another source of anxiety was 'whether Anglo-Saxon qualities had deteriorated in such a hot land south of the equator'. It seems laughable now, but there was a feeling that Australians might 'revert to the aboriginal type' in the southern climate; the *Australasian* of 14 October 1871, noting the incidence of short people on the streets of Melbourne, said: 'So far as present appearance can be trusted, the Anglo-Australians in this colony promise to be as stunted in their growth as the former possessors of the soil'.

Victory against England showed that 'convict origins did not necessarily prove morally disadvantageous'. It provided 'an emphatic refutation of the theory that there is a tendency to decay among the descendants of the early colonists'. It proved, said the *Sydney Morning Herald* on 24 January 1874, that British blood has not yet been thinned by Australian summers'. This line of reasoning had its critics: James F. Hogan asserted that Australians had an 'inordinate love of field-sports' and decried a society where sportsmen 'are to be cheered and lauded . . . whilst men of brains . . . are to be treated with cold neglect'. But, as Bill Mandle says, 'There is a case for arguing that Australian nationalism and self-confidence was first and most clearly manifested in the late 1870s because of the feats of its sportsmen and particularly of its cricketers'. Towards the end of the century an article in the *Bulletin* claimed that 'this ruthless rout of English cricket will do — and has done — more to enhance the cause of Australian nationality than could ever be achieved by miles of erudite essays and impassioned appeal'.

CHAPTER 18

Down, but not out

To gloss over the years from 1882 to 1900 is not to say they were not interesting years for cricket in Australia, nor to belittle the many great players of that era. But by 1882 the game had established its place in the Australian sporting calendar and in the hearts of the Australian people. A pattern had been set of visits to and from England which, from the 1880s until 1977, was interrupted only by the two world wars. The game's initial development was complete.

Cricket has changed since then; the wrong 'un had not been developed at that time; fast bowling has become faster and more consistent as batting has become more scientific and fieldsmen more mobile and uninhibited. In all the sports where performance can be measured, standards have improved, and I have no doubt that, with the intensity and professionalism of the game today, the same applies to cricket. Test players last century stayed in the game until they were much older, commonly into their forties and sometimes into their fifties. Playing top sport at that age is virtually impossible by today's standards of fitness. But conventions and skills had been established 100 years ago which would make the cricket of the 1880s quite recognisable today. While the best players of the 1850s would have been completely out of their depth in modern cricket, the best players of the 1880s, Spofforth, say, or Murdoch, Turner, and Blackham, could turn up at a first-class game today and hold their own, or better.

The 1882–83 series in Australia, during which the actual Ashes were presented, was squared two Tests each. In 1884 two

Tests were drawn and England won the only Test completed. Australia's chances in the 1884–85 series were reduced by disputes over finance; the players wanted 50 per cent of the gate money and when this was refused they declined to play. As a result there were new caps in the Australian team for the second Test, five of whom had their first and only game for Australia. England won by 10 wickets, which put them 2–0 up in the series. The Australian team for the third Test looked more familiar, although it was without Murdoch, who did not play for Australia again until 1890. Australia won the third and fourth Tests to level the series, but England, who fielded the same team throughout, won the fifth Test by an innings and 98 runs.

Then Australian cricket suffered a five-year slump. Three Tests were played in England in 1886, three again in 1888, and two in 1890. In Australia, two Tests were played in 1886–87, and only one in 1887–88, when the two English touring parties in Australia that summer combined for a match against Australia in Sydney. Of the 11 Tests played over that five-year period, Australia won one, England 10. There were a number of reasons why England should have became so dominant for a period. Murdoch, so often the cornerstone on which Australian innings were built, was absent. The first Test of the 1886–87 series was Spofforth's last; it was also C. T. B. Turner's first Test, but although Turner and Ferris were to form a bowling partnership which nearly matched the greatness of Spofforth and Boyle, for a period they did not get the support they deserved from the Australian batting.

This relative weakness came at a time of great strength in English cricket. W. G. Grace was still going strong. Although he did not tour Australia again until 1891–92, he was influential in several of England's wins at home. Arthur Shrewsbury was as consistent as he was brilliant and the bowlers Lohmann, Peel, Briggs and Barnes usually had the measure of the Australian batting.

As the Test team's results declined, so did public interest in the game. In 1882–83 total attendance for the four-Test series was 170,000, an average of more than 42,000 per Test. In 1884–85 the average attendance per Test fell to 19,000 and the total crowd for the five Tests was only 94,000. In 1886–87 only 17,000 people attended the two Tests and total attendance for the one Test of the 1887–88 season, which was badly affected by rain, was 1971.

Dr W. G. Grace and W. L. Murdoch. Despite the doctor's highly-publicised antics on and off the field, he and Murdoch were firm friends.

The Australian revival began with the 1891–92 series. The English team was managed and financed by Lord Sheffield and captained by W. G. Grace. Apart from the absence of Shrewsbury and Gunn, it was as strong a side as England could muster. The team for the first Test included nine men who had played in Tests against Australia in England, and another, A. E. Stoddart, who became a regular member of the England XI. Australia was without Ferris, who had gone to England to play for Gloucestershire and later played for England against South Africa. Australia won the first Test, played in Melbourne, by 54 runs and the second, in Sydney, by 72. England won the final Test, played in Adelaide, by an innings and 230 runs. Rain ruined Australia's chances in this Test, but as England had made 499 (Stoddart 134) in the first innings, the only chance Australia had was to force a draw.

Grace was paid £3000 plus expenses for the tour, on which he topped the first-class batting averages. Roads and transport had improved considerably since the doctor's first visit, but again he managed to stir up a reasonable amount of controversy; he insulted an umpire in Sydney and carried on a long and bitter correspondence with the New South Wales Cricket Association about the incident. But the tour was a reasonably happy one, even though it lost money for Lord Sheffield, whose expenses included a donation of £150 to the cricket associations, to be put towards a trophy for competition between the colonies. The newly formed Australasian Cricket Council commissioned a silver shield containing 5·6 kilograms (200 ounces) of silver, with a batsman depicted on one side and a bowler on the other. We know it today as the Sheffield Shield. The first competition was played in the 1892–93 season, between New South Wales, Victoria and South Australia.

The 1893 tour was an unhappy affair. England was again clearly the better side. Two Tests were drawn, one on even terms and one in England's favour. England won the only completed Test by an innings. The leading Australian cricketers of the day were widely criticised for their performances, their drinking habits, and for the 'shamateurism . . . which claimed the right to the prefix "Mr" on the scoreboards . . . yet went there to obtain as great share of gate-money as possible'.

But the revival was completed in 1894–95, in the first five-Test series between fully representative teams. The summer of 1894-95 produced drama, big scores and sensational collapses.

George Giffen wrote: 'I had trained specially for that season's play. During Lord Sheffield's tour, being unwell, I did not do myself justice, and there were plenty of critics who said that, though I could score in intercolonials, it was significant that I had not done so in the great Test matches. Determined to vindicate myself, I went through a severe course of winter training, and began the season in as fine fettle as ever I was in.' Giffen made 475 runs and took 34 wickets in the series, more runs and wickets than anyone else on either side.

The first Test was played in Sydney. Blackham won the toss and Australia batted on a perfect wicket, but the first three wickets fell for 21. Giffen then put on 171 with Frank Iredale and 139 with Syd Gregory, who went on to make 201. The crowd of 30,000 were so appreciative of the innings that a collection raised £103. Blackham hit out against a tired English attack for 74, before he split a finger. Australia's total was 586. England were 3 wickets for 130 at stumps on the second day and went on to make 325. Following on, they batted with great determination and reached 425. 'One was bound to admire the

English batting in the second innings,' Giffen said. 'One by one they went in and played "keeps", and gradually wore down the bowling, and in the end we were left with 171 to make . . . when, at the close of the fifth day, we had scored 113 for 2 wickets, the match seemed as good as won. All of us thought so that night save Blackham, who feared rain. I know I turned in to rest with an easy mind on the subject. When I awoke the next morning and found the glorious sun streaming into my room, I was in ecstasy. But the first man I met outside was Blackham, with a face as long as a coffee-pot. The explanation of his looks came with the remark, "It has been pouring half the night, George".'

Bobby Peel and Johnny Briggs were unplayable and 15 runs were still needed when the injured Blackham went in with nine wickets down. Four runs later he gave a return catch to Peel and England had won by 10 runs. Giffen lamented: 'Did ever a team have such cruel luck? To make 586 and then be beaten by the wicket! Some one said the rain beat us, but Blackham was nearer the mark when he rejoined, "No, it was the sun that did it". However we could not entirely begrudge our opponents their victory, for against tremendous odds they had fought magnificently.' Blackham's injury ended his long first-class career.

The second Test, in Melbourne, started on a wet wicket. England were dismissed for 75 and by stumps on the first day the Australians were all out too, for 123. By Monday the wicket was perfect. England made 425 and Australia could only manage 333, losing by 94. Australia won the third Test, played in Adelaide in scorching heat, by 382 runs and justice was done in Sydney in the fourth Test when Australia, sent in on a wet wicket, made 284 as a result of some brilliant hitting by Harry Graham (105), and Albert Trott (85). A violent storm then presented an impossible wicket for the Englishmen, who were out for 65 and 72. Two-all and one to play!

'By the time the first of March came round, thousands of people had poured into Melbourne from all parts of the colonies,' George Giffen wrote. 'Special trains brought human freight in hundreds from Sydney and Adelaide. What wonder, then, that during the five days over which that great game extended, 63,469 people paid for admission, and that the receipts amounted to £4003 and 14 shillings—records not only for Australia, but for the world! The total attendance, including members, exceeded 100,000. The play which followed was worthy of the mammoth attendance.

'The excitement extended to the players, and not least to the captains. I know that when Stoddart and I went into the ring to toss and arrange preliminaries, he was as white as a sheet, and I have been told that the pallor of my own countenance matched his. It was a trying moment, for both knew that with two such strong batting sides, much depended on the toss. I won it, and I felt as though a great burden had been lifted from my shoulders. Poor Stoddart gave me a despairing look, which said as plainly as words, "I'm afraid it's all over, George".'

Australia made 414. Joe Darling top-scored with 74 and most of the team contributed reasonable scores, even tailenders Fred Jarvis and Tom McKibbin putting on 47 for the last wicket. England replied with 385, due mainly to a stand of 162 between A. C. MacLaren (120) and Bobby Peel (73). George Giffen expected Australia to make at least 350 in the second innings, but 'a terrible dust storm on the fourth morning made the light bad, and a gale blowing across the ground caused Richardson's bowling to be very awkward'. Richardson took 6 wickets for 104. The Australian total was kept to 267, Giffen 51, Joe Darling 50. England needed 297 to win.

England was 1 wicket for 28 at stumps on the fourth day and lost Stoddart, lbw to Harry Trott, to the first ball of the fifth day. Rain was threatening, which would have ruined the wicket and with it England's chances. J. T. Brown came to the wicket with orders to score as many as possible before the rain, took 50 runs in his first 28 minutes and reached his hundred in 95 minutes. In the event, the rain held off, Brown went on to 140 in 145 minutes while the opening batsman Ward defended, and this pair took the score to 238. England eventually won by the comfortable margin of six wickets.

Giffen, despite his personal success, was disappointed at the loss of the series: 'Nothing but cruel luck in the first match prevented us from repossessing the Ashes,' he said. But his disappointment must have been tempered by a public subscription which raised 400 sovereigns in recognition of his services to Australian cricket.

The game's popularity was firmly re-established in both Australia and England, where on the first day of the 1896 series play at Lord's was hampered by a rowdy crowd of 30,000 which spilled onto the field. They saw Australia collapse for only 53 on a good wicket, destroyed by Richardson, who took 6 for 39, and Lohmann, 3 for 13. Although Giffen was still in the Australian team, Harry Trott was now the captain, and his 143 in the

G. H. S. (Harry) Trott, the Victorian all-rounder who played 24 Tests and captained Australia from 1896 to 1898. His younger brother, Albert, played three Tests for Australia and two for England.

Hugh Trumble, the Victorian off-spinner who took 141 wickets in Tests between 1890 and 1904, including two hat-tricks. Tall and gangling, Trumble was the master of flight and deception.

second innings gave Australia a chance of saving the match. It was not to be; England won by six wickets, but Australia won the second Test, played at Old Trafford, by three wickets, despite a superb innings of 154 from K. S. Ranjitsinhji, playing in his first Test. England retained the Ashes by winning the third Test. In Australia in 1897–98, after losing the first Test, Australia won the next four.

The final series of the century, in 1899, was the first five-Test series played in England. It produced four draws, with Australia winning the only completed match, the second Test, at Lord's, by 10 wickets. The first Test was W. G. Grace's last. Aged 51, he scored 28 and 1. Victor Trumper, 22 years old, playing in his first Test, was bowled by Hearne for 0 in the first innings and by F. S. Jackson for 11 in the second. The selectors stuck with him. In the second Test he made 135 not out.

CHAPTER 19

Real Australians

Until the 1890s economic progress had been virtually unchecked, spurred on by the opening up of new lands, the population explosion of the gold rushes, the export of agricultural products and the building of cities and towns. Progress had come of its own accord and it was assumed that it would continue. Money was lent to Australian investors for speculation in real estate, mainly in Melbourne, then the financial capital of the nation, where property was being bought and sold at well above its real value. The colonial governments raised loans in London in excess of their needs and of their capacity to repay.

After 1890, as a result of a financial crisis in Argentina, British investors needed funds at home and started withdrawing their money from Australia. In 1893 there was a run on the banks; within a few months a dozen banks were forced to close and the Melbourne financial system collapsed. Several Victorian politicians were found to have lent themselves public money at concessional rates and terms. The Victorian government stopped all public works, interest rates rose and at the same time there was a dramatic fall in the price of Australian farm products. Added to this was a period of drought throughout the eastern colonies during the 1890s. Unemployment was widespread, immigration was halted. There was an obvious need for a federal system of economic management.

From the times of convict labour, working people had been exploited harshly. The gold rushes had brought people with experience of trades unions in Europe, and from the 1870s there was a movement for action to prevent the exploitation of labour. There were a number of strikes for better pay and conditions in the early 1890s, but following the financial collapse, unemployment was high and there was no shortage of labour and 'scabs' to act as strike-breakers. Unions had little in the way of funds to keep their men out on strike; with the opposition of the colonial governments and the press, the strikes were broken or collapsed. The unionists turned from strike action to political action. The first members of the Labor Party were returned in the New South Wales elections in 1891 and by 1899 Queensland had a Labor Government.

By now, although England was still called home, large numbers of the population were second or third generation Australians. They regarded themselves as Australians, with no thought of living elsewhere, unlike earlier generations who had been sent here as soldiers or convicts, or had come here to make money to retire on 'at home'. Australian sportsmen provided the first focus for national unity and pride. Artists, writers and journalists continued the theme; the main newspapers of the day, magazines like the *Bulletin*, writers like Henry Lawson, Adam Lindsay Gordon and Henry Kendall and painters like Arthur Streeton, Tom Roberts and Charles Conder reflected and reinforced the new nationalism.

The Germans and the French were active in the Pacific; a national defence policy was needed. Other factors in the drive for a national identity and administration included the clumsiness of having immigation, tariffs, transport and posts and telegraphs administered by six colonial governments. In 1889, Henry Parkes, Premier of New South Wales, had called for 'a great national government for all Australia'. Over the next two years discussions between the colonial governments and a national convention recommended the founding of a 'Commonwealth of Australia' and a draft constitution. The idea then languished for a time, due to intercolonial rivalries and bickering. A second convention was held in 1897. It sat for more than three months in Melbourne, Adelaide and Sydney, producing 5000 pages of transcript and a second version of the constitution. At this time the colonial governments in Western Australia and Queensland did not favour federation, so in 1898 a referendum was put to the voters of New South Wales, Tasmania, Victoria and South Australia. It was rejected by the voters of New South Wales, who feared a loss of power to Victoria. In 1899 New South Wales was offered better terms and was joined by Queensland in a second referendum, which was passed, and the draft constitution was submitted to the British Parliament. Western Australia finally agreed to join, Queen Victoria gave her assent, and on 17 September 1900, the proclamation was made, constituting the Commonwealth of Australia from 1 January 1901.

Edmund Barton, Australia's first Prime Minister, was a keen cricketer and a respected umpire. He stood in a number of intercolonial matches and was the umpire at the other end when George Coulthard gave the decision against Murdoch which led to the 'Lord Harris riot' at Sydney in 1879.
Illustrated Australian News.

The constitution provided for a Senate with six members from each State, and a House of Representatives with as near as possible to twice the number of members as the Senate, elected in proportion to the population of each State. At the election in 1901, the Liberal Protectionist Party, led by Edmund Barton, won 32 seats in the House of Representatives, the Conservative Free Traders won 27 seats, and Labor 16 seats. In the Senate, the Liberal Protectionists had 11 seats, Conservative Free Traders 17, and Labor 8. Up until 1910, none of the three parties was able to win an absolute majority in the House of Representatives, but reasonably stable government was provided by a 'working association' between Liberals and Labor. Their differences were of degree rather than ideology; the historian Manning Clark says Labor was a 'reformist rather than a radical' party, and, while it put 'itself forward as the party of the working classes it was careful to include in its programme points that appealed to other classes'. The Liberals were committed to 'careers open to talent, and material well-being for all, but were prepared to use the state to ensure a minimum standard of living and to protect the weak against the strong'. The Conservatives drew their support from 'the pastoral area, traditionally devoted to free trade, the more opulent suburbs in the capital cities, the chambers of commerce, and the large importing firms'.

All parties were agreed on 'the wish to preserve a predominantly European society in Australia by prohibiting the immigration of Asiatics and Pacific Islanders . . . Under section 3 of the Immigration Restriction Act of 1901, any person who failed to pass a dictation of fifty words in a European language could be declared a prohibited immigrant'.

CHAPTER 20

A champion
on the cheap

Victor Trumper was born in the Sydney suburb of Darlinghurst in 1877 and brought up in a terrace house in nearby Paddington. His parents had nine children; two of his sisters died in infancy, another at the age of three. Like Monty Noble, who was a few years older, Trumper went to Crown Street Superior Public School. Boys at the school played cricket at every opportunity. The rules were simple: the batsman was replaced by the boy who got him out. The story goes that Trumper once batted for six weeks; the first thing he said to his mother when he came home from school in the afternoon was 'I'm still in'. His father, Charles Trumper, was born in New Zealand but settled in Sydney in the 1870s. He had a business making slippers and the family was comfortably off. When his son's extraordinary ability became evident, Charles Trumper gave him every encouragement. Early in the morning father and son used to go off to Moore Park for a couple of hours practice before Victor went to school. As a boy, Trumper's bowling was on a par with his batting.

Later he had some coaching from Charles Bannerman at the Sydney Cricket Ground. Bannerman eventually refused to coach him because he kept chasing balls wide of the stumps. Jack Blackham wrote in 1915 that, when he first saw Victor Trumper, he said to Tom Garrett, 'My word, Tom, isn't he like Charles Bannerman', and Garrett replied, 'That's who he reminded me of'.

Victoria won the first Sheffield Shield competition, played in 1892–93 and South Australia won the following year. Trumper made his first appearance for NSW in 1894–95, but scored only

22 in four innings. Although he made 67 for New South Wales Colts against Stoddart's English side that summer, he was still regarded as too flashy and was not selected for New South Wales for another two seasons.

In 1896 Trumper made 113 for the Next Fifteen against New South Wales. In 1897–98 he made a series of big scores in Sydney club cricket and scored double centuries against Tasmania and New Zealand. But when the three selectors, Syd Gregory from New South Wales, Hugh Trumble from Victoria and Joe Darling from South Australia, met to select the team to tour England in 1899, only Gregory was in favour of picking Trumper and he was not included in the original selection. The touring team played a series of matches before leaving for England and in one of these, in Adelaide, Trumble and Darling saw Trumper make 75. 'Trumble and I were then convinced that Trumper was a coming champion and we realised we had made a mistake in not selecting him,' Darling said. It was decided that an extra man should be added to the team, but as profits for the tour were shared between the players, his late selection was conditional on him agreeing to help with the laundry and accepting half the normal share of profit from the tour.

Trumper did not start well on tour in England but his form in the nets was good enough to gain him selection in the second Test, at Lord's. England made 206, fast bowler 'Jonah' Jones taking 7 wickets for 88. Australia then made 421, with Clem Hill and Trumper both scoring 135, the latter not out. Australia went on to win the match by 10 wickets. England had the advantage in the remaining three Tests, but could not force a conclusion and all three were drawn.

What film there is of Trumper shows him practising at Lord's, in a session set up for the camera, playing a few short-pitched balls down the leg side. He looks relaxed and it is obvious that he had an easy, wristy style. C. B. Fry, the English cricketer and scholar, said: 'He had no style, and yet he was all style. He had no fixed canonical method of play, he defied all orthodox rules, yet every stroke he played satisfied the ultimate criterion of style—the minimum of effort, the maximum of effect.' The Australians who played with him were more laconic; Joe Darling, who captained the Australian team from 1899 to 1905, said 'What do I think of him? I thought I could bat', and Clem Hill, who also captained Australia and in fact had a better

A sequence from the only remaining film footage of Victor Trumper in action. Taken at Lord's in 1905, the film shows him playing a couple of short-pitched balls down on the leg side. It does little to explain his reputation, although it is evident that he had a natural, relaxed style with a rather wristy flourish. **Cinesound Library.**

career record than Victor Trumper, said: 'I wasn't fit to lick Victor's boots.' Neville Cardus, regarded as the greatest of cricket writers, wrote: 'God no doubt could create a better batsman than Victor Trumper, but so far He hasn't.'

Trumper had the natural ability and instincts which are the essential equipment of all great athletes. He had style and grace and the temperament to play attacking cricket so that his natural abilities were most attractively displayed. Australians wanted heroes, but they liked their tall poppies to be of the people; Victor Trumper was self-effacing to a fault. He took no care with his appearance: 'It did not worry Trumper in the slightest that his cricket gear was disgracefully creased,' Monty Noble said. There are many stories of his generosity to others, although he was not well-off himself. According to Frank Iredale, 'His unselfish nature was of such a breadth that at times it became embarrassing to his many friends'.

He was, in short, revered as a saint. But, as Philip Derriman points out in *True to the Blue*, 'There was another side to him which over the years seems to have escaped comment. Selfless though he may have been, Trumper was a proud man who appreciated his own worth and was ready to stand on his dignity'. When he heard that a bowler in Sydney grade cricket claimed to have his measure, he took 50 runs off 10 balls the next time they met. He was frequently unavailable to play for New South Wales in Sheffield Shield games, but when in 1909–10, after Noble's retirement, he was not appointed captain of the State, he wrote to the secretary; 'not doing so is an injustice to me, and leaves me only one course to adopt, and that is to withdraw from the eleven'. He was appointed captain the following season and was conscientious in his role as a delegate to the association and as a State selector, but his relations with officials, and in particular with the ambitious Billy McElhone, were often strained.

They started badly; in 1899, McElhone recommended that a request by Trumper for expenses of 10 shillings per match be refused. Later McElhone was the leading advocate of the suspension of 10 New South Wales players who had agreed to play against England for the Melbourne Cricket Club in 1906–07. This was the beginning of the power struggle which led to the withdrawal of the 'Big Six', including Trumper, from the 1912 England tour. It may be that these incidents reflect more on the administrators than on the character of Victor Trumper, but to be fair it should be recorded that his sports store had useful contracts with the association and that his benefit match at the Sydney Cricket Ground in February 1913 raised £3086, which included a donation of £105 from the association.

Victor Trumper and Australian wicket-keeper James Kelly

were married to sisters; Trumper married Annie Briggs in 1904 and they had two children, Annie Louise, born in 1906, and Victor Trumper II, born in 1913. Trumper was not robust; after a bout of scarlet fever in 1908 his health was always suspect. He first became seriously ill in October 1914 with what he described to his wife as 'a cold on the kidneys'. He spent part of the next eight months confined to bed and was hospitalised on 21 June 1915. A week later, aged 37, he died of nephritis, a disease of the kidneys known in those days as Bright's disease. Victor Trumper II played six matches for New South Wales as a fast bowler in the 1940–41 season.

The first Test series after Federation was played in Australia in 1901–02 against an English team which included MacLaren, Hayward, Tyldesley, Lilley, Jessop, Gunn, Barnes and Blyth, some of the great names of English cricket. England won the first Test but Australia won the remaining four, due mainly to the batting of Clem Hill, who made 521 runs during the series and the bowling of Noble and Trumble, who took 60 wickets between them.

Trumper did nothing of great merit, although he played some useful innings, with a top score of 65 in the third Test. He had his best season in England in 1902. Despite the wet summer, he scored 2570 runs in the season including 11 centuries. Australia saved the first Test after England scored 376 and Australia collapsed for 36 on a wet wicket. Rain limited play in the second Test to 105 minutes. Australia won the third, due mainly to a century from Hill and 62 from Trumper on a difficult wicket in the second innings and the bowling of Monty Noble, who took 5 wickets for 51 and 6 for 52.

Then came two classics. At Old Trafford, the ground was sodden at the start; Darling won the toss and chose to bat while the wicket was easy and the bowlers' footholds were slippery. Trumper attacked from the first ball, putting on 135 in 78 minutes with Duff for the first wicket and going on to 104 in 115 minutes. Hill (65) and Darling (51) continued to hit and Australia totalled 299, with the pitch starting to play tricks. England lost 5 wickets for 44 and were 5 for 70 at stumps. But on the second day F. S. Jackson and L. C. Braund took the score to 185 before the sixth wicket fell. Jackson went on to 128 in a total of 262. Then it was Australia's turn to collapse; 8 wickets for 85 at stumps on the second day, all out for 86 early on the third, after more rain overnight. England, needing 124 to win, were 36 without loss at lunch. The sun began to work on the pitch, Saunders and Trumble began to get some bite and wickets fell at 44, 68, 72, 92 and 97. But with England's first innings heroes at the crease and Lilley, Lockwood, Rhodes and Tate to come and only 27 runs needed, England's position seemed secure. Jackson went for 7, caught by Gregory off Saunders. Six for 107. Trumble had Braund stumped by Kelly for 3 then he bowled Lockwood for 0. Eight for 109. Lilley thrashed, Rhodes played calmly. They took the score to 116 — two boundaries needed — when Lilley hit Trumble hard and high to leg, for what seemed to be four runs until Clem Hill, diving one-handed on the boundary, took the catch.

Rain sent the players off the field for 45 minutes. When they returned Tate edged a boundary off Saunders. Four to win when Saunders beat Tate's bat and broke his wicket. The fifth Test was almost a repeat performance. Australia made 324 and 121. England, with 183 in the first innings, needing 263 to win, lost 5 wickets for 48. Jackson and Jessop went on the attack, but still 15 runs were needed when Rhodes joined Hirst with 9 wickets down. The two Yorkshiremen made the runs, but Australia went home with the Ashes. On the way home through South Africa the Australians won a three-Test series 2–0.

CHAPTER 21

Practise, practise, practise

The only truly new technique which has been brought into the game this century is the off break which looks like a leg break; the 'wrong 'un', the 'googly', or the 'bosie' as it used to be called, because it was brought into big cricket by a man named Bosanquet. Born in 1877, B. J. T. Bosanquet was a versatile cricketer. He made 120 for Eton against Harrow at Lord's in 1896. Up at Oxford, he was picked for his fast-medium bowling but developed into the university's best all-rounder. During intervals in play, or when it was raining, they used to play a game with a tennis ball over the pavilion table; the object of the game was to deceive the man at the other end of the table with the bounce. Bosanquet first developed his reverse leg breaks indoors and under-arm. Then he took the technique outside, first with a tennis ball, then with a cricket ball, over-arm. He gave up fast bowling and learnt to bowl leg breaks. He spent a winter practising at an indoor net with a stump and a dozen cricket balls. G. D. Martineau, in *They Made Cricket*, says that the game's most subtle trick was at first regarded as something of a joke, suitable only for demonstrations during the luncheon interval. An opposing batsman would be brought out and offered a couple of leg breaks before being deceived with an apparently identical ball which, if it landed on the spot, would break back and rap him on the knee. Then, as Bosanquet described it, 'everyone shrieked with laughter and I was led away'.

Bosanquet first came to Australia early in 1903 with a team led by Pelham Warner, which played three games here after a tour of New Zealand. After the game against Victoria, Warner wrote in

Joe Darling leads the 1905 Australians onto the field at Lord's. Syd Gregory follows Darling, with Frank Laver clearly visible behind. **Cinesound Library.**

Cricket Across the Seas, 'Bosanquet's slow "googlies" as they were called in New Zealand, made me blush, for over and over again the ball pitched three or four times before reaching the batsman, and once he bowled one so wide that Graham (Harry Graham, the Australian batsman) ran almost to deep point in order to reach it'. Then against New South Wales, Trumper cut loose in the second innings; 'Our bowlers seemed helpless, and it really looked as if the two batsmen would be in at the drawing of stumps . . . after 72 runs had been made off twelve overs, Bosanquet went on with his slows, and with his first delivery clean bowled Trumper with a ball which the great Australian batsman thought was breaking from leg, but which came back, and to which he played forward.'

Charles Bannerman prophesied that Bosanquet's bowling would one day win a Test match for England. After the team arrived home, C. B. Fry wrote to Warner urging him to 'persuade that Bosanquet of yours to practise, practise, practise those funny googlies of his'. Bosanquet was picked to come to Australia with Pelham Warner's side in 1903–04, after four successive series had been lost to the Australians. Despite criticism of the team, which was the first touring team selected and managed by the MCC, England won the first Test, in Sydney, by five wickets, when R. E. Foster made the then record score in Tests of 287. They won again in Melbourne, where Hirst and Rhodes dismissed Australia for 122 and 111, by 185 runs. Bosanquet took three wickets in the first Test, but did not play in the second. In Adelaide, where Trumper made 113, Bosanquet took seven wickets, but Australia won by more than 200. Back in Sydney for the fourth Test, Australia needed 329 to win in the fourth innings, on a good wicket. Bosanquet took 6 for 51, including a spell of 5 for 12. Although he did not always bowl well, the uncertainty he generated in the Australian batsmens' minds is regarded as one of the main reasons for England's 3–2 series win. His best performance was in the first Test in England in 1905. He took 8 for 107 from 32.4 overs, winning a Test which would otherwise have ended in a draw.

Bosanquet's example was first followed by the South Africans, who played four googly bowlers against England in 1906 and won the series four Tests to one. In Australia Bosanquet set the scene for Hordern, Mailey, Grimmett, O'Reilly, McCool, Benaud and more recently John Gleeson, Jim Higgs, Kerry O'Keeffe, and Bob Holland, who won a Test at the Sydney Cricket Ground against Clive Lloyd's mighty West Indies in the 1984–85 season, ending their record sequence of 27 Tests without a loss. Australia won its only Test of the 1986–87 season, also in Sydney, when, with England trying to force a draw and only six balls remaining, the leg-spinner Peter Sleep bowled John Emburey. It would be nice to be able to say it was a wrong 'un. It wasn't. It spun from leg and kept low. But perhaps Emburey played for the wrong 'un and . . . such are the subtleties of the leg-spinner's art.

CHAPTER 22

The power struggle

Tours to and from England had been privately sponsored until the 1903–04 season, when the English team came for the first time under the management of the MCC. In Australia, although the Australasian Cricket Council was set up in 1892 to organise and manage Australian cricket, it proved ineffectual and had been disbanded by the turn of the century. The Melbourne Cricket Club had been involved with most of the overseas tours by Australian players and as the tours had generally been successful, both from a playing and financial point of view, the players were happy with this situation.

But Federation had done little to reduce interstate rivalry in the new Commonwealth. Given the ambitions of the States' administrators, it was not likely that the system in England, where the MCC virtually ran cricket, would succeed in Australia. At a meeting of representatives of the New South Wales, Victorian and South Australian Cricket Associations held in Sydney on 6 January 1905, the New South Wales representative, Billy McElhone, a Sydney solicitor, proposed the appointment of a Board of Control. This was carried and a constitution was drafted which proposed wide powers for the board, including the control of tours to and from England. The South Australian association refused to join the board unless the constitution provided for the players to be represented, so the board, representing only New South Wales and Victoria, held its first meeting on 6 May 1905, led by the secretary of the Victorian Cricket Association, Ernest Edward Bean. Queensland joined the association in September the same year.

The leading players did not like the idea. Apart from the fact that they had in the past been able to share in profits from tours, they saw themselves as the people who knew the game and drew the crowds and the proponents of the board as men who wanted power at the players' expense. Joe Darling, the Australian captain from 1899 to 1902, and a representative of the South Australian Cricket Association in 1905, had strong feelings about administrators; recalling a game in Sydney played in very hot weather he said: 'When we adjourned for tea we found McElhone and some leading notoriety seekers present with some dead head friends who had rushed the afternoon tea provided for the players. The waiters were very busy and with this crowd we could not get a look in sideways. I got up and walked over to the large tea urn, called two mates I could rely on at a pinch, and we took possession of the tea urn, and served the players and kept the dead heads waiting.'

The Melbourne club had taken the precaution of approaching 11 of the leading New South Wales players to get their written agreements that they would play against England if the club was able to bring out an English team in 1906–07. When members of the New South Wales association found out about this arrangement they called a special meeting, which was held in May 1906. McElhone led the attack for the association and Monty Noble, the Australian captain, represented the players. McElhone recommended that the players should be suspended unless they renounced their agreements with the Melbourne club. Noble said they wanted to play for their State, but were bound to honour the agreement and, as the board did not provide for representation by the players, they did not regard it as properly constituted. He added that the players would not make any further agreement with the Melbourne club if they were represented on the board.

The meeting recommended the suspensions. Only one player renounced his agreement, so 10 players, including Noble, Trumper, Duff, Cotter and Hanson Carter, were suspended from the New South Wales team. The association also required that the 10 players should be suspended by their clubs and when Paddington, for whom Noble and Trumper played, refused, the association threatened to suspend the club.

As Philip Derriman says in *True to the Blue*, 'The Association's dispute with the NSW players ought to be seen in perspective, for it was but one dispute in a whole tangle of disputes bedevilling Australian cricket at the time. At the centre of it all was

Joe Darling.

the power struggle between the Board of Control and the Melbourne Cricket Club. The board was supported by the NSW and Victorian Cricket Associations, each of which had its own feud with the Melbourne Cricket Club. The Melbourne Club was supported by the South Australian Association, then at odds with the board, and by the Sydney Cricket Ground Trust, which had been in conflict with the NSW Association for more than twenty years'.

The board invited the MCC to send a team to Australia in 1906–07, but the invitation was declined on the grounds that the board 'was not fully representative of Australian cricket'. As a result the board declared a truce with the Melbourne club in order to discuss their problems and the banned players were reinstated with a spiteful proviso that they be disqualified from holding office in the association for three years.

The episode set a standard for dealing with Australian cricketers which was still having an effect 70 years later.

CHAPTER 23

The public gaze

The Australian team which sailed for England via New Zealand on 1 February 1905 was the last team organised by the players and the Melbourne Cricket Club before the Australian Cricket Board asserted its authority over the game. The team was captained by Joe Darling and had Frank Laver as player-manager, both elected by vote of the players as was the custom. The team arrived in England at the end of April after several games in New Zealand, one in Fiji, and stops in Hawaii, Canada and the United States.

Frank Laver was an unattractive but effective all-rounder. Thought not a talented cricketer, he was immensely popular with the players. His book *An Australian Cricketer on Tour*, illustrated with 'photographs by the author' reflects the atmosphere and thinking of the times: 'A large crowd awaited our arrival at Liverpool, many of whom were reporters desiring an interview. A Liverpool friend pointed them out, and I tried to dodge them by holding down my head and bustling past. But I was not very successful, for they stuck to me like leeches and questioned me pertinaciously, as I worked our way through the crowd. So many spoke at the same time that I could not distinguish one question from another. They followed me to the Customs sheds and to the station platform, where I finally evaded them by slipping on to a departing train.

'One morning was devoted solely to photographers, and twenty-four availed themselves of the privilege. Whilst the twenty-four photographers were at work on us a cinematograph photographer was busy with them as well as with us with a curious result. I was unaware of his presence and it was only

Left: *Frank Laver. Right: Monty Noble, Australian captain in 1903–04 and from 1907 to 1909, with Warwick Armstrong, captain in Australia in 1920–21 and in England in 1921.* The Argus.

later on at the Palace Theatre that I knew he had been there. We were highly amused at some of the antics we cut while being photographed. When reproduced at the Music Hall our movements looked particularly funny. Some of the photographers, however, were a perfect nuisance. They appeared to think we were in England for their special benefit and did not seem to realise we had come here to play cricket, with little time for ourselves beyond the hours for playing and travelling. We required from each a guarantee that he would give each member of the team a copy and would not use the photo in any form whatever for advertising purpose or on postcards.' (The 'cinematograph' film which Laver refers to has been preserved and is included in the documentary film which accompanies this book.)

The Australians had a disappointing tour on the field. Trumper did not produce the form of previous tours, making only 125 runs in eight Test innings. Even Clem Hill managed only 188 runs in the Tests and Noble also was not at his best. The bulk of the work was done by Duff, with 335 runs in Tests, and Armstrong, who made 252 runs and took 16 wickets. Laver also took 16 wickets during the series. A feature of the Australian attack was the fierce, short-pitched bowling of Cotter, who bowled a mixture of yorkers and bumpers which wicket-keeper

J. J. Kelly, standing deep, sometimes had to take high over his head. Cotter missed the second and third Tests through injury and bowled without distinction in the fourth Test. But in the fifth he bowled 40 overs in the first innings and took 7 wickets for 148 in an England total of 430. England won the first and fourth Tests, the others were drawn.

During a match at Lord's, the MCC arranged a meeting to discuss the Australian Cricket Board. Darling, Noble, Hill and Laver met a group including Lord Harris, Pelham Warner and F. S. Jackson, who agreed that the Australian board 'did not represent the true interests of all parties concerned, and until it did the Marylebone Club felt they could not recognise it. They further stated that they would not send a team to Australia . . . until the present trouble with the Board of Control had ended'. In the meanwhile 'they would welcome visits of Australian cricket teams to England, under the same conditions as have existed in the past'.

Many of Laver's thoughts and comments are reflected in modern cricket; lamenting the arrangements in England under which Tests were played over only three days, he wrote: 'I shall not be surprised if, one day, a rule is brought into force abolishing the second innings altogether. Football, baseball, lacrosse, and nearly all national games are decided on two or three hours' play. These games have a great advantage over cricket for that very reason. Life is too short for long contests.' He also foresaw the covering of wickets: 'At present too much depends on the spin of the coin and the vagaries of the weather . . . attendances, too, would improve.' Over the fence only counted for four runs in England; Laver suggested that 'If 6 or 8 were registered for a hit over the chains, and 10 for one out of the ground, many a batsman would be tempted to try the stroke'. (In Australia, before the 1907–08 season, over the boundary counted as five runs and out of the ground as six runs. Since 1907–08 all hits over the boundary have counted as six. In England, before 1912 the general rule was that over the boundary counted as four runs and out of the ground counted as six runs. Since 1912 all hits over the boundary have counted as six.)

Domestic arrangements are dealt with in some detail: 'The dressing rooms, as a rule, are small, and contain insufficient pegs for hanging up clothes. In some instances they were also not nearly secluded enough from the public gaze; the ladies seated in the Reserves were now and then able to see us putting on our flannels. This was, however, quite interesting to a number of them . . .' and 'Shower-baths — an Australian's delight — were conspicuous by their absence on the majority of grounds. English crowds, 'Though not so demonstrative as an Australian crowd . . . are perhaps fairer in their treatment of erring cricketers. . . they do not tell delinquents to "get a bag" or "get off the field" and "give somebody else a show" as the Australian crowds do'.

Laver was outspoken about the distinction between amateurs and professionals: 'The English custom of amateur cricketers entering the field from one gate, and professional cricketers from another seems, to all Australians, priggish and out of place . . . what is more ridiculous than seeing two batsmen from the same side enter the field from gates a hundred yards apart.' He was less liberal in his view on players writing for the press: 'The practice in England of players writing articles in newspapers on the game in which they are taking part struck us as being questionable in the interests of the game . . . one of the clauses in our agreement was as follows: "No member of the team shall correspond for any newspaper by letter or cable during the tour. A breach of this clause renders the culprit liable to a fine of £100."' This didn't stop the papers from trying — one editor was so anxious to get articles from one of the Australian players that he offered to pay the fine.

Finally, there is no doubt the players were given a good time: 'We were the recipients of numerous presents in the form of knives, books, razors, medicine chests, gold match boxes, pipes, bats, cricket material, whisky, champagne, tobacco, cigars, underwear, eucalyptus, and other things . . . The proprietors and managers of nearly all the theatres and music halls were very obliging and thoughtful, giving us free entry to all their performances whenever we chose, besides treating us occasionally to refreshments behind the scenes, taking us to the dressing-rooms of the leading actors and actresses for introductions, and allowing us to watch the various scenes from the wings of the stage. Usually boxes were at our disposal, but we were generally at liberty to choose our seats. Some of the music halls gave us passes for all time. One had a metal pass specially struck in our colours of green and gold, and when we visited a special performance at the theatre the whole of the exterior was lit up by electric lights of green and gold. The interior, too, was suitably decorated, and as the team sat down three cheers were given by the assembled audience.'

CHAPTER 24

Personal differences

Noble resumed the captaincy when England toured in 1907–08 and continued as captain in England in 1909. The nucleus of the team remained much the same although Reg Duff and Joe Darling had retired from Test cricket, Darling to a farm in Tasmania. Their places were filled by Charles Macartney and Warren Bardsley. Australia won the series in Australia by four Tests to one and retained the Ashes in 1909 by winning two and losing one, with two drawn.

Clem Hill was unavailable for the 1907–08 season and for the tour to England in 1909, but he returned to captain Australia against the touring South Africans in 1910–11. The series was dominated by the resurgence of Victor Trumper, who scored 661 in the five Tests at an average of 94.4, and the fast bowling of Tibby Cotter. The cricket writer J. C. Davis wrote of Cotter: 'Those who have never gazed upon Albert Cotter stripped often marvelled how he got the tremendous pace into his bowling when he was at his top. But if they could have seen his deep chest, powerful shoulders, thick, clean-muscled arms, the strength and symmetry of his body and limbs, they would no longer wonder. He was a model for the sculptor.' Cotter bowled with a side-on, slinging action, similar to Jeff Thomson's. Like Thomson, he was inclined to spray the ball, but was capable of searing pace and was not shy about dropping the ball short. South Africa had a quartet of googly bowlers but only R. D. Schwarz lived up to his reputation. Australia introduced its first exponent of the art, H. V. Hordern, who had recently completed his qualification in dentistry in the United States. Hordern played in the fourth and fifth Tests and took 14 wickets at 21.07. Australia won the series 4–1.

The Australians did not fare as well against the brilliant

England team led by J. W. H. T. Douglas in 1911–12. Australia won the first Test after a century by Trumper and 90 from the newcomer Roy Minnett gave them a first innings total of 447. Then the bowling combination of S. F. Barnes and F. R. Foster, on a series of helpful wickets, was able to counter the strong Australian batting, while Jack Hobbs, 'the Surrey Master', made centuries in the second, third and fourth Tests, all of which were won by England, along with the fifth Test, which gave them the Ashes by a 4–1 margin.

Meanwhile, the relationship between the players and the Australian Cricket Board, which had begun so badly in 1905, continued to deteriorate. Frank Laver played for the East Melbourne club and until 1905 had a long friendship with another member of the club, the batsman Peter McAlister. McAlister had missed selection for the 1905 tour, managed by Laver. He blamed Laver for his omission and their friendship turned sour. When in 1909 the Australian Cricket Board, which had gained the approval of the MCC and was rapidly gaining control of the game in Australia, selected the side to tour England, Laver again went as manager. But for reasons which had more to do with politics than with performance, the board included McAlister and appointed him treasurer, vice-captain and Australia's delegate to the Imperial Cricket Conference in London. This was not a popular or effective move; McAlister proved not to be up to Test class and when he was asked to produce his books for the tour, he had to reveal that he had kept no records. He claimed that his brief as treasurer was undefined and that in any case Laver had prevented him from obtaining information. Laver, who had kept financial records, refused to produce them on the grounds that they contained information which was personal to himself and the other players.

McAlister was clearly the board's man and, as a sub-plot to the growing split between players and administrators, he was a member of the selection committee during the 1911–12 season. So were Clem Hill, the Australian captain and very much a players' man, and Frank Iredale. McAlister and Hill had already argued over the selection of the team for the third Test against Douglas's team. Hill wanted Macartney in the team in place of Roy Minnett. McAlister disagreed and cabled Hill, 'If Iredale agrees with you as to Macartney's inclusion, I favour yourself standing down, not Minnett'. This was obviously provocative; although Hill had failed in the second Test with 4 and 0, he had made 46 and 65 in the first Test. And he was, after all, the Australian captain.

The affair came to a head a few weeks later when the selectors met in Bull's Chambers in Moore Street, now Martin Place, to select the team for the fourth Test and to discuss the selections for England. The meeting had not been going for long when their personal differences got the better of them. According to Frank Iredale, Hill got up and punched McAlister on the nose. McAlister retaliated and with blood everywhere from McAlister's nose, they wrestled each other around the room, upsetting a table, before Iredale and Syd Smith, the secretary of the board, were able to pull them apart.

Hill resigned from the selection committee and Iredale and McAlister proceeded with the selection of the team for England, a process which quickly degenerated into farce. The question at issue was the appointment of the manager for the tour. Six of the senior players — Armstrong, Cotter, wicket-keeper Hanson Carter, Hill, Trumper and the Victorian batsman Vernon Ransford — wanted the right to choose their own manager. They wanted Frank Laver, who was unacceptable to the board. The board appointed a Queenslander, G. S. Crouch. The six players said they would not make the trip but the board refused to back down. They picked six replacements and sent away a much weakened team to take part in a triangular tournament with England and South Africa. Three Tests against England were played for two draws and a loss. The Australians defeated the South Africans twice, with one draw. Of the newcomers selected to replace the 'Big Six', only the NSW all-rounder Charles Kelleway was to make a reputation in Test cricket when it resumed in 1920 after the First World War.

Albert 'Tibby' Cotter was killed in a cavalry charge during the war.
The Australasian.

CHAPTER 25

Death of a cricketer

In 1909, Alfred Deakin, who succeeded Edmund Barton as Prime Minister, merged the Liberals with the Conservatives. 'Office is his vice,' wrote the *Australian Worker*, 'and it is as indispensable to him as opium to the Chow, and grog to the drunkard.' The merger backfired; in 1910 Labor won 41 seats in the House of Representatives and 22 in the Senate and Andrew Fisher became the first Labor Prime Minister. The Liberals won back control of the lower house, by one seat only, in 1913 but Labor used its power in the Senate to have both houses dissolved in 1914 and won both houses by a substantial margin. A year later Andrew Fisher resigned as Prime Minister and accepted the post of Australian High Commissioner in London. His place was taken by William Morris Hughes. By this time domestic issues had been overtaken by events on the other side of the world.

When in August 1914 Britain declared her intention of opposing German and Austrian aggression in Europe it was clear that Australia would soon become involved; 'Labor and Liberal leaders tried to outdo each other in offering Australia's last man and last shilling,' according to historian Donald Horne. Although there were some voices of caution raised from the growing ranks of the unionists, the common view was that the war would be a romantic adventure, that 'war was the greatest of the Australian sporting events'.

The Australian navy was placed under the control of the British Admiralty. An expeditionary force of 20,000 men was promised. Recruiting offices were jammed. Within a year 50,000 men had enlisted. They were clothed in woollen uniforms with slouch hats bearing the badge of the rising sun, armed with Lee-Enfield ·303 rifles with long bayonets, and trained in camps in the country and on sports fields in the city. Their pay was six shillings a day. Saddles and harness, tents and supplies were manufactured, rations and medical supplies were collected and ships were refitted as troop transports.

Australians saw their first action on 14 September 1914 when a small force seized bases in German New Guinea. On 1 November the first Australian and New Zealand troops embarked for Europe, escorted by warships of the Australian and British navies. As training camps in Britain were overflowing with English and Canadian troops, and because of the growing threat from the Turks who had entered the war on the German side and represented a threat in northern Africa, the Anzacs were disembarked in Egypt. They spent several months camped on the outskirts of Cairo, where they were joined in February 1915 by a second force.

In Britain, the General Staff, including Winston Churchill, was formulating a plan to relieve pressure on the Russians by attacking Turkey. If Constantinople was taken, so the reasoning went, the rest of Turkey would follow. The key to Constantinople was the Straits of the Dardanelles, which were strongly fortified and defended by the Turks. A naval bombardment of Constantinople by the British and French failed. It was clear that if the plan was to succeed, troops would have to be landed to overcome the Turkish forces. The landing place was to be the Gallipoli Peninsula.

Early in April 1915 the Anzacs were taken by train to Alexandria. They boarded ships which took them north to the Greek islands where they joined the main Allied force, including British, French and Canadians, and set sail for Gallipoli on the evening of 24 April. The first party left the convoy to row to shore before dawn the next morning. Their destination was a relatively safe cove near a promontory named Gabe Tepe but strong currents swept them past to a beach which became known as Anzac Cove. It was surrounded by steep cliffs and overlooked by the Turkish defences.

They stayed there until December, gained a little ground from time to time, but never looked like achieving their objective of over-running the Turkish defences. In August, when they were reinforced by British troops, the beach and surrounding hills were jammed with more than 100,000 Allied soldiers living in trenches, constantly under attack, short of water, clothing and supplies and nearly all suffering from dysentery. When Lord Kitchener visited the lines he quickly realised that the task was hopeless; the Allied force was ordered out of the Dardanelles. The Anzacs slipped quietly out of the cove under cover of darkness on 19 December, having never moved more than a few kilometres inland. More than 10,000 men had been killed and 24,000 wounded. The French force also lost 10,000 men killed; the British lost almost 30,000. The Anzacs returned to Egypt.

Early in 1916 the General Staff decided to send them to the Western Front in France, where the British and French had already lost more than 100,000 men. By May the Anzacs were in position near the village of Armentieres and on the night of 19 July the Fifth Division tried to break through the German lines at Fromelles. By morning 5533 were dead. On 23 July the First Division attacked German positions at Pozieres. They took the town but lost 5285 men under a German counter-attack which reduced the town to rubble over three days. They were replaced by the Second Division, which made some progress, but lost 6846 lives. The Second Division was replaced by the Fourth, which lost 4649 men, then the First Division was thrown back into the battle and another 2650 men were killed. This one battle went on for seven weeks over two kilometres of hillside. Nineteen attacks were mounted, 23,000 Australians died before they were withdrawn to recuperate at Ypres. Then it was on to Bapaume, Bullecourt, Messines, Villers Bretonneux. A total of 330,000 Australians enlisted for the war, almost seven per cent of the population of just under five million. Sixty thousand died and 152,000 were wounded. A third of those who enlisted came through the war physically unscathed.

The Australian Light Horse Brigade had been left in Egypt to prevent the Turks from controlling the Suez Canal and to drive them out of Palestine. In October 1917, en route to Jerusalem, the Light Horse mounted a cavalry charge on Beersheba, which they needed for its water. 'Tibby' Cotter, the Australian fast bowler, was a stretcher-bearer with the Light Horse. He took part in the charge and was hit by machine gun fire at close range as the Australians went through the Turkish lines. Cotter was still alive when the Australians returned, to tend the injured and bury the dead, but he died soon afterwards.

If the war caused suffering and hardship in Australia, its

effect in Britain was devastating. England 'lost the flower of its youth'; more than 900,000 young Englishmen were killed during the 1914–18 war.

They don't make them like that any more! Charlie Macartney and the left-handed Jack Gregory leaning out to drive. Gregory usually batted without gloves. He was a right-arm bowler. **Herbert H. Fishwick, courtesy of the Sydney Morning Herald.**

A tour of England in 1919 by a 'Services' team made up of Australians who had served in the war was promoted by Field Marshal Birdwood, commander of the Australian forces, and supported by the MCC and the Australian Cricket Board. Charles Kelleway, who had served as a captain in France, was the only member of the team who had played Test cricket before the war, and was made the captain. It soon emerged that Kelleway, conservative by nature and a batsman who concentrated on defence, was not the right man to lead a goodwill tour where bright cricket was essential. Field Marshal Birdwood asked him to step down. Herbie Collins was the players' choice and he emerged from the tour as a reliable opening bat and a capable captain. Collins later took over the Australian captaincy when Warwick Armstrong retired in 1921. Other players discovered on the tour were the all-rounder Jack Gregory (a nephew of Australia's first Test captain, Dave Gregory) and Bert Oldfield, who was to be Australia's wicket-keeper for nearly 20 years. The tour was a great success on and off the field. They played exciting cricket, winning 15 of their 34 games in England, with only four losses. On the way home they played 10 games in South Africa, where they were undefeated.

The first Test series after the war was played in Australia in 1920–21 and England's weakness was immediately evident; Australia won all five Tests. In the fifth, Charles Macartney, returning after missing three Tests through illness, made a superb 170, watched by a 12-year-old named Don Bradman. Under Warwick Armstrong, Australia won the first three Tests of the 1921 series in England, with the last two drawn. When Australia won the first three Tests of the 1924–25 series, England had lost 11 out of 13 Tests, with two drawn. England won the fourth Test of that series, lost the fifth, then in 1926 after four draws with honours even, won back the Ashes in the final Test at the Oval, where Hobbs and Sutcliffe made an opening stand of 172 in England's second innings. In Australia's second innings Wilfred Rhodes, in his 49th year, took 4 for 44 from 20 overs and a youngster named Harold Larwood took 3 for 34 from 14 overs. By the 1928–29 season, 10 years after the war, a new generation of England players had emerged and Australia was thrashed 4–1 at home. This was the first series for young Don Bradman who, after being dropped for the second Test, made centuries in the third and fifth and watched in the field while Walter Hammond made 905 series runs at an average of 113.

CHAPTER 26

Out of a job again

Hunter Hendry, better known as 'Stork', was born in Sydney in 1895. I spoke to him in December 1986 in the comfortable cottage where he lives with his wife Vida in the Sydney harbourside suburb of Rose Bay.

'I started playing cricket almost when I was in kindergarten and played right through my school days. We lived in Double Bay, and at the back of our house there was a lane with a great big coral tree just about 22 yards from the street. We played cricket there, my father and uncles and a couple of neighbours and their kids, at every opportunity. If it wasn't every day, it was every other day in the cricket season.' Hendry went to Sydney Grammar School, played in the All-Schools Eleven and went straight into Paddington firsts: 'how privileged and lucky I was that Alf Noble was captain. Alf took me under his wing and that was the greatest opportunity anyone who wanted to play cricket could have had.

'My first job was with the Westinghouse Brake Company at Concord and they were very good to me and let me off for a lot of Sheffield Shield matches. But eventually the time came when they said, "Look, you'll have to decide whether you are going to stay with us or play cricket". There was a very important match in Adelaide and they were just about to pick the team for the 1921 tour of England. Well, I thought I had better take the risk, so I gave up my job and went to Adelaide. But I wasn't in the first touring side they chose, so it looked as if it had been a wasted trip. Then Charlie Kelleway dropped out of the side and I was picked to go in his place.

'I was lucky, too, that Warwick Armstrong was captain on

Left: *Hunter Hendry in 1921.* Sydney Morning Herald. Right: *Arthur Mailey, leading leg-spinner of the 1920s and Australia's foremost cricket comedian. Mailey made the ball hum through the air but was not always able to pitch it on the spot. In a New South Wales v South Australia Sheffield Shield match he bowled Vic Richardson with a ball that landed halfway down the pitch and bounced three times before it hit the wicket. As everyone, including Richardson, laughed, Mailey called out, 'Bad luck, Vic, the last bounce was a yorker'. A plumber before he became a Test cricketer, Mailey was also a talented writer and cartoonist. His book* 10 for 66 And All That *is one of the game's classics.*

that tour. Warwick stood up to the officials. He always put his players first. That side was responsible for getting the players a three-day break before the Test matches. They used to arrange the fixtures, whether by design or just a fluke, so that it seemed we always played the strongest counties on the eve of a Test match. For example we'd be playing Yorkshire on Wednesday, Thursday, Friday, and we'd finish on Friday night and have to go back to London and start a Test match next morning. So you might have your fast bowlers bowling in Yorkshire on Friday afternoon and if you lost the toss on Saturday morning they'd be out there again. We had a meeting and Warwick went and saw the MCC and said that the team should have a break before the

Test matches. They didn't like it very much but eventually they had to do it. That's something Warwick did that I have never seen any publicity about. He was a very strong man and he knew what he was doing; he knew the game inside out.

'That's how he became the only man to bowl two consecutive overs in a Test match. It was the Manchester Test in 1921. We'd won the first three Tests very easily, so we had already held on to the Ashes. We were a very strong side, with Warren Bardsley and Herbie Collins, then Charlie Macartney, and Gregory and McDonald and Arthur Mailey to bowl them out. At Manchester it rained as usual—they say it never stops raining there—and rain washed the first day out completely. Now that altered the rules of the match, so the batting side could not close after ten minutes to five on the second last day. We were in trouble too, no doubt about that. England were over 300 with only a few wickets down and we were anxiously watching the clock. At the tea break Warwick and old Sammy Carter, who was an encyclopaedia on cricket, had the rule book out, so we knew what the situation was. When it passed ten to five we heaved a great sigh of relief. About an hour later the Honourable Lionel Tennyson, captain of England, waved out of the dressing room with a grand air and he said "Close" and Warwick tried to call out to him that he couldn't do it, but he'd gone, so we had to come off the field and Warwick told the English people they didn't know their own rules. There was no option; we had to go back out.

'Now Warwick had bowled the last over before we went off the field. And when we went back on the noise was so bad that it was necessary to get Tennyson and the umpires to go round the ground and say that it was the English who were at fault. Warwick parked himself down on the ground near the pitch and when everything was normal again, or comparatively normal, he picked up the ball and had another over. And nobody took any notice! Anyway we struggled out of that and made a draw of it, but they had us in the cart properly, or would have if Warwick and Sammy hadn't known the rules.

'I was fortunate to tour with some of the great names of Australian cricket in 1921. Arthur Mailey used to bowl full tosses and long hops, but he could bowl a ball when you were a hundred that would knock you over. Although they were both leg-spinners, Grimmett was quite a different type of bowler. If you were prepared to play Grimmett straight down the line all the time, you'd still be there at six o'clock. You could only score in ones and twos, but you could play him all day. Grimmett got you by wearing out your patience, but Mailey could bowl the unplayable ball and he was cunning as a fox. In the Lord's Test in 1921, Frank Woolley had made 90-odd in the first innings and he was 90-odd in the second innings too, and hitting us all over the place. Arthur was bowling and I was fielding at square leg, and he said to me, "Get back about ten yards. On the fourth ball, if he's still up that end, you might get a catch". Well he bowled an absolute long hop, Woolley obviously thought "Here's four penn'orth", and he certainly hit it hard, but he hit it straight at me. Mailey bowled some rubbish, but he bowled with his head.

'I've got a great admiration for Jack Gregory, he was a wonderful all-rounder, but I reckon where Gregory got his great success as a bowler wasn't so much his pace, but because he was such a big, athletic fellow. He used to follow through to such an extent with that huge kangaroo jump that he had, that he was practically on the batsman by the time the ball got to him, and that distracted you a bit. I don't mean to detract from him in any way, but purely as a bowler he wasn't really in the same class as someone like Larwood.

'Ted McDonald wasn't all that fast, but he had such a perfect action that on his day he could do anything with the ball. McDonald had to do all the dirty work. Gregory used to bowl with the wind behind him and Ted had to bowl into the wind all the time. He went and played in England later, so he could play cricket and still earn a living. It was a terrible thing the way he was killed. It was in 1937, he had a car accident on the Yorkshire Moors one night; he wasn't hurt, but when he got out of his car to go and see if the other fellow was all right, he was run over by a truck.

'Charlie Macartney was the greatest stroke-player of my time. He used his feet so well. There's no way he would be tied down by the spinners the way they do now with two men close in on the bat. He would have just come down the wicket and hit them out of the way.

'We came across Douglas Jardine for the first time on that 1921 tour. We took an instant dislike to him and I think he felt the same about us. I think he had it in for all Australians from the time we played against him in 1921 at Oxford. He made 90-odd, but he was an unattractive bat and we didn't want him to get a hundred because there was a young chap called Hubert Ashton who played a magnificent innings. We just didn't want

Charles Macartney, known as 'The Governor-General'. Neville Cardus wrote: 'You could not in any circumstances have had dull cricket with Macartney. Dullness at cricket comes out of the souls of the players. On and off the field Macartney was the same vital man; his jaw was strong, his mouth firm and humorous; and out of his eyes shone temperament that was accustomed to being expressed'. **Sydney Morning Herald.**

Ashton's hundred to be belittled by Jardine getting one too, so we made sure we kept him out of it.'

The 1921 Australian team came home through South Africa, where the first Test was drawn. Australia made 450, including a century in only 70 minutes by Jack Gregory, in the first innings of the second Test, but again they were held to a draw. They won the series by winning the third Test, played at Newlands, by 10 wickets. They were paid £500 each for the tour. 'That was quite a good sum of money in those days, but remember we were away for nearly nine months,' Hunter Hendry said, 'and we weren't allowed to make any money from the game. Later on they fined Bradman £50 because extracts from his book were published during the 1930 tour, and they left Arthur Mailey out of a Test match because he wrote for the papers without their permission. We generally had as little to do with the administrators as possible, and they were pretty stand-offish too. They were a severe lot of blokes; when we were on tour we weren't even allowed to have our wives in the country we were playing cricket in.

'The fellows on the board then, we felt with a lot of them that they were there for themselves rather than for cricket or the cricketers. The same thing applied right through to the World Series bust-up; I thought the board came out of that very badly. Financially, it was a pretty hard life being a cricketer in my playing days. I had to find temporary jobs a lot of the time but I was asked to go down to the Melbourne Cricket Club in 1923 and I worked as a clerk down there. The Melbourne people looked after the players pretty well. I had a marvellous time down there; I captained the side for five years and it was a great help to me too, because of the practice I got. It helped my game a lot, apart from the wonderful friends I made. What a club it is. A member there can play bowls, cricket, football, baseball, lacrosse. It's a pity they've never made anything of the Sydney Cricket Ground like that.

'The difference between Sydney and Melbourne was pretty much the same then as it is now. Sydney is open-handed and everybody greets you as if you were an old friend. In Melbourne they take time to find out about you, but once you are a friend there, you are a friend for life.'

Australia was again too strong for England in 1924–25. England had Hobbs and Sutcliffe, who had good tours, and Patsy Hendren and Frank Woolley, but apart from Maurice Tate they didn't have the bowlers for Australian conditions. Australia batted to number nine or 10 and had bowlers Mailey and Gregory and Clarrie Grimmett, who made his debut in the fifth Test with 11 wickets.

Hunter Hendry did not play in the Tests in 1924–25, but was picked to go to England in 1926. He started the tour well but caught scarlet fever and was out of the game for four months. After four drawn Tests, England won back the Ashes with victory in the fifth. Hobbs, Sutcliffe and Tate again were England's strength, and Harold Larwood played in the second and fifth Tests. Charlie Macartney had his best tour, with successive centuries in the second, third and fourth Tests. At Leeds, in the third Test, he went in first wicket down when Bardsley was out for a duck and made his hundred in 103 minutes. At lunch he was 112.

The Australians saw Larwood for the first time in a festival match at Folkestone. 'I thought he was a great bowler when I first saw him,' Hendry said. 'He had such a perfect action, and so much control. His great feature was his accuracy and length. He could put it on a two bob piece and he moved the ball a bit in the air. I reckon he is the best fast bowler I have seen.

'By the time the 1928–29 series came around the tables had turned on us. England had the experience of Patsy Hendren, Hobbs, Sutcliffe and Tate. They had a real express bowler, Harold Larwood, and they had Walter Hammond, who was the best bat in the world then, by a long way. He had a wonderful summer. England won the first and second Tests easily. Then they won the third Test by three wickets and the fourth by only 12 runs. We finally got one back on them in the fifth Test, when Bradman got a century, his second of the series. That was a "timeless" Test, there was no limit to the number of days the Tests could go on for during that series. It finished on the eighth day. I was out of the team by then; I played in the first four Tests and I got a hundred in the second, but I had been dropped. But when I heard people say they play too much cricket these days, I often think of that game that lasted eight days in Melbourne in March 1929.'

The opening Test of that series was the first Test match played in Brisbane. It was played on the Brisbane Exhibition Ground. It was also Don Bradman's first game for Australia. Bradman made 18 in Australia's first innings. 'It rained after our second innings started,' Hunter Hendry told me, 'and we had a sticky wicket. I remember some of the old timers like Hugh Trumble, Warwick Armstrong and Clem Hill came into the dressing room and they were talking about it, and one of them said "It'll be all over in half an hour". They weren't far wrong, although if we could all have batted like Bill Woodfull, who opened, and carried his bat for 30, it might have been a different story. At any rate I was getting changed next to Bradman and he said to me, "What do they mean by a 'sticky', Stork?" "Well Don," I said, "you'll probably find the ball will do unexpected things. It'll probably turn a lot, and it'll jump straight up at you." "That'll suit me", he said, "I'll hook them". Anyway we only got 66 and England won by nearly 700. "Farmer" White got Bradman for 1, but what confidence he had. I reckon that's the secret of Bradman's success, his confidence in himself, and his marvellous eyesight. That first Test might have made an impression on him too, and affected the way he played the game later on when he was captain. England made 521 in their first innings and then we went in late on the second day and lost four wickets for 40 odd before stumps. On top of that, Jack Gregory had hurt his knee and couldn't bat — in fact it finished his career. We were all out for 122, 399 behind, then, because it was a timeless Test, England batted again and they finally declared at 8 for 342, a lead of 700-odd. Really, it was a hopeless task, even before it rained, and I think it may have coloured Don's attitude later in his career, when he had the chance to turn the screw the other way.

'Maurice Tate was the greatest medium-pace bowler in my memory. He only took four yards, but he came off the wicket as fast as any of the so-called fast bowlers and he could move the ball both ways. He could bring one back at you; he was on his own. He and Larwood were a great combination in 1928–29. I could never forgive Jardine for the way he treated Tate in 1932–33. Maurice stood up to him over the bodyline business, so Jardine kept him on the outer, hardly even gave him a bowl. During that tour half-a-dozen of the English players who didn't like Jardine's tactics had a private dinner to talk about what they could do, and Douglas Jardine barged in on them, wanting to know what was going on. Now Maurice Tate was the nicest, gentlest man you could ever meet. He was quietly spoken and a great sportsman. But that dinner ended up with Tate picking up a glass of beer and emptying it over his captain.

'I tell everyone not to blame Larwood one scrap for bodyline. He was a professional cricketer, and Jardine was a very strict amateur, so Larwood was practically a servant to him. If Jardine had told him to jump over the bloody moon, he'd have had to try and do it. He wasn't to blame at all. It was different for someone like Gubby Allen, who was an amateur and so was allowed to make up his own mind about how he bowled. That was the way it was in those days. It wasn't so many years before that the professionals couldn't change in the same dressing room as the amateurs.'

Hendry had temporary jobs most of the time during his playing days: 'That was all you could get then, unless you were lucky enough to get a job like the one I had at the Melbourne Cricket Club. But there weren't too many of them around. There were a few employers prepared to put well-known sports-men on as salesmen — that sort of thing — but that became more common later. And of course there was never any thought of making decent money from actually playing the game, as the players do now, so it was hard to make a living. On the way to England in 1926, I met a chap on the ship called Webb, of H. H. Webb and Company; they made handles and all the equipment for coffins. He told me that he was going to England to get the agency for the London Paint and Varnish Company and that he'd been looking round for somebody to run that side of the business and he said, "I'm offering it to you. Think about it, and you can tell me what you decide at the end of the tour". Well I was very happy to join and the Melbourne Cricket Club were very good to let me go. A director of the London Paint and Varnish Company came out to start the business off and we'd just got it organised, we had a demonstration car — it took three weeks to do a car with paint and varnish — when duco came in and put us out of business.

'So I was out of a job, and of course the depression was starting, so I was on the dole for a while. As a matter of fact I was working on the roads, but only for about two hours, because someone who knew me saw me and got me a job in the office. Then I went back up to Sydney to work for an American firm that put tomato juice on the market. They did a good job too, with all the market research and advertising, but, you wouldn't believe it, that went bung too and I was out of a job again.'

Stephen Harold Gascoigne, one of the great characters of Australian cricket, although it is not known whether he ever set foot on a cricket field. Better known as 'Yabba', he was cricket's most celebrated barracker. **Cinesound Library.**

CHAPTER 27

The Bradman
phenomenon

During the 1920s, Australia's population grew from 5·4 million to 6·4 million. More than 320,000 immigrants were settled in Australia, most of them from Britain. The increase in population, and housing, and progress in transport and communications led to a boom in the economy.

By the 1920s cars were becoming a common means of transport. Bitumen roads were built in the suburbs and main roads snaked out into the country. Construction of the Sydney Harbour Bridge, built to cope with the increasingly mobile urban population, was started in 1923.

The brothers Keith and Ross Smith made the first flight from England to Australia in 1919 and claimed the £10,000 prize offered by the government. Commercial airlines were started; Western Australian Airways began operations in 1921 and in November 1922 Qantas (Queensland and Northern Territory Aerial Services) made its first flight, from Charleville to Cloncurry in Queensland. In 1928 Charles Kingsford Smith commanded the first flight across the Pacific, via Hawaii and Fiji; it took three days and 11 hours. At that time the sea voyage took nearly three weeks.

The Australian theatre and film industry were active and prosperous. The world's first full-length film, *The Kelly Gang*, was made in Australia in 1905. By 1920 several classic silent films had been made, including *For the Term of his Natural Life*, *The Sentimental Bloke*, *On Our Selection*, and *While the Billy Boils*. But by the late 1920s the 'talkies' had replaced silent films and our popular heroes were stars of the American screen: Rudolph Valentino, Charlie Chaplin, Greta Garbo and Mary

Pickford. Later, Australian radio personalities like Jack Davey adopted the American style and accent.

Perhaps when our childrens' children look back on the 1920s they will say that the move towards mass communications was more significant than the purely physical progress. Before the 1920s exploration and expansion had discovered and created diverse societies and cultures. Mass communication, with one source speaking directly to a huge audience, reversed that trend. The first Australian radio broadcasts were made from Victoria to Tasmania in 1905, on radio stations set up by the Marconi Company for communicating across the Tasman. The first commercial radio stations were established in the early 1920s and the first radio broadcast of a cricket match — Charles Bannerman's benefit match — was made in November 1922. By 1930 there were more than 300,000 radio licences issued. The Australian Broadcasting Corporation was established in 1932.

A young man named Charles Bradman came out to Australia from Suffolk in 1852 and found work, probably as a farm labourer, in the highlands south of Sydney. Eleven years later he was able to take up land in the developing pastoral district near Cootamundra and he went to live there with his wife Elizabeth Biffen of Mittagong. Their youngest son George also married a girl from Mittagong, Emily Whatman. George owned a wheat and sheep farm at Yeo Yeo in southern New South Wales. Three years after their fifth child, Donald George Bradman, was born in 1908, George Bradman's family moved back to the highlands where they bought a house in Bowral.

The Bradmans had no particular sporting ability but the Whatmans were keen sportsmen, devoted to cricket. Don's uncles, George and Richard Whatman, provided the enthusiasm for the game and what little coaching was needed for a boy with quite extraordinary natural talents. (Bradman was said to be as good at tennis as he was at cricket. He won the 1939 South Australian amateur squash championship and after he retired from cricket, reduced his golf handicap to scratch.) By the time he was 18 a number of big scores in the local competition, including 300 against Moss Vale and 234 against a Wingello side which included Bill O'Reilly, had attracted the attention of the New South Wales selectors. He made his debut for St George in Sydney first grade in November 1926 with an innings of 110 against Petersham.

The following season in his first game for New South Wales

Bradman's aggression and power are well illustrated in this photograph taken by Herbert H. Fishwick during the 1928–29 series. Fishwick, who worked for the **Sydney Mail,** *was one of the world's first great sports photographers.*

he made 118 against South Australia on the Adelaide Oval. After further success in grade and Sheffield Shield games he was picked to play for New South Wales against Percy Chapman's 1928–29 English team. The MCC declared at 7 for 734. Bradman made 87 in the first innings and, when New South Wales followed on, he made 132 not out in the second innings in a stand of 249 with Alan Kippax. He was chosen for the first Test against England. Tate deceived him with a slower ball in the first innings; he was lbw for 18. In the second innings, on the Brisbane 'sticky', he was caught by Chapman off 'Farmer' White's bowling for 1. He was twelfth man for the second Test, but was brought back into the team for the third Test, and made 79 and 112. In the two remaining Tests he scored 40, 58, 123 and 37 not out. His scores later in the season included 131 and 133 not out against Queensland, 340 against Victoria and 175 against South Australia. In 1929–30 he started the first-class season with 157 against an MCC side on its way to New Zealand. Then came a trial match in Sydney, to help the selectors assess talent for the team which was to tour England in 1930. Jack Ryder's team made 663, Bill Ponsford 131 and Archie Jackson 182. Bradman, for Woodfull's team, was 54 not out at the end of the third day and went on to 124. But Woodfull's side had to follow on; Bradman opened the batting in the second innings and was 205 not out at stumps. Later in the season he made the then world record first-class score of 452, against Queensland, in 415 minutes with 49 fours.

In his first game in England in 1930, at Worcester, he made 236 and followed that with 185 against Leicestershire. In his first Test in England he made 8 and 131 and in the remaining Tests he scored 254, 1, 334 (a record in Tests), 14 and 232. He made 974 runs in the series at an average of 139.14. The quiet, good-natured country boy, who four years before had seldom been far away from his home town, was lionised and feted in England and became a national hero in Australia.

It is said of Bradman that he brought to cricket an emphasis on huge scores, the inferred criticism being that, by relentlessly seeking double- and triple-centuries, he took some of the sportsmanship out of the game. A fairer interpretation might be that he brought to the game the ability to make big scores on a regular basis. After all, the incomparable sportsman Victor Trumper made the first triple century by an Australian in England, 300 not out against Sussex in 1899. Trumper once carried on to 335 (scored in 180 minutes) in a Sydney grade game, and he had nine scores of more than 200 in first-class cricket.

But it is no criticism of Bradman to say that he brought nothing new to cricket. Like W. G. Grace, his genius was in his synthesis of all the existing skills, mental and physical, into an incomparable whole. His unusual grip, with the left wrist turned more towards the back of the handle than is common, is said to have been the key to his ability to keep the ball on the ground when he played the hook or the pull. But his footwork—early, quick, and decisive—enabled him to play any shot from perfect position. And in common with the other legends of the game Bradman had the desire to impose his will on events while he was at the crease. He could hit the ball terribly hard. Occasionally, at the end of an innings, he 'had a slog'. During the bodyline series, he sometimes abandoned science against the English spinners because runs were so difficult to come by against the fast bowlers when they were bowling 'scone theory', as the Australian players called it. But for the most part his method was pure science, almost percentage cricket. He liked to get off the mark first ball with a push towards midwicket. Then he would get his eye in, get a feel for the wicket and assess the bowling before he started to exploit the gaps.

In the course of making documentary films, I have seen most of the film of Bradman which still exists in Australia. After the initial wonder at the spectacular shots, the lasting impression is of the finest of late cuts at the MCG, made possible because he had gone so far back and across that he could caress the ball almost out of the 'keepers gloves; and of him coming two paces down the pitch to play a ball gently to cover for a single. He ran like lightning between the wickets.

A non-drinker, and quite short (under 165 centimetres, or five feet five inches on the old scale), Bradman was diligent, courteous and thoughtful. There is hardly a photograph of him taken off the field which does not show a pleasant, open smile. In his younger days, by all accounts, he was outgoing and friendly, sure of himself but not an extrovert. The glare of publicity and the events of the bodyline summer of 1932–33 may have changed his outlook, but in all the writings about him I have never read an account of his being rude, unpleasant or arrogant. He may not have been the typical Australian of legend, the bronzed Anzac or the 'dinkum Aussie', but he was probably typical enough.

Don and Jessie Bradman in the late 1930s.

CHAPTER 28

Don't get hit

On 9 May 1927, 40,000 people gathered in Canberra for the opening of the newly-built Parliament House by the Duke of York. A solitary Aboriginal who wanted to watch the ceremony was led away by police on the grounds that he was 'inadequately clad for the occasion'.

William Morris Hughes had formed the Nationalist Party in 1917 from elements of the Labor and Liberal Parties and he led the new party to a comfortable win in the federal election held that year. They won again in 1919, but in 1922 Labor won 30 seats and the Nationalists only 28. The Country Party, with 14 seats, held the balance of power. When Earle Page, leader of the Country Party, announced that he would not serve with Billy Hughes, Stanley Melbourne Bruce became leader of the Nationalist Party and the Country and Nationalist Parties formed a coalition.

Despite the material progress since Federation, traces of the divisions in Australian society which had existed since its settlement by Europeans were still evident in the 1920s. Wages and working conditions were generally better than in England but the proud notion that Australia could 'show the world how to live' was replaced by the realisation that the Nationalist and Country Parties were becoming more and more the representatives of special interests. There was a spate of strikes; looters took over the centre of Melbourne when the police went on strike in 1923; seamen and waterside workers brought the waterfront to a standstill in 1925; the coalfields saw further strike action in 1928. The government decided to confront the unions and at the 1928 elections Stanley Bruce introduced proposals for industrial reform. The coalition won the election, but Billy Hughes, eager for revenge, engineered the defeat of the proposals in parliament. The election which followed, in 1929, was won by the Labor Party.

The new Prime Minister, James Scullin, insisted on the appointment of Isaac Isaacs, a judge of the High Court, as the first Australian-born Governor-General. But Scullin had little opportunity to devote to ideological issues; following the collapse of the international financial system in 1929 the price of Australia's main exports, wool and wheat, fell by 50 per cent. British capital was again withdrawn from Australia and it was almost impossible to borrow money to replace it. Public works were postponed or abandoned, the demand for goods and services declined, production and profits fell, investment ceased. Unemployment rose from six per cent in 1926 to 19 per cent in 1930 and to 29 per cent in 1932. An army of unemployed roamed the country. Most of them knew they could not find work and would settle for something to eat.

No government was equipped to deal effectively with personal hardship on such a scale. The Labor Party split in January 1931 and was defeated in the house in November. At the election which followed in December 1931 Labor won only 16 seats. The Country Party held four seats and the United Australia Party, formed by a merger of Nationalist and Labor members under the leadership of Tasmanian-born Joseph Lyons, won 37 seats.

Left: *Douglas Jardine, as drawn by Arthur Mailey.* Above: *1930s style promotion, from the* Adelaide Advertiser.

Douglas Jardine, who disliked Australians, was chosen to captain the English team to Australia in 1932–33. It is hard to find a good word in Australia for the perpetrator of bodyline, but Douglas Jardine has his defenders. Bill O'Reilly played for Australia in all five Tests of the bodyline series. He finished the series with the conviction, due to Jardine's tactics, that there were not many Englishmen that he 'would want to spend the time of day with'. Twenty years later, as a journalist covering an Australian tour of England, O'Reilly had dinner with Douglas Jardine. In his book *Tiger*, O'Reilly says 'I was overjoyed to find that Douglas Jardine was human. Even shyish . . . there had been a strange but moving change. I liked him, and I told him so'.

Jardine's duty as captain of the 1932–33 side was to win back the Ashes. The only way to do that was to curb Bradman, who had proved that he was the master of the English attack when orthodox tactics were used. If England was to win, if Jardine was to do his duty, unorthodox methods had to be adopted. Bodyline was devised; it was systematic short-pitched bowling on the line of the batsman's body, with eight of the nine fieldsmen on the leg side. Five men were placed close to the batsman so that a defensive shot at a rising ball was likely to produce a catch. In case the batsman tried to attack the short ball, men were placed at deep square and deep fine leg, positioned to catch the hook or pull. It was a fine piece of logic. Larwood was the key; he had the speed and control to make it work. Though less than express, Voce was sharp enough and accurate enough to act as a foil for Larwood. Bowes was less effective. Allen, the amateur, refused to bowl bodyline, although he fielded close in on the leg side and took several catches off Larwood's bowling. Tate would have nothing to do with it and was not selected for the Tests. The Nawab of Pataudi, one of the best batsmen in a strong batting side, told Jardine of his disapproval and was dropped after the second Test, having made a century in the first.

Australia had played two series since the England tour of 1930. The West Indies, who had played their first Test series against England in 1928, came to Australia in 1930–31. They had plenty of ability but not much experience. Despite the spectacular all-round ability of Learie Constantine and the brilliance of the batsman George Headley, Australia won the first four Tests. The West Indies won the fifth Test, their first Test victory against Australia, at the Sydney Cricket Ground in March 1931, when Grant declared leaving Australia 250 to win on a difficult wicket. Australia failed by 30. South Africa had their second tour of Australia in 1931–32, losing all five Tests.

The exuberance and style of the West Indies is evident in this photograph taken during their tour in 1930–31. The batsman is the Victorian Keith Rigg and the fieldsman at left is Learie Constantine.

The bowling of Clarrie Grimmett, who took 33 wickets in the Tests against both touring sides, was perhaps the decisive factor in both series. Bill O'Reilly played his first game for Australia in the fourth Test against the South Africans. Stan McCabe, Archie Jackson, Alan Kippax, Bill Ponsford and Bill Woodfull furthered their reputations.

Bradman confirmed his brilliance with a double century and a century against the West Indies and scores in successive Tests against the South Africans of 226, 112, 169 and 299 not out. He married Jessie Menzies in April 1932 and three weeks later left with the Australian team which toured the United States and Canada, playing 51 matches in 100 days. The tour was organised by Arthur Mailey and remains the only tour of the United States organised with the involvement of the Board of Control. Among the board's stipulations was a requirement that no player should receive more than £100 from tour profits and that any amount in excess of this should be handed over to the board. For this tour, the board dropped its ban on wives touring with the team; Jessie Bradman went with the team and acted as their hostess when they entertained.

Bradman started the 1932–33 season with 238 in 219 minutes against Victoria. Jardine's team arrived in Perth in October 1932 and swept impressively eastwards. Very strong in batting, they made 334 for 8 wickets against West Australia, 583 for 7 against a combined Australian team in Perth, 634 for 9 in Adelaide and 408 for 9 against Victoria. Larwood had been fast, but not especially menacing. Then, in Melbourne, in a game against an Australian XI—not a Test match—the MCC, batting first, were all out for 282. Although Douglas Jardine was not playing in the match, the Englishmen chose this moment to unveil their tactics. Arthur Mailey, in *And Then Came Larwood*, wrote of this game: 'Larwood was the spearhead of the English attack . . . there is no doubt that in this match he set up a complex in the minds of the Australian batsmen that was not really shaken off throughout the whole tour.' Bradman, who used his brilliant footwork to try to score runs without being hit, was lbw to Larwood for 36 in the first innings. The Australian XI made 218. Then Lisle Nagel, who could swing the ball prodigiously in the right conditions, took 8 for 32 from 10 overs. The MCC were dismissed for 60. In the short time remaining before the match ended in a draw, Larwood unleashed some more of his thunder-bolts. He had Woodfull caught behind for a duck. Bradman made 13 before he was bowled by Larwood, stepping away to leg to try to cut a ball which hit the top of his off stump. In the one remaining match before the first Test the MCC defeated New South Wales by an innings. Bradman, who was unwell and unable to eat, played in this game without success. Larwood did not play, but Jack Fingleton, who made 119 for New South Wales in the first innings, wrote in *Cricket Crisis* that Voce 'bowled with studied intent at the body, the ball pitching at the half-way mark and sometimes shorter; he had four to five short legs with two men covering them in the deep. Voce bowled Bradman, but for the main purpose the stumps were intended to serve, they could well have been left in the pavilion'.

Bradman's ability was such that, despite occasional failures, his success had been relatively easily won. It had come quickly and had peaked at a level which approached the physical limits of batsmanship. Bodyline threatened his supremacy. It also threatened him with serious injury. In the long run, it gave the batsman the choice of getting hurt or getting out, which repre-sented an attitude which people were not used to. This had come about because of Bradman's dominance.

Bradman had other worries at the time. There was little money to be made from playing cricket for Australia. The previous year an English club had made him an offer which would have given him more money in a season than he would have made in Australia in several years. He was tempted, but in October 1931 a consortium of newspaper, radio and retail interests made him a counter-offer to write and talk on cricket and sell sportsgoods, which he accepted. At the start of the 1932–33 season the board ruled that he could not write on cricket and play for Australia. Bradman said he would honour his contract with Associated Newspapers, even if it meant that he could not play for Australia. The board then asked Associated Newspapers to let Bradman out of the contract. After Associated Newspapers had agreed to do this, Bradman had an offer from an English paper to cover the coming series for a fee of £3000. Bradman again told Associated Newspapers that he was willing to honour his contract with them, but was asked by R. C. Packer, the editorial head of the group, to play for Australia, and 'to forget writing for the time being'. (R. C. Packer was Kerry Packer's grandfather.)

So play he did, but not before his health had broken down. He was unavailable for the first Test, played in Sydney, where Stan McCabe played his marvellous innings. Larwood and Voce bowled bodyline from the first over and, despite an unresponsive wicket, Australia was 3 wickets for 82 when McCabe came to the crease and 4 for 87 when Victor Richardson, the last recognised batsman, joined him. Gradually this pair broke down the bowling, getting on top of Voce first, and then hitting a tiring Larwood temporarily out of the attack. They put on 129 before Richardson went to the new ball late on the first day.

Bill O'Reilly went in to bat the next morning when the eighth wicket fell: 'It was an experience I will never forget. Larwood had just bowled Lisle Nagel first ball. Nagel's bat hadn't come down from its backlift at the time the middle stump went hurtling. I walked out to be met by my mate Stan McCabe, who was then 127, during the greatest Test innings I've ever seen played on this ground. He met me halfway and he said: "Don't worry Tiger, he won't bowl a bouncer at you". I had enough intelligence to say to him "I know, he won't waste one". So I took block as if I really meant to stand up and give him larrydooly. I had a good look around the field, which is what everyone does who wants to look like a batsman, and then this little man came running in from the distance. I say little; he was about five feet eight, he had a chest on him as big as the village blacksmith and I thought as he came up of what my captain, Billy Woodfull, had said to me: "Whatever you do Tiger, don't get hit." I thought that was pretty reassuring, but as he came up I thought of my friend down the other end; I'd better do the right thing by him. So I got in behind the bat, and it seemed that the ball hit the middle of it at the same time as Larwood had let it go. I looked down at Stan and I just shook my head. He nodded, and from that time onwards I took a very advantageous step to the rear every time I faced Harold Larwood.' McCabe went on to make 187 in an Australian total of 360. A diagram of McCabe's scoring strokes shows that he made only 16 runs in front of the wicket during his innings. Such were the restrictions of bodyline.

England, batting slowly, reached 360 with only two wickets down. Arthur Mailey wrote: 'Generous applause was accorded to the Englishmen when they had passed Australia's first innings score. This appreciation is doubly pleasing when it is considered that the batting during the day was dull and un-interesting . . . there is something wonderful about the Australian cricket crowd, despite the fact that one section of it throws oranges at another section.' England's total was 524, with centuries from Sutcliffe, Hammond and the Nawab of Pataudi. Larwood, bowling to his packed leg-side field most of the time, dominated the batsmen and took five wickets during Australia's second innings, which totalled 164, leaving England one run for victory.

Bradman returned for the second Test, in Melbourne, where the wicket suited the spin bowlers. Australia made 228 in the first innings, Fingleton 83. Bradman, who had apparently decided that the way to handle the English bowlers was to attack at all costs, was bowled first ball trying to pull a shortish ball from Bill Bowes. O'Reilly and Wall then had the Englishmen all out for 169. The first two Australian wickets fell cheaply. Mailey said, 'The scene was set for Bradman, who came in with a smile playing around his mouth. The 65,000 people packed like sardines, hanging on to balcony, railing posts, trees, and every other vacant spot, forgot their discomfort for a while and looked forward to seeing the young champion stop the rot'. Against tight bowling on a difficult wicket, Bradman started slowly, but gradually got on top. He had support from Bill Woodfull (26) and Victor Richardson (32) but as he approached his century, only the tailenders were left. 'People could hardly restrain their anxiety. Barmen, gatekeepers, waitresses, groundsmen, cashiers, policemen joined the big crowd, which was ready to burst into one mighty cheer.' Finally, facing Voce, 'Bradman shut his teeth, and, crash, the ball went soaring over the leg fieldsmen . . . the deafening roar which followed held the game up for minutes. Fresh outbursts in different parts of the crowd broke out and were joined by the whole crowd time after time'. England needed 251 to win. O'Reilly took five wickets for the second time in the game. He and Ironmonger made sure they went to Adelaide with the series square.

It seemed that Bradman had mastered bodyline and when four English wickets had fallen for 30 on the first morning in Adelaide, Australia seemed set to go 2–1 up. But Leyland, Wyatt, Paynter and Verity held them out and England made 341.

Then the simmering bodyline business came to the boil. Larwood bowled his first over to an orthodox field. Gubby Allen, bowling with terrific pace from the other end, had Fingleton caught behind in the second over of the innings. With the last ball of his second over Larwood hit Woodfull over the heart. Woodfull staggered away from the pitch. Film of the incident shows him doubled up in agony as Bradman and several of the fieldsmen run to his side. The crowd hooted and counted Larwood out. At the start of Larwood's next over, Jardine further antagonised the crowd by moving his men into their leg-side positions. Woodfull was struck several times on the body; Bradman weaved, ducked and tried to play attacking shots on both sides of the wicket. Eventually, playing a defensive shot to a ball coming at his chest, he propped a catch to Allen at short backward square leg. Larwood then attacked McCabe, who soon edged a catch to Jardine in the leg trap. Woodfull was bowled by Allen when the score was 51 and left the field still distressed by the hit over the heart from Larwood. Pelham Warner, the English manager, came into the Australian dressing room to sympathise with Woodfull, who made his famous remark: 'There are two team out there on the oval. One is playing cricket. The other is not.'

Richardson (28) and Ponsford (85) then held out for 80 runs and Oldfield batted quite confidently against orthodox bowling. Soon after the new ball had been taken Oldfield, who had made 41, tried to hook a shortish ball from Larwood. He deflected it into his head and collapsed beside the pitch. There was

Bert Oldfield escorted off the field by Woodfull after Oldfield had deflected a short ball from Larwood into his head. **Cinesound Library.**

pandemonium in the crowd. Woodfull, in a suit, came onto the ground to escort Oldfield off. Bill O'Reilly, who was the next man in to bat, says it was about 10 minutes before the crowd had settled down enough for the game to resume.

Woodfull's remark to Warner was reported in the papers, which put the Board of Control in the position of either having to back him publicly, or ignore the incident, which would have implied lack of support. They chose to cable the MCC:

'BODYLINE BOWLING HAS ASSUMED SUCH PROPORTIONS AS TO MENACE THE BEST INTERESTS OF THE GAME MAKING PROTECTION OF THE BODY BY THE BATSMAN THE MAIN CONSIDERATION. THIS IS CAUSING INTENSELY BITTER FEELING BETWEEN THE PLAYERS AS WELL AS INJURY. IT IS OUR OPINION IT IS UNSPORTSMANLIKE. UNLESS STOPPED AT ONCE IT IS LIKELY TO UPSET THE FRIENDLY RELATIONS EXISTING BETWEEN AUSTRALIA AND ENGLAND.'

The MCC replied, deploring the board's cable, denying

Bradman tries to glance Larwood but is bowled behind his legs in the fifth Test of the 1932–33 series. **Cinesound Library.**

unsportsmanlike play and offering to cancel the remainder of the tour. The tour went ahead; England won the Adelaide Test by 338 runs and the remaining two Tests by six wickets and eight wickets. Larwood and Voce continued to bowl at the body and although all the Australian batsmen made reasonable scores at one time or another, overall the Englishmen were much too good. In the fifth Test, played in Sydney, Larwood, sent in as nightwatchman on the second day, went on to make 98 before being caught off the attempted big hit which would have given him a century. The crowd gave him a huge round of applause. In Australia's second innings he broke down at the start of his eleventh over and bowled the last few balls of the over at less than medium pace to Bill Woodfull, who patted them gently back down the pitch without making any attempt to score. Larwood's feet were bruised and painful, but Jardine would not let him leave the field until Bradman had been dismissed. When Verity bowled him for 71, Bradman and Larwood both left the ground. Larwood did not play Test cricket again.

The Australian Board of Control asked for an assurance that bodyline bowling would not be used on the scheduled tour of England in 1934. There was discussion as to whether the tour should proceed if the assurance was not given. The MCC were naturally reluctant to take steps to outlaw bodyline, as this would have inferred criticism of Jardine's tactics in 1932–33. At home in 1933, England saw some bodyline tactics from Larwood and Voce and from the touring West Indians. Before the 1934 series started it was made clear to the Australians that intimidatory bowling to a leg side field would not be allowed. It was an unwritten agreement; the umpires, apparently, were to be the enforcers. Larwood played county cricket in the 1934 season but was not picked to play against the Australians for Nottinghamshire.

Cricket returned to normal. In England in 1934, after an uncertain start, Bradman returned to his usual brilliant form. He made 304 in the fourth Test at Leeds and 758 runs in the series at an average of 94.75. Ponsford, with 569 runs at 94.83, was almost as prolific and McCabe (483 at 60.37) was consistent and reliable in a crisis. Australia's only real fast bowler, Tim Wall, did not succeed in English conditions and his partner in the opening bowling department was Stan McCabe, who bowled accurate medium pace. Fortunately, what Australia lacked in quantity of bowlers it made up for in quality; O'Reilly and Grimmett bowled two-thirds of the overs in Tests and took 53 of the 71 English wickets to fall. Australia won the first Test, England the second; the third and fourth were drawn. Australia won back the Ashes at the Oval, where Ponsford (266) and Bradman (244) put on 451 for the second wicket in a total of 701.

CHAPTER 29

A whale of a time

The first English team to visit Australia after the bodyline series was the women's team led by Betty Archdale. This was the first international tour by a women's cricket team. Miss Archdale now lives just north of Sydney at Galston, in a cottage with an uninterrupted view of the Australian bush.

'That was after the bodyline summer, which caused so much ill-feeling, and I think that one of the reasons that we got such a warm welcome was that our cricket was so completely devoid of anything like that,' Betty Archdale told me. 'It was a happy-go-lucky, "let's have a bit of fun" sort of game, even in the three-day Tests, and I think the press and a lot of other people thought, "Isn't it wonderful to see cricket played without all that animosity that had come into the men's game".

'Cricket in England was started by what you would call the leisured class and the code of behaviour was very much the leisured class code of behaviour. Women's cricket was still played very much that way. Each club made up its own list of fixtures, and if we didn't like another club, we didn't play them. It was absolutely amateur of course: there was no form of competition and it very much played by the cricket code. If you were out and you knew you were out, you didn't wait for the umpire to say so, you just went. As for disputing with the umpire, you wouldn't have dreamt of it. You would have been sent off and not asked again. This wasn't so strong here and I don't think it is in England now. I mean, you can't very well say it's not cricket these days, can you. There was a time when you knew what that meant, but of course things change. When we were young we were still very much dominated by that code, but that's all gone by the board now. But they still play very nicely. I enjoyed the last lot when they came out. They were fun.

Betty Archdale in Australia in 1934. Cinesound Library.

'The Australian girls were much more regimented and organised than we were, and I think that's an Australian trait. We were much freer in what we did. It seemed to me that their team was very much more controlled. We all wore the same uniform to play in, but that was it. What we wore when we weren't playing was nobody's business but ours. I think Australians do rather like to regiment and organise things. Of course I can remember the days in England when the professionals came out of one door and the amateurs the other. That's just laughable now, ridiculous. But it was a different world in those days, and in many ways England has changed much more than Australia.

'But the trip here was a real eye-opener to us English girls then, and we learned a lot about not worrying who we were or where we came from. I know we were all terribly impressed by the open-handedness of the Australians. They were your friends from the word go, as soon as they met you. And the friends I made then, I've still got. In those days we were much slower in England to become friendly with people. The Australians were gloriously open and friendly right from the word go. They liked us and they expected us to like them. And we did of course. There was also more of an egalitarian atmosphere here than there was in England, but I think that's probably broken down a bit in England now. I think we are all getting to be more the same, I think that's one of the sad things in some ways, because you can go from country to country, and you might just as well stay at home. One of the things that surprised us about Australia was that you could go all the way from Perth to Sydney, 3000 miles, and the people were much the same; that was very strange to us, coming from England, where you travel 50 miles and you are in another county, with different accents and ways of doing things, and you might as well be in a different country.

'There were class divisions here, but nothing like as obvious as they were at home. The Australians were very competitive — they still are — and I think this may have been due to the lack of class divisions in Australian society. There are exceptions of course, like Douglas Jardine, but in England the upper class were generally non-competitive. They started cricket, and their standards and attitudes dominated the game. In Australia there was more of the working class ideology that you had to win, that it was a hard life, and you went for it.

'I was finishing training as a barrister, I had done my degree but I hadn't been called to the Bar. I was doing my degree at London University at night and I was doing various secretarial and office jobs to keep me going during the day. In those days you couldn't just come out here casually as you can now. Never in one's wildest imagination would you have thought of a trip to Australia. And suddenly this invitation came: "Would we go and play out there?" Of course we leapt at it.

'The cricket we played then in England was Saturday afternoon 2.30 to 6.30 and we'd often get through two innings without any trouble. Occasionally we played in London from six to nine in the evening and we had one England versus The Rest match each year which went on for two days. I remember we laughed our heads off because they sent a timetable with the matches against the States, and the Tests, and some very nice country areas. But the Tests were to go on for three days and we looked at this and thought about our 2.30 to 6.30 sprees and wondered how in the name of creation we would last for three days. Of course when we came out we found we did. The wickets were better than the club wickets we played on in England, and it's quite extraordinary how, the longer you allow, you spin the game out. These days the women are playing four-day games and there is talk of five-day Tests. But if you only have one day, you finish in one day.

'We paid our own fare, which was £99, and that took us right round the world; Australia, New Zealand and home again. Once we docked at Fremantle the Australians paid for everything; they put us up in hotels or in private homes and paid all the expenses. I thought it was a marvellous effort on the part of the Australians to risk it. We were terribly lucky. We started in Perth, and played on the WACA. We didn't play in Adelaide; they had women's cricket, but didn't feel they were up to the standard. But we played on the Melbourne Cricket Ground and the Sydney Cricket Ground and of course we got an enormous thrill out of that. I can still remember the excitement of walking out onto those famous grounds. It was just beyond any expectations that any of us had. They were miles better than most of the grounds we played on, although to be fair we did play on the Oval and some of the county grounds.

'We had a whale of time, and we thought the tour was highly successful. We got good crowds, a terrific press, and I think we did a lot of good for the game here. I think a lot of people came to scoff, but stayed to watch when they saw that we could play cricket and that we enjoyed it so much. We played three Tests. The first was in Brisbane, which we won very easily. I always thought the Australians individually were slightly better than we were, but by the time we got to Brisbane we were already a team. We'd travelled out on the ship and been all round Australia, thank you very much, and the Australians didn't know what had hit them. They were 11 good players, but they hardly knew each other. We played Tests in Sydney and Melbourne, too. We won two Tests, and drew one and we didn't lose a match on the tour.

Leg-spin bowler Peggy Antonio. Cinesound Library.

'We travelled by train and bus, of course, and we didn't just see the capital cities; we went into the country and saw some of the outback. There was great excitement when we thought they were going to fly us to Newcastle, but something went wrong and it didn't happen. I remember on the train trip up to Brisbane, in those days the train stopped at Coffs Harbour at about breakfast time, and we all jumped off the train and went for a swim. That was wonderful to us, it was just quite outside our experience, coming from England, to think you could just get off a train and go for a swim.

'The best Australian players at that time were Nell McLarty, a beautiful bowler, medium pace; she wasn't very fast, but she was very clever. She was a good field too. Molly Flaherty — I was terrified of her. And little Peggy Antonio, who bowled googlies, gave us some problems; "The girl Grimmett", they called her. Hazel Pritchard was a beautiful bat. And Margaret Peden, who opened the batting, was a good all-rounder and a very good captain. She was captain of the Australian team that came to England in 1937. They did very well, too. They only lost one match and that was one of the Tests.

'I find it very hard to tell whether the standard has improved. The fielding is considerably better; we always had one or two players who we couldn't put out in the deep because they wouldn't be able to get it back. Now they can all throw and the fielding is very good. But it's very hard to tell whether the batting and bowling are better. I suppose they are, but you can't really compare one era with another. The girls now are certainly more correct, more intent on playing the right stroke. We were more like cricket on the beach; have a whack, you know. I don't think we ever practised before a match; we just went out and played. I was very impressed the last time the English girls were out here. I went over to the Perth Test. They were very good. There was a nice atmosphere too, but it has changed, it's more serious than in our cheerful, carefree days.'

Betty Archdale returned to Australia during the Second World War. 'They announced that Wrens were going overseas and called for volunteers and the director of the WRNS called in on us and I asked rather nervously: "Where's overseas?" We thought overseas might mean Iceland, which was in the news at the time and I didn't really feel I wanted to go there. I was actually up in London playing cricket against the army and halfway through the afternoon there was a phone message to

The Australian women's team that went to England in 1937. They played 19 matches and lost only one. **Cinesound Library.**

ring headquarters, which I did, and they asked me would I be ready to go to Australia next week. I said "Yes ma'am. No trouble". We didn't actually get away for another month or so as it turned out, and by the time we got here the war was just about over. It was a lot of fun to catch up with old friends, and at the end of the war the job of principal at the Women's College in Sydney University became vacant and some of my cricketing friends said "Put in for this, it'll be fun". I thought about it for a long time; I was a barrister by then, but I was in my mid-thirties, and at that time in England, even for a man, if you went to the bar it was 10 years before you went anywhere. So I thought, "If I've got any sense at all I'll grab this job". I had to go home to get things in order, but I've been here ever since.'

In Betty Archdale's scrapbook are instructions to go with a sample of Bulli soil which she was given by George Garnsey, coach of the New South Wales Cricket Association: 'If you care to make an entire polished ball of the soil it is only necessary to pound it up with a hammer, moisten sufficiently to roll into shape, dry thoroughly and polish with an old blacking brush.' Garnsey also wrote: 'I am sorry I could not be of more assistance to your eleven, but I am sure your visit will do an immense amount of good. We all know of the brotherhood, and I should add sisterhood of cricket, and it will take more than a piffling dispute on bodyline to upset that fellowship. With kind regards . . .'

CHAPTER 30

Cricket by correspondence

In 1935–36 Victor Richardson captained a successful side in South Africa, Australia winning the series 4–0, with one Test drawn. McCabe, Brown and Fingleton made big scores consistently. Grimmett took 44 wickets in the Tests, O'Reilly took 27, and Ernie McCormick emerged as a talented fast bowler.

Bradman was not available for the South Africa tour. His health had not been good and he was involved with a new career in Adelaide, where he had taken a job with a firm of stockbrokers. But when the Englishmen returned in 1936–37 Bradman took over the captaincy. England was led by Gubby Allen, who was determined to repair the damage done by bodyline. All five Tests produced results and, as in 1894–95, the series was level with one Test to play. Attendance at the fifth Test, in Melbourne, was 350,534; total attendance for the series was 948,498. Both these records still stand.

Australia lost the first Test, in Brisbane, when they were caught on a wet wicket and skittled for 58 in the second innings. Worse was to follow; in Sydney, England was 6 for 426, Hammond 231 not out, when rain came. Allen declared and on a wet wicket Australia was soon 3 wickets for 1, with O'Brien, Bradman and McCabe back in the pavilion. After being 7 for 31, they managed a total of 80 due to some big hitting late in the innings from Bill O'Reilly. Following on, Australia made 324, leaving England an innings and 22 runs clear. In Melbourne the weather favoured Australia. When we were 5 for 129 at tea on the first day it seemed the Ashes were lost, but McCabe (63) held the batting together and after heavy rain overnight Bradman declared at 9 for 200. England collapsed for 76. Half an

161

The Sydney Cricket Ground scoreboard during the second Test of the 1936–37 series. Cinesound Library.

hour remained on the second day and the wicket was impossible. Bradman sent the tailenders, O'Reilly and Fleetwood-Smith, out to open the Australian innings. The following day, with the pitch improving but wickets continuing to fall, Bradman juggled the batting order. When the fifth wicket fell at 122, Bradman joined Fingleton. They put on 346, Bradman 270 and Fingleton 136, and put the game beyond England's grasp. So Australia went to Adelaide 1–2 down and when England led Australia by 42 on the first innings the Ashes again seemed at risk. Another double century from Bradman left England with 392 to win. Fleetwood-Smith, in his second Test, took 6 for 110 with his left-arm wrist spinners to wrap the game up for Australia.

The teams went to Melbourne for the fifth Test with the Ashes in the balance. Australia won the toss. After a couple of early wickets Bradman and McCabe put on 249 runs in 163 minutes and Australia was 3 for 342 at stumps on the first day. Bradman was out early the next morning but Jack Badcock and Ross Gregory put on 161 for the fifth wicket to put the game, and the Ashes, beyond England's reach. Australia made 604. O'Reilly, who took five wickets in the first innings and three in the second, dominated the English batsmen throughout. Australia won by an innings and 200 runs. Relations between the two sides had improved so much since the bodyline tour that after the game, during a speech from the grandstand of the Melbourne Cricket Ground, the chairman of the Board of Control, Dr Alan Robertson, said he was sorry England had not won the Test and the Ashes!

Bill O'Reilly's columns in the *Sydney Morning Herald* and Melbourne *Age* are famous for their bias in favour of spin bowling. He comes across in print as irascible, almost outlandish. As a cricketer he was famous for his persistence, his loathing of all batsmen—which was forgotten the moment stumps were drawn—and his appealing, which was loud, frequent and said to be 'more in the nature of demands for justice'. Bradman, who described O'Reilly as 'the greatest bowler I ever saw', also observed that 'hitting O'Reilly for four was like disturbing a hive of bees'. In person Bill O'Reilly is full of provocative opinion and good humour. I spoke to him at the Sydney Cricket Ground early in 1987.

'Fundamentally I was a leg-spinner. I ran 13 paces which, for a leg-spinner, is a long way, but I bowled at close to medium pace. And I bowled the wrong 'un very frequently. They used to say to me when I came to the city: "Don't bowl your wrong 'un more than about once every two years, because once they get used to it they'll hit it for four every time." I didn't agree with

Bill O'Reilly in action in 1936–37.
Cinesound Library.

Clarrie Grimmett in England
in 1934. Cinesound Library.

that—I used to bowl it every time the inspiration came to me. Quite often I would bowl it three times in an over and I didn't ever find anybody, except perhaps Lindsay Hassett, who could pick it regularly. Immediately, as soon as a new batsman came in, if I hadn't played against him before, I would test him out on the back foot. I would push him back and see how he went; whether he was awkward or clumsy, or whether he did it with style. If he went back with style and got me in the middle of the bat I would say to myself, "There's a job here O'Reilly, get stuck into it". But if he came forward, if he wasn't game to go onto the back foot, I couldn't get the ball back quite enough. I reckoned I could get rid of anyone like that at least once an over. The secret of being able to do that is to have absolute mechanical control of length and direction. I drilled that into myself hour after hour, day after day, when I was a boy and without that I would never have taken a wicket in Tests. I would never have played Test cricket.'

Ernest Peter O'Reilly, Bill's father, was the first teacher at White Cliffs, near the South Australian border about 800 kilometres west of Sydney. 'My father opened the school there in 1895. He was the first teacher, a young man of 21, and he had to deal with the offspring of 8000 "gougers", who were working in the cliffs getting opal. He met a beautiful girl out there called Myna Welsh and he married her and I was the fourth of their seven children. My father was a very industrious and ambitious young man and to get on in the Education Department he had to sit for the teachers' examinations, which were held each year in Hay, nearly 500 kilometres away, at the end of December. So he went to Sydney and bought a bike and he rode it back to White Cliffs. And every year, just after Christmas, he rode from White Cliffs down to Wilcannia, crossed the Darling River there, then rode south through Ivanhoe and all those old western towns and finally found his way to Hay, where he would sit for his examinations. Then he would get on his bike and ride home again. So he had a round trip of about 1000 kilometres, in the middle of summer.'

Ernest O'Reilly was transferred to Marengo, in the central west of New South Wales, in 1908 and to Wingello, in the southern highlands near Bowral, in 1917. 'It was there I discovered that cricket was a real game and that I loved it,' O'Reilly said. 'I walked seven miles, there and back, to attend my first match, for Wingello Public School versus Tallong Public

School. We walked along the railway line, killing snakes as we went.

'As I got older most of my practise was done solo. My particular hero when I began to realise that I wanted to be a spin bowler was Arthur Mailey, who was sitting pretty then as the best spinner in the world. He bowled leg breaks, not very consistently — he bowled a fair few long-hops — but I followed his deeds closely through the papers and I read about this ball he bowled called a "bosie". It was a wrong 'un of course, but I had never heard of either expression before and of course I didn't have the foggiest idea of how it was done. I learnt to bowl it by correspondence. That came about because my eldest brother, Jack, had gone to Sydney to live and he became a member of the North Sydney District Cricket Club. There he had the good luck to see Arthur Mailey bowling his wrong 'uns in the nets. He watched it so very carefully that he was able to sit down that night and write me a letter about it and from that letter, I reckon within a day and a half I was bowling bosies at our front gate post there at Wingello. I never had any coaching; I think I was very lucky to have been born so far away from the system of coaching that I had no option but to work things out for myself. In fact there wasn't very much coaching in those days. Bradman was never coached, nor was Stan McCabe and I think they were lucky boys too.

'So I learnt the mechanics of bowling on my own and by correspondence. When I got into big cricket, I was certainly influenced by Clarrie Grimmett. He could bowl line and length for 48 hours in succession if required. He was the greatest mechanical machine I've ever seen bowling leg-spinners. He gave the no-hoper no hope. There was no way in the world you could handle him if you couldn't use your feet. Those that could use their feet battled with him day-long and he was prepared to go day-long too, never giving a run away, until they lost their patience. I'll never forgive the Australian selectors for not picking Grimmett in 1936. They just didn't know what they were doing.

'In my view spin bowling is essential to the game because it does two things; it gets the batsman out and it satisfies the spectators. You find that the bloke who can deal with leg-spinners is hitting them attractively through the covers and that's the best shot in cricket, the one that goes beautifully along the ground through the off-side field. Now you hardly ever see that in one-day cricket, because the emphasis is on short-pitched bowling. What very few people realise is that one-day cricket is actually becoming more and more of a defensive game and as it becomes more defensive it will become less attractive. That's why we have to keep spinners in the game, as a concession towards the future. If you've got no spin in the game then it has got no hope whatever of prospering, because people will eventually say: "We'll go and find something more interesting to watch". A team without a spinner is like a man without a soul.

'I played my first Test against South Africa at Adelaide in 1932. I got paid £30 for a game which could, if required, have gone on indefinitely, because they were timeless Tests. It could have lasted for a week or a fortnight, they were played till the finish. My career ended in New Zealand in 1946, when I threw my old worn out cricket boots out the window of the Basin Reserve at Wellington, to signify the fact that the game and I had parted company because of a knee that had gone bust. For that tour of New Zealand, about 21 days, we got £21. In their wisdom the Board of Control knocked back a suggestion which came from the New Zealand Cricket Council, who said they would like to raise the ante for each player by one pound a day; they were getting tremendous crowds at the matches over there and they thought that was the best way to show their gratitude. But our board, God bless them, said "No, they're contracted to play for a pound a day and that's what they'll get". That was their form, and it had been that way since 1905, it seems to me. The board was formed in trouble with the players; remember that six of the greatest players ever to play for Australia pulled out of an Australian team after a row with the Board of Control only a few years after it was formed. That attitude carried forward until 1977, and that's why they got into so much trouble then. They lost control of the game and they ended up having to sell it. Now I have to be a bit careful here, because there were a few good blokes on the board, in my time and after, but our attitude, the players of my time, was that most of the Board of Control were what you would call "coat-minders".'

In England in 1938 the first two Tests were drawn. In the first Test, at Trent Bridge, two of England's new players, Len Hutton and Denis Compton, made centuries. Barnett also made a hundred and Eddie Paynter was not out 216 in a total of 658. Australia was in trouble with half the side out for 151, but

En route to England in 1938. From left: Ernie McCormick, Lindsay Hassett, Bill Brown, Charlie Walker, Jack Fingleton, Ted White. **Cinesound Library.**

McCabe played one of cricket's classic innings to save the game. He was 105 when the seventh wicket fell at 263. In the next 80 minutes 148 runs were scored, 127 of them by McCabe. Australia had to follow on but avoided defeat comfortably. In the second drawn game, played at Lord's, Walter Hammond made his last big score against Australia, 240 in a total of 494. Australia's stylish opener, Bill Brown, carried his bat for 206 in the Australian first innings of 422. The Manchester Test was washed out without a ball being bowled, then at Leeds, on an under-prepared wicket, O'Reilly took five wickets and England were all out for 223. In bad light on a difficult wicket, Bradman played one of his best innings for 103 in a total of 242. O'Reilly, with another five wickets and support from Fleetwood-Smith, put England back in the pavilion for 123, leaving Australia 105 to win. At 4 for 61, in bad light with rain threatening and Bradman and McCabe out, it was anybody's game. Some judicious big hitting by Lindsay Hassett (33) settled the issue in Australia's favour. At the Oval, Hammond won the toss for the fourth time in succession. Len Hutton made his record score of 364, Leyland and Hardstaff also made centuries and England's total was 903 for seven wickets. With Fingleton and Bradman injured in the field and unable to bat, Australia was never in the race. England won by an innings and 579 runs.

A year later the world was at war again.

CHAPTER 31

One before the roller

Ray Lindwall was still at school when the war started. 'We were certainly afraid that Sydney would be attacked,' Lindwall told me. 'Later on, when Darwin was bombed, we thought we would be next, and when the Japanese submarines came into the harbour, well we didn't know what would happen. When I left school I had a job with a company called Commercial Steel; they were making bombers, guns, fuse caps and other war materials. Then in 1942 I was called up and I joined the army and went to New Guinea and the Solomon Islands. I was up there for about three years in the signal corps. I was a telephone mechanic; I spent a lot of time clinging to trees and posts, putting up wires for the communications up there. I wasn't involved in the actual fighting, but we had a few nasty experiences. When we were at Lae, the Japanese used to raid our camps at night, because they were short of food, I think. One morning we found that the kitchen had been raided and five of our blokes had had their throats cut. Another night I was on duty as a picket — we had orders to shoot on sight — and we heard a noise near our picket tent and we thought it must have been the Japanese, so we went out in the bush and circled round looking for them. I actually had a bloke in my sights, only a few yards away, and I was just about ready to pull the trigger when he said, "It's only me, Ray". It was a mate of mine. "Don't worry" I said, "the safety catch is on". It wasn't though.

'While I was up there I had dengue fever four times. I went to hospital four times and when I came back and played cricket, every now and again I'd get an attack of the shivers and get sick. I put it down to malaria at first, but after about a year I had a

168

blood test and there was no sign of malaria, so it must have been the dengue fever recurring. I had dermatitis too, so when cricket started again after the war I was playing under difficulties for a while. By about 1947, a couple of years after the war, everything seemed to come right and I was fully fit again, or pretty close to it.'

When German troops invaded Poland on 1 September 1939 the British and French governments told Hitler that they would declare war on Germany if the troops were not withdrawn. Hitler took no notice and war was declared on 3 September. On the same day the Australian Prime Minister, Robert Menzies, announced: 'In consequence of a persistence by Germany in her invasion of Poland, Great Britain has declared war upon her, and as a result, Australia is also at war.' Menzies had become leader of the United Australia Party, and Prime Minister, when Joe Lyons died in 1939. He was a lover of England and all things English and a gifted and witty speaker. Menzies had considerable appeal to the middle classes, but not much sympathy with or understanding of the union movement. He was not popular with his peers, many of whom had felt the sharp edge of his tongue. After the general election in 1940 he had to rely on two independents to survive in parliament, and he was forced to resign from the leadership of the coalition in August 1941. His replacement was Arthur Fadden, leader of the Country Party, but within a couple of months the independents crossed the floor of parliament. Labor took over the government and won the ensuing election.

The new Prime Minister, John Curtin, was a quiet, dedicated man, a lapsed Catholic and a reformed alcoholic. He had worked his way up through the union movement but had abandoned hardline socialism, although he still sought a more equitable society. Curtin had actively opposed conscription during the First World War, but he realised that he had to delay his plans for a new social order; 'We have to concentrate on the one supreme task which the enemy has imposed on us. We have to defeat him or die'.

Early in the war Australian troops were in action in North Africa and Greece. The threat from Japan arrived with appalling suddenness; on 7 December 1941, carrier-born aircraft attacked and destroyed a significant part of the United States fleet anchored at Pearl Harbour in Hawaii; on the same day the

Japanese army landed in northern Malaya; three days later Japanese planes sank the British battleships *Repulse* and *Prince of Wales* off the Malayan coast. They occupied Guam and Wake Island, north of New Guinea, and on 26 December the British garrison in Hong Kong surrendered. As the Japanese prepared to enter Singapore, the last post of British military strength in Asia, John Curtin said in a New Year message: 'Without any inhibitions of any kind, I make it quite clear that Australia looks to America.'

The Japanese landed at Rabaul in northern New Guinea on 23 January and began advancing down the chain of islands which led from Singapore to northern Australia. On 15 February Singapore surrendered and the 37,000 Indian, 19,000 British and 15,000 Australian troops were taken off to prison camps, or to work on the Burma Railway. On 3 February Port Moresby was bombed. The Pacific War Council in London requested that the Seventh Division be directed to Burma, but Curtin replied: 'Australia's outer defences are now quickly vanishing and our vulnerability is completely exposed.' He rejected the request, insisting the troops were needed at home. Churchill urged Curtin to reconsider: 'We could not contemplate that you would refuse our request,' Churchill said, but Curtin remained firm. On 19 February 1942 Japanese planes bombed Darwin. They sank eight ships and destroyed 23 aircraft, killing 238 people. In the following months 55 raids were conducted on Darwin, and Broome, in Western Australia, was also bombed. Java was invaded on 28 February and 20,000 Allied troops surrendered. On 8 March the Japanese landed at Lae and Salamaua on the north coast of New Guinea and began to move overland along the Kokoda Trail towards Port Moresby, while others sailed from the Solomon Islands.

General Douglas MacArthur was appointed Commander-in-Chief of the South-west Pacific and arrived in Australia during March. The United States Navy moved into the Pacific in force. Australia had almost 500,000 men in uniform, many of whom had very little equipment or training. Equipment poured in from the United States, along with 88,000 US marines, some 14,000 of whom were housed in temporary barracks at the Melbourne Cricket Ground. It was acknowledged that the Australian coastline was indefensible. The first line of defence was from Sydney to Brisbane, where MacArthur had his headquarters.

On 7 May Curtin announced to parliament that the Japanese fleet, bound for Port Moresby, had been intercepted. The following day, although the United States and Australian navies suffered heavy losses, the Japanese had three carriers sunk or disabled and were forced to turn back. The Battle of the Coral Sea, as it was called, turned the tide. Two Japanese midget submarines entered Sydney Harbour on 31 May and sank a ferry before being destroyed. A few days later the Japanese fleet suffered a major defeat off Midway Island near Hawaii, where they lost four more aircraft carriers.

In New Guinea, Australian troops stopped the Japanese advance along the Kokoda Trail and at Milne Bay east of Port Moresby the Japanese suffered their first defeat on land, at the hands of the Australians. At the end of 1942 American and Australian troops began the job of driving the Japanese out of Guam, the Philippines, Wake Island, Malaya and Borneo.

In Europe, Hitler's army was trapped outside Stalingrad and forced to surrender. By May 1943 the German forces in Africa had also surrendered. The war in Europe dragged on until 7 May 1945. By this time American troops were fighting, and still suffering heavy losses, close to the Japanese mainland and bombing Japanese cities including Tokyo. On 6 August 1945 an atomic bomb was dropped on Hiroshima and a second on Nagasaki three days later. The two bombs killed more than 100,000 people and injured and maimed another 100,000. Japan surrendered immediately. Almost 35,000 Australians died in the fighting or in prison camps during the war.

Ray Lindwall's grandfather emigrated from Sweden, married an Australian girl and settled at Bega, on the south coast of New South Wales, where they raised eight girls and seven boys. Lindwall's mother's family came from Ireland. Ray was brought up in Hurstville, a southern Sydney suburb. 'My brother Jack was a couple of years older than me; he was a keen cricketer and he taught me how to play when I was very young,' Lindwall told me. 'We used to play cricket and football at school. After school we used to play in the parks or on the roads; there was nothing else we could afford to do in those days.

'Bill O'Reilly lived up the top of our street. He was a school-master and every day when he came home from work, he walked past the corner where we played cricket and I used to try to make sure I was bowling when he went past. He didn't seem to take

The final stride of the perfect fast bowler's action. Ray Lindwall in 1947. **Cinesound Library.**

any notice of us, but years later he told me he knew what we were up to. I played junior cricket in the St George district and when I was about 14 I was recognised as a possible chance to play in club cricket, so I went up and tried out with St George. The next year I had three games in third grade. I went up to the seconds for another three matches, and then I was picked in the firsts and Bill O'Reilly was our captain. We had a young side, most of us were 16 or 17, and Bill did a wonderful job with us. We used to have to get up at half past five to practise, because it was very hard to get away from school in those days and Bill organised nets for us three mornings a week, Monday, Tuesday and Wednesday, at six in the morning.

'I was lucky enough to see Larwood bowl, during the Sydney Test in 1932. That was the start of bodyline of course, but it didn't really make much of an impression on me, for a number of reasons; we hadn't heard anything about it, it wasn't called bodyline then, and anyway Stan McCabe gave it such a hiding that it didn't seem to be very effective in that Test. And most of

172

our cricket was played on coir matting; you got plenty of lift on the matting, so we were used to seeing plenty of bouncers. I was impressed with Larwood though. I thought he had a beautiful action. People say I copied his action, although I think I probably had a similar action before I saw him. But I suppose I did copy him, even if it was unconsciously. He had a wonderful rhythmic run-up and I remember being very impressed by that. It must have been an influence.

'I was never coached officially. When I was 10 or 11 I used to play with the men and some of the senior players used to help me and give me tips. We had matches at school on Saturdays, but we didn't practise at school, not officially. Of course I used to practise at home, with my brother and the other kids in the street. I suppose in the cricket season we used to play for about five hours most days; an hour before school, at lunchtime, then for two or three hours after school, every day except Sunday. We had to go to church and stay home for Sunday dinner; by the time we'd had Sunday dinner we were too tired and full to play cricket.

'When I first played for St George under Bill O'Reilly, Arthur Morris was a bowler and I reckoned I was an all-rounder. When I got picked in the first grade side, I thought I was in the team as a batsman. I had been bowling medium pace into the wind and the first match I played in under Bill O'Reilly — it was over at Manly — Bill came up to me and said, "Well, son, which end do you want to bowl?" I said, "Well I've been bowling swingers against the wind". Bill said a word that I won't repeat, then he said, "From now on you lengthen your run two yards and bowl fast". That was when I became a fast bowler again. The next week we were batting and when I went to have a look at the order to see where I was going in, there I was, one before the roller. So there went my batting career.

'Arthur Morris was a left-arm wrist spinner at that time. A very good spinner, too, with a good wrong 'un. But during the same year one of our opening batsmen didn't turn up and Bill said "Righto Arthur, put the pads on, you're opening". He got 60-odd, I think. It was a beautiful innings and after that he didn't bowl very much. But he became one of the best batsmen I've ever seen.

'Another thing Bill O'Reilly did was to teach me to drink beer. I was picked in the Australian team that went to New Zealand in 1946, and played one Test. I was a teetotaller until then. When we played Christchurch I had to bowl about 30 overs one day, and I was sitting on the floor at the end of the day—it was very hot for New Zealand—drinking a pint of lemonade. Bill saw me and said, "What are you drinking, son?" So I told him, and he said, "That'll rot your gut". Then he gave me a pint of beer: "Drink this", he said, "and I want to see you drink three of these every day after the game". That was my first drink, except when the war ended, and I became a beer drinker after that. Bill reckoned that what you took out of yourself in energy during the day, the beer put back in again.

'I first got to know Keith Miller on that tour to New Zealand in 1946. He came back after the war with the Services side which toured England and India and then came home and played against the States. I played for New South Wales against them and after that we were picked to go to New Zealand with the Australian side. We've been friends ever since then. Keith had plenty of interests outside cricket, including the ponies. I never got involved with them, although he used to get me to hold his money if he had a big win and tell me not to give it back to him. But he always changed his mind and made me hand it over, then he would tell me it was my fault when he lost it again. Keith loved music too. We used to room together on tour and I used to take a portable radio. I was interested in jazz, but I didn't get to listen to much jazz because Keith loved classical music; I got to learn quite a lot about Beethoven and Schubert on those tours though. In 1948 we stopped at Naples on the way to England and we went on a sightseeing tour. Keith had to see the Opera House of course, and when we got there it was open, but there was no one around. We heard some people practising away up in the top somewhere, so we went up the stairs to have a look. It was a choir; we listened to them for a while, then we had a look around. By the time we got back to the front door it was closed and the whole place was locked up. We couldn't get out and the boat was due to leave, so we pushed and shoved, and eventually I gave the door a good bang and it opened. We just made it back to the boat in time.'

In the 1946–47 series against England, which Australia won three Tests to nil, Lindwall was the leading wicket-taker. He also topped the bowling averages and made an even 100 in the second innings of the third Test. After the 1947–48 series against India, which Australia won 4–0, he was picked for the 1948 to tour England. 'The 1948 tour was the best tour I ever

went on. We had such a strong team—we went through undefeated of course—and it was my first major tour. Australians
were very popular after the war and we were treated like royalty;
everywhere we went we were feted and we mixed with all the
high society. I don't think there has ever been a tour like it since.
They have changed the format now, they don't have the dinners
and functions we used to have; they don't have the time or the
opportunity to meet people.

'Bradman was certainly the best captain I played under.
Apart from his batting talent, he had a complete command of the
game. The next time I went to England it was under Lindsay
Hassett and he was a very good captain, too, and a lovely chap,
on and off the field. He was a very good mixer, with the players
and with all sorts of people and was a born entertainer. There is a
well-known story about him at the Park Lane Hotel in London,
during the 1953 tour. We had a dinner, it was after a cocktail
party one night, and we were all dressed up in our dinner suits
and Lindsay had some ice cream spilled on his coat. The head
waiter came over and said, "I'm sorry sir, I'll get that cleaned for
you" and he took Lindsay's coat off and started to walk away.
He'd only gone a few paces when Lindsay called out, "Hey, just
a minute. I've got some on my trousers too". So he stood
up—this is in the dining room of course—slipped his trousers
off and said "Here, take these too and he sat down in his

**England 1953. Keith Miller, Lindsay Hassett and the Duke of
Edinburgh, with Don Tallon and Ray Lindwall in the background.**

175

underpants. About an hour later, they were all pressed and cleaned, and he stood up and slipped them back on again.

'We had a lot of good times, but it was a difficult sort of career, being a Test cricketer. There was no question of making a living from it. Most players had to have jobs, but it was hard to get a job where they would give you time off to play or practise. I lost a job when I came back from the army; I got the same job back as I had before I went in, with the aircraft factory, but after a while they said to me: "Do you want to play cricket, or have a future in business?" I decided I wanted to play cricket. I didn't have a job for a while, but then with the help of Bert Evatt, the federal Attorney-General, who was a great cricket fan, I got a job as assistant secretary to his brother, Clive Evatt, in a government department. I was there for about 18 months, then Stan McCabe offered me a job in his sports store. After that I got time off to play and to practise.

'Our pay was very poor. On the 1948 tour, we got paid £715 for a nine-month trip. We had to buy our own gear and equipment; a firm in England gave us two pairs of cricket trousers each, but everything else we bought ourselves. And we had to pay all our own expenses in England except hotels. If we went out anywhere we had to entertain ourselves. The only time I came back from a tour with any money in kitty was 1956, when I'd had hepatitis, so I couldn't drink for 18 months. We never complained though. We were pretty much in awe of the officials. We were treated—not quite like schoolboys—but every time we were selected to play a State match we were given a talk by one of the officials of the New South Wales Cricket Association. They told us what to wear, how to behave and what to do and we respected all that. We didn't think much about the money—we just didn't think like that—we thought we were lucky to be playing at all and we thought the regular thing to do was to get that much money. We would have loved to have had a lot more, but there it was, we didn't think the money was in it, so we just played for the love of the game. That was the way the world worked then. In my view, Kerry Packer did a wonderful service for the players. I wish it had been going in my day. I would have been in it.

'But I was very lucky with my career, to be able to play for so long, and the people I played with. I started in 1946 in New Zealand, with Bill Brown as captain and I finished playing under Richie Benaud in 1959–60. I even captained Australia for

Lindwall to Bradman, during Bradman's testimonial match at the Melbourne Cricket Ground in 1948. Cinesound Library.

one Test, in India 1956–57, when Ian Johnson was sick, and that's something I'm very proud to have done.'

'After the 1948 tour Australia toured South Africa, where we won the Tests 4–0 with one drawn. Then we lost one Test to both Freddie Brown's England team in 1950–51 and to the West Indies in 1951–52, but won both series 4–1. South Africa came to Australia in 1952–53 and the series was tied 2–all with one Test drawn, but then consecutive series were lost against England in 1953, 1954–55 and 1956. 'That was the low point, I suppose, when we were cleaned up by the English spinners in 1956,' Lindwall said. 'That came about because of the wickets, really. I don't think it was done with the Test series in mind, but at that time in England there were some very good batting wickets and there had been some very high scores. The idea was to make the games more interesting by making the wickets less in the batsman's favour. So they used to put 'marl' — it's like a red sand — on the wickets and it affected the wickets so they favoured the spinners. I don't think it was aimed at us, but it certainly didn't help us, because we didn't have finger spinners like they had, we had wrist spinners and the wickets were made to suit finger spinners. Anyway it certainly suited Laker and Lock. Mind you they were very good bowlers, and they had a good batting side too.

'The only real setback I had in my own career, apart from getting old, was in 1947 when I was called for dragging in Sydney in a Shield match against South Australia. It set up a big problem with the officials; they asked me to change my action, but the only thing I could do was go back a couple of feet behind the bowling crease. I couldn't stop the drag, that was completely natural. Anyway the association got a coach to try to change my run up and my action; he was very sincere and he was trying to help, but I couldn't do it, so I went to Bill O'Reilly and I said, "Look, I can't do this. What will I do?" He said, "Just tell them you've changed, and when you get five wickets in the next match say thanks very much to the coach". Which I did, and that was the end of the problem in Australia. There was lots of publicity about it when we got to England in 1948 and there was a suggestion that I would be no-balled by the English umpires.

'Bradman sorted it out this time; before the first match at Worcester he said to me, "Look, it doesn't matter, if you don't get any wickets at all, just make sure you don't upset the umpires. Stay back behind the line as far as you can and once you pass the first few matches they'll get used to it and let you go". So I was very careful for a while and as a result I passed every umpire's test and again the problem went away. Another thing that helped was a newsreel that was made of Miller, Bedser, Pollard and me, the four fast bowlers of the time. It actually showed that I was the least offender with the front foot. I was dragging more with the back foot, but my front foot landed way back behind theirs on the wicket, so in fact I wasn't as close to the batsman as they were. From 1948 onwards my front foot was on the popping crease, so it would have passed the test under the present laws.

'I suppose I relied mainly on my experience to get wickets. When a new batsman came in I would usually give him a yorker first up, or very early in his innings; sometimes I would give him a short ball. With someone I hadn't bowled to before, I would watch him for a while and just try to work out where he might be vulnerable and concentrate on that. If it didn't work, then I would try something else.

'Later, when Richie Benaud became captain, I developed a great deal of respect for him because of the way he used to work things out. I suppose it was a bit different with Richie, because when I first played under Bradman he was already a legend, and Lindsay Hassett was a contemporary and a friend, whereas when Richie Benaud became captain I was a senior player and I had seen him come up through the ranks in club cricket. But we started to win Tests regularly again after Richie took over and, of course, he became a great captain. His father was a good slow bowler before him and Richie was a good bat as well. He took quite a long time to reach his best but by the time he did he had a very good knowledge of the game. Richie was always very keen and he worked things out more on paper before the game than anyone else I knew. He used to have a theory about how to do things and he carried it out on the field.'

Lindwall was married in 1951 and in 1953 he went to live in Queensland. 'After the 1953 tour of England I was offered a job in Queensland. My wife Peg was a Queenslander and as I was going to be travelling around playing cricket a lot of the time, we reckoned it would be better if she was near her mother. Peg was a florist, and when I retired from cricket I was looking for a business. I was looking at a sports goods business but when we went into the details there wasn't much profit in it at the time, so we started with the florist shop. Peg started the shop — I still had a job — but when she settled in and the business started to look promising after six or eight months, I left my job and joined her.'

CHAPTER 32

Take it or leave it

Australian society changed dramatically in the 20 years after the Second World War. The population grew from 7·4 million to 12 million. Migration schemes brought two million people, 40 per cent from non-British countries, mainly the Mediterranean countries and central Europe. They were, at first, crowded into migrant camps, called 'dagos', 'reffos' and 'New Australians', and generally treated as second-class citizens by the Australian-born. They survived and prospered and eventually changed Australia's racial mix and cultural outlook.

Ben Chifley's Labor Party lost the election in 1949; during the election campaign the Liberal Party, led by Robert Menzies, made much of the inconvenience of postwar rationing and controls and the threat of socialism. Menzies promised to ban the Communist Party and the Communist Party Dissolution Bill was passed in October 1950. When the bill was declared invalid by the High Court, on the grounds that it interfered with civil liberties, Menzies proposed constitutional powers for the ban and called a referendum. The proposal was rejected by a narrow margin.

The economy, fed by the wool boom of the 1950s and the growing international demand for Australian wheat and mineral resources in the 1960s, was the Liberal Party's greatest ally. Australians were among the most affluent people on earth and also among the most conservative. Menzies remained in office until 1966, when he handed over the leadership to Harold Holt.

On radio and television, which was first broadcast in 1956, the dominant influence was increasingly American. Most popular music and a good deal of television was aimed at teenagers, who were identified as having access to the new affluence and were encouraged to see themselves, and be seen, as an important element of the new consumer society. There were a thousand things for young people to do. In summer, surfing became a minor cult. Many teenagers spent their weekends at the beach, or driving around in the car, or just watching television.

At a time when selling to a mass audience involved spending increasingly large sums of money on advertising and promotion, it seemed as if the cricket administrators' attitude was, 'This is how cricket is, you can take it or leave it'. Their relationship with the players continued to be that of servant and master.

Sid Barnes was perhaps the only player of the immediate postwar era who did not accept the conventional wisdom that the players should be grateful that they were playing for Australia, that they should not rock the boat. Barnes's father died before he was born and his family moved from a sheep station in Queensland to suburban Stanmore in Sydney. He grew up tough, talented and very ambitious.

He was a natural showman. On his first trip to England with the Australian team in 1938, his enjoyment of shipboard life was

Sid Barnes. **Sydney Morning Herald.**

marred by the fact that he could not dance, so he took lessons from a professional dancer on board; by the time they arrived in England he was giving dancing exhibitions. In *It Isn't Cricket* Barnes wrote: 'I was very impressed by the King's suits. They were the best I had ever seen. I asked one of the coves who was in his party if he could tell me where the King got his suits made, but he looked pretty blank and didn't reply. For all that, I soon became known as the best-dressed cricketer in England.' Barnes bought expensive suits in London and a set of midnight blue tails. He broke his hand in 1938 and could not play for much of the tour, so he bought a 16mm camera and learnt to use it. In 1948, he made a film of the tour, which he took on the road around Australia when they came home. His film nights are described in *It Isn't Cricket*: 'The opening announcement, flashed right across the screen, was "Sid Barnes Presents . . ." And then would come "The 1948 Australian Cricket Tour of England". On the next flash would be:

Production	*Sid Barnes*
Direction	*Sid Barnes*
Camera	*Sid Barnes*
Commentary	*Sid Barnes*
Projectionist	*Sid Barnes*
Electrician	*Sid Barnes*
Labourer	*Sid Barnes*

'That always got a good laugh, and I got another one, too, when the first flash showed me walking from a pitch, just dismissed with the stumps spread-eagled. "Hullo," I'd say, "something's gone wrong here".' Part of the proceeds of the screenings went to charity.

Barnes made 1072 runs in Tests at an average of 63.05. As an opener in Sydney grade cricket he sometimes hit the first ball of an innings for six and on one occasion he hit four sixes and four fours off an over from the State fast bowler, Ginty Lush. But when the job of opening for Australia demanded different tactics, he took the elimination of risks to extremes, becoming, as the writer Ray Robinson said, 'Bricked up inside his own run factory'. He irked the crowd, he sometimes irked the people he played with and he certainly irked the officials.

Barnes was captain of the New South Wales Sheffield Shield team for a short period following the war, but after a series of wrangles with officials he declared himself unavailable for the

1949–50 tour to South Africa, saying that the £450 allowance was insufficient and he could not afford to go. The climax came during the 1951–52 season; he was chosen by the selectors for the third Test against the West Indies, but was rejected by the board. Barnes threatened legal action and when a letter defending the board was published in the *Daily Mirror*, he sued the writer for defamation. In the court case which followed board members were called as witnesses and interrogated by his barrister. Barnes won the case, several members of the board were made to look foolish in court, and the board was exposed as dictatorial and out of touch with the players. Members of the New South Wales Cricket Association, supporters of Barnes in this affair, were also hurt. E. A. Dwyer, who along with Bradman had opposed Barnes's rejection, was dropped by the board from the selection panel and for a time New South Wales was not represented on the selection committee.

Barnes, no doubt, was provocative and self-centred, but as Philip Derriman says in *True to the Blue*, 'First-class cricketers in Barnes's day were treated with a high-handedness which ought not to have been tolerated, even in 1952. In his own case, the board's conduct had been inexcusable. It had imposed on Barnes a terrible penalty — indefinite exclusion from international cricket — without allowing him a hearing or any right of appeal. It had even refused to tell him why he was being penalised. Yet Barnes's confrontation with the board in 1952 was not the landmark in player-administrator relations it might have been'.

Sid Barnes had a few more Shield games before he retired. As a journalist, he further alienated himself from the world of cricket by sniping at both players and officials. He died of an overdose of sleeping pills in 1973. In 1946, Arthur Mailey had said of Sid Barnes, 'If I were a cricket dictator I would shackle his rebellious spirit with responsibility. When Bradman walks off the stage Australia will be looking for a strong personality to take his place'.

In one of those accidents of fate which may have changed the course of the game's history, Richie Benaud spent the first of many days at the Sydney Cricket Ground in 1939. The game was New South Wales versus South Australia, the crowd was 30,400, the drawcard was the clash between Bill O'Reilly and Don Bradman. Benaud recalls in *On Reflection* that he and his

'I can still hear the impact and see the look of horror on Lindwall's face': Frank Tyson ducks into a short ball from Ray Lindwall. The next day Tyson took 6 Australian wickets for 85. **Sydney Morning Herald.**

father caught a bus to the Parramatta railway station, a train to the city and a tram to the ground, where they sat in an aisle in the Sheridan Stand. Unfortunately for young Richie Benaud, New South Wales won the toss: 'I didn't see much of Bradman, because New South Wales batted the whole day, but I did see Grimmett bowl and take 6 for 118. I went home that evening and started thinking about bowling leg breaks.' No doubt Richie's father, who bowled leg breaks with a good deal of success in Sydney grade cricket, gave him some encouragement.

If South Australia had won the toss and Bradman had been 200 not out at stumps, young Benaud might have gone home and started thinking about double centuries. His talent was such that he would have made it into Test cricket anyway; if he had not concentrated on leg spin, he was a good enough batsman to have played for Australia and he was an exceptional fieldsman. But he may not have become captain. Whatever the administrators may have done wrong over the years, they did the right thing by sticking to Benaud. First picked against the West Indies in 1951–52, it was his all-round ability, rather than any outstanding performances, which kept him in the side through the mid-1950s, when Australian cricket went through a slump, as it had done before in the 1880s and the 1920s.

Benaud played in four Tests in the drawn series against Jack Cheetham's South Africans in 1952–53 and in three Tests in

England in 1953, when we lost the Ashes 1–0, with four draws. He had a permanent place in the team in 1954–55, when England under Hutton clearly had the better team. England lost the Brisbane Test by an innings after Australia, put in to bat by Hutton, made 601. In Sydney, with Ian Johnson injured, Arthur Morris won the toss, asked England to bat, and seemed to have got it right when they were all out for 154. Australia replied with 228 and needed 223 to win after England made 296 in their second innings. Then Tyson struck a purple patch, as Larwood had done 22 years before. Tyson had been taken from the ground half conscious the previous day after turning his back on a short ball from Lindwall, which hit him on the back of the head. (I was there that day; I can still hear the impact and see the look of horror on Lindwall's face as Tyson fell.) Tyson was back on the ground the next day, bowling as fast as any man had ever done, and the Australians had no answer. They were all out for 184, Tyson 6 for 85 from 18.4 overs.

In Melbourne, when Australia, needing 240, were 2 for 75, he struck again, with 7 for 27. Australia lost their last eight wickets for 36 runs. England won again in Adelaide and the fifth Test was drawn in England's favour. Tyson shared the bowling honours with Statham, Wardle and Appleyard in the fourth and fifth Tests. With Hutton, Graveney, May, Cowdrey, Compton and Bailey, England were very strong in batting, too. The Australian team had some great names: Lindwall and Miller, Morris, McDonald, Harvey and Ron Archer. Alan Davidson played three Tests and Peter Burge came into the side for the fifth Test. They played very well in Australia's first tour to the West Indies, where they were immensely popular with the crowds and won the series 3–0. But England's superiority was confirmed in 1956 when, after a draw and an Australian win at Lord's, England, now led by Peter May, won successive Tests by an innings. The second of these, at Old Trafford, was 'Laker's match': he took 9 for 37 and 10 for 53. Laker and Lock between them took 38 of the 40 wickets to fall in the two Tests. There were charges of doctored wickets; in *The Game Is Not The Same*, Alan McGilvray recalls how, after Laker had taken his 19 wickets, 'The Lancashire president invited Don Bradman, Bill O'Reilly and me to take a look at the pitch. "What pitch?" boomed O'Reilly. "There's no pitch out there".'

On the way home the Australians played three Tests in India and one in Pakistan. In Karachi, Fazal Mahmoud was virtually unplayable on the matting and the Pakistanis won their first Test against Australia. The Australians won the series in India 2–0. Ian Craig led a successful tour of South Africa in 1957–58 and Richie Benaud, with 30 wickets and two centuries in the Tests, emerged as a world-class all-rounder. Australia won the series 3–0. Ian Craig, who had started his Test career at the age of 17 and was appointed captain when he was 22, seemed secure in the position, but he came down with hepatitis and was not available for the tour by England in 1958–59. Harvey was the senior player, but the board chose Benaud to lead a balanced and experienced Australian team. Lindwall and Harvey remained from the immediate postwar era; McDonald, Burke, Davidson and Grout were by now experienced and at the height of their powers; the newer players still on the way up included fast bowlers Ian Meckiff and Gordon Rorke, who was picked for the fifth Test, and the exciting young batsman Norman O'Neill.

Although Australia won the first Test, it did nothing to enhance Benaud's reputation as an advocate of brighter cricket. In England's second innings Trevor Bailey occupied the crease for seven and a half hours for 68. Then, with Australia needing only 147 to win, Jim Burke batted just as slowly for 28 not out. Australia won by eight wickets. In the second Test Peter May hit a fine century for England, but 167 from Harvey took Australia to a first innings lead of 49. Meckiff and Davidson, aided by some brilliant catching, took 18 wickets between them, and the margin was again eight wickets in favour of Australia. The Sydney Test was drawn after defensive cricket from both sides. Australia won the fourth by 10 wickets and the fifth by nine wickets, amid cries from the English press that Gordon Rorke and Ian Meckiff were throwing, and that Rorke was bowling off 18 yards and should be consistently no-balled for dragging his back foot over the bowling crease before he had delivered the ball.

Despite the brilliance of some of the players, Test cricket was becoming a war of attrition, with occupation of the crease being the prime object. Jack Fingleton said, 'the original purpose of the game had been perverted by several generations of "total cricket", in the evolution of which my own Australia must certainly accept her full share of responsibility'.

This was all changed one afternoon in Brisbane in December 1960. The West Indies had produced many brilliant cricketers

Jack Fingleton interviewing Harold Larwood, on Larwood's arrival to live in Australia in 1950. Fingleton, the opening batsman of the 1930s, was later a political journalist and a most thoughtful and authoritative writer on cricket. **Sydney Morning Herald.**

since the 1920s; they won home series against England in 1934–35 and 1947–48 and won the series in England in 1950, when the 'three Ws', Worrell, Weekes and Walcott, got the runs and the young spinners, Sonny Ramadhin and Alf Valentine, took the wickets. Since then they had not won a series against England and, although they had defeated India 3–0 with two draws in 1958–59, they had never looked like winning a series against Australia.

In the early games of the West Indies 1960–61 tour it was evident that Frank Worrell had some very talented young players in his team, but it seemed they would live up to their reputation of being erratic and not at their best in a crisis. In the lead up matches to the first Test, after an easy win against Western Australian Country, they lost by an innings against Western Australia and New South Wales, beat Victoria by an innings and drew with South Australia, Queensland and a Combined XI.

They played typically at the start of the first Test; Hunte slammed Davidson's third and fourth balls to the fence, Cammie Smith was caught by Grout trying to smash Davidson through the off side field. Hunte went in similar style, caught by Benaud at third slip. Sobers flicked Davidson to the fence at square leg from the first ball he received. Kanhai went the same way as Smith and Worrell joined Sobers with 3 wickets down for 65. Benaud came on soon after, was treated with respect for a couple of overs, then hit by Sobers for three fours in four balls.

Sobers's 50 took 57 minutes, the 50 partnership came up in 41 minutes and at lunch the West Indies were 3 wickets for 130. In the previous Brisbane Test, against England in 1958–59, the daily totals for the first four days were 142, 148, 122 and 106. Sobers century took 125 minutes. The West Indies were 7 for 359 at stumps on the first day and all out for 453 after 90 minutes play on the second. There is a great deal of chance in cricket. Sobers was within inches of being caught by Benaud at third slip, slashing at Davidson, before Worrell came in. As it happened the shot brought four runs. The permutations of what could have occurred between then and the end of the Test are infinite, but as it happened, 10 minutes after the scheduled time for stumps on the final day, Joe Solomon gathered the ball at square leg with the scores tied and the batsmen on their way for the winning run. It was the seventh ball of the over, which had started with Australia needing six runs to win with three wickets in hand.

The first ball had hit Grout high on the pad, dropped into the blockhole and resulted in a bye. Benaud had been caught behind from the second ball, trying to hit it out of the ground. Ian Meckiff played the third to mid off; no run. The fourth went down the leg side to the wicket-keeper, Alexander, as the Australians stole another bye. Grout swung at the fifth and skied a simple catch to midwicket, where Hall, after brushing Kanhai out of the way, dropped it. Another single; three runs needed with three balls left.

Wesley Winfield Hall pounds in, shirt tails flying. Meckiff swings, connects. The ball flies towards the square leg boundary. From the Australian dressing-room Conrad Hunte is obscured behind the sightscreen; it looks like a certain four. As it is about to hit the fence Hunte emerges and, running at full speed, drops a hand on it. But it doesn't matter. Look! They've run two and are on their way for the third. Hunte has no time to aim. He has to throw like a bullet and hit the stumps, or Alexander's gloves, from 80 metres away. He does. Grout dives full length from five yards out and skids along the wicket on his belly. The dust settles. Australia has won! No! He's out! The scores are tied. Two balls to go.

Lindsay Kline, last man in for Australia, a fine slow bowler with no pretensions as a Test batsman, has been sitting in the dressing room 'pale and quite unable to speak'. He steps out onto a chaotic stage. There is pandemonium in the crowd. Can this really be happening? All over Australia, work has stopped as people gather round radios. On highways, traffic pulls into the side of the road as drivers adjust the tuning. Hall trudges back, pounds in again, every nerve screwed with tension, every fibre strained to breaking. Kline, a left-hander, deflects the ball towards square leg and runs for his life. Meckiff has already started to run. Joe Solomon picks the ball up and throws left-handed from about 10 yards away, side on to the stumps . . . you know what happened, of course. You've seen the photograph; Solomon, on the left, with his arm still extended after the throw; Hall halfway down the wicket with his arms raised in relief and disbelief, Kanhai and Sobers at the striker's wicket, arms raised in triumph, Kanhai screaming his appeal to square leg; Alexander, backing up the throw, far to the right; Worrell backing up at the bowler's end, poised over the stumps, apparently relaxed, possibly not yet aware of the result. The batsmen know, though. Meckiff, running towards the broken wicket, is well short of the crease. Kline is two-thirds of the way down the pitch, looking back at Solomon. An inch either way and Australia would have won the Test. Of course, Solomon need not have thrown down the stumps; if he had lobbed the ball gently to the bowler's end, Worrell would have had plenty of time to take the bails off.

Underneath the photograph, in his copy of Jack Fingleton's book *The Greatest Test of All*, my father wrote: 'The beginning of the end of cricket.' He was right of course; after a game like that a time must come when that sort of excitement would have to be created to retain interest in the game. My father saw, and played cricket as a game for amateurs, played as hard as possible, by the letter of the law, but played to win. The game was for the players, not the crowd; any suggestion to the contrary meant that it was something other than a game, not cricket. But for younger people that game and the cricket played that summer reflected what was happening in the rest of the world. It changed our expectations.

The West Indies looked a fairly ordinary side in losing the Melbourne Test by seven wickets. But in Sydney, Sobers's 168 and the finger spin of Gibbs and Valentine won the game for

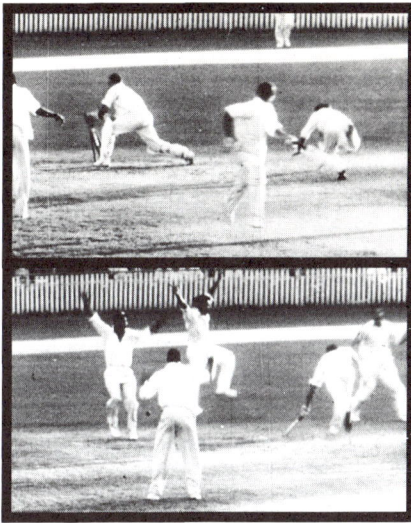

The most exciting over in the history of Test cricket started with Australia needing six runs to win with three wickets in hand.
First ball: Grout and Benaud run a bye.
Second ball: Benaud caught behind off Alexander.
Third ball: Meckiff drives but Hall cuts it off. No run.
Fourth ball: Meckiff and Grout set off for a run as the ball goes through to Alexander. Hall misses the stumps with Meckiff yards out of his crease.
Fifth ball: Grout skies the ball high to midwicket and Hall drops the catch. Three runs to win with three balls remaining.
Sixth ball: Meckiff swings the ball towards the square leg fence. They run two and set out for the run which will win the match, but Hunte's throw is right on target and Grout is run out. The scores are tied.
Seventh ball: Kline turns the ball to square leg and they set out for the winning run, but Solomon's throw hits the stumps. **All Cinesound Library.**

them by 222 runs. They should have gone 2–1 up in Adelaide, where Kanhai made two blazing centuries and Australia was 252 behind with nine wickets down and more than 100 minutes left to play. An extraordinary stand by Kline and Mackay denied them victory. So they went back to Melbourne for the decider, and with four runs needed by Australia, with three wickets in hand, another tie seemed possible. Grout might have been out bowled; a ball from Valentine apparently grazed the stumps, a bail wobbled and fell, but it was not clear what had happened and two byes resulted. Grout gave his wicket away; Martin and Mackay looked most uncertain. Then Valentine beat Mackay and Alexander, thinking it would hit the stumps, threw his hands in the air. The ball missed the stumps and byes won the Test for Australia.

Australia had never seen a series like it. The crowd was 90,800 on the Saturday of the Melbourne Test. Attendance for the Test was 274,424. Attendance for the series was 734,892, which compared with 395,798 during the previous West Indies tour in 1951–52. A huge crowd turned out to cheer Worrell's team through the streets of Melbourne when they left for home a week later.

'From something which seemed inexorably headed for the textbooks of the antiquarians,' Jack Fingleton wrote, international cricket emerged as a game 'for the enjoyment of the players themselves and the enormous delight of the cash customers'. The series, he said, had 'caused Australian crowds to reassess the merits of their country's rivals. Who can blame them if they assess merit in terms of the entertainment they receive for the cash they pay at the turnstiles to keep the game alive?'.

The change was a long time coming. In England in 1961 Richie Benaud knew he had a reputation to live up to. It was a good series in the traditional mould but Australia's reputation for brighter cricket was not helped by the fact that our most prolific batsman was Bill Lawry. England had the most exciting batsman in either side, Ted Dexter. The series was square at one-all after the third Test. Benaud, suffering from fibrositis which made bowling painful, had missed the second Test. England looked likely to go 2–1 up when Australia was only 157 ahead with 9 wickets down in the second innings, but Davidson (77 not out) and McKenzie put on 98 for the last wicket. Then, when Dexter had ripped the Australian bowlers to pieces with 76 in 84 minutes, Benaud had him caught behind and went on to clinch the match with 6 wickets for 70 from 32 overs. The fifth Test was drawn. In Australia in 1962–63, both sides had a pair of great fast bowlers; Trueman and Statham for England, Davidson and McKenzie for Australia. But the wickets were flat throughout and both sides had depth in batting. The series was drawn, one Test each.

The result was the same the following summer against South Africa. The controversy over Ian Meckiff's action was resolved during the first Test, when he was no-balled four times in his first and only over. Meckiff announced his retirement and

Richie Benaud in action against the West Indies in 1960–61.
Cinesound Library.

Richie Benaud relinquished the captaincy, although he played
out the rest of the series under Bob Simpson.

In England in 1964 four Tests were drawn, but Australia
retained the Ashes by winning the third Test, at Leeds, after
Peter Burge (160) had taken the score from 7 wickets for 178 to
389 with one of the great innings of Test cricket. In 1964–65
Australia played three Tests in India for a win, a loss and a draw,

and one in Pakistan, which was also drawn. Ian Chappell made his debut against Pakistan in Australia during the same season, in another drawn game. He failed and was not selected for the 1964–65 tour to the West Indies, which was marred by allegations of throwing. Led by Garfield Sobers, the West Indies won the series 2–1, but Charlie Griffith's action was widely criticised. Simpson had no doubt that Griffith threw and he was supported by Benaud, who covered the series for the press. Alan McGilvray and Keith Miller said that Griffith bowled within the law. The previous year, when the West Indies were in England, the umpire and former player Cec Pepper stood for an exhibition game in which Griffith played. After the game he wrote to the MCC saying, 'Had it been other than an exhibition game I would have had no hesitation in calling him for throwing'. The MCC replied, thanking Pepper for his letter, and adding that they 'entirely approve of the steps you have taken in this matter as it would have caused unnecessary unpleasantness'.

CHAPTER 33

Crash through or crash

President Kennedy first committed United States troops to the civil war in South Vietnam in 1961. His intention was to stop the spread of communism in South-east Asia. In 1964, Prime Minister Menzies announced a return to conscription by ballot for military training. In April 1965 the Australian government decided to send troops to South Vietnam to support the United States; a battalion of 1500 men arrived at Bien Hoa during May and June. Menzies retired in January 1966. His successor, Harold Holt, privately believed it was essential for Australia to build a closer association with South-east Asia, but he found that his options were either to support the Americans in a war in South-east Asia, or to back away from the alliance formed with the United States during the Second World War. By 1967, some 6300 Australians were serving in Vietnam.

Despite increasingly vocal opposition to the war, Harold Holt had considerable support. In the 1966 elections he won a record majority of 82 seats to 41 in the House of Representatives. Soon after, Gough Whitlam replaced Arthur Calwell as leader of the Labor Party. Holt was drowned in the surf near Portsea in December 1967 and was replaced by John Gorton. Gorton increased Australia's commitment to 8000 soldiers, 40 per cent of whom were conscripts. At the October 1969 elections, Gorton had a majority of only seven seats. Withdrawals of Australian troops from Vietnam started, but Gorton fell out with some of the senior members of his party, including Malcolm Fraser, and in March 1971 Gorton was challenged for the leadership by William McMahon. When the leadership vote was tied, Gorton gave his casting vote to McMahon.

McMahon, 63-years-old, had been a competent Treasurer under Harold Holt but he had little of the popular appeal of Holt or John Gorton. Meanwhile Gough Whitlam was reorganising the Labor Party and appealing to the new mood of independence and social reform. In December 1972 Labor was elected with a majority of nine. In the first few weeks, Whitlam withdrew Australian support from the government of South Vietnam, abolished conscription, recognised the People's Republic of China and announced sweeping changes to health, education and social services. Spending on education at all levels was to be increased, university fees were to be abolished, free health care was to be provided in return for compulsory medical insurance, land rights were to be granted to Aborigines. Much of it was overdue and much of it was done.

Perhaps it was done too quickly and without adequate understanding of the effects on the economy. The public sector became the pacesetter for salary levels, which doubled in the space of a few years. Unemployment and inflation increased rapidly and interest rates reached double figures, unheard of in Australia since the depression. For all his admirable ideals, Whitlam had little grasp of the realities of administration; many of his cabinet ministers had less.

Gough Whitlam's attitude was described as 'crash through or crash'. He did both. The incompetence of the older generation was exposed for the younger generation to see, as the focus of the consumer society continued to move towards the young. Whitlam survived an election in 1974, but in November 1975 he was brought down by the apparent arch-conservative, Malcolm Fraser, who professed a wish to see sport, rather than politics, on the front pages of Australian newspapers. As the administration of cricket fairly accurately reflected the national administration, his wish was soon granted.

In the opening chapter I quoted the start of an interview with Ian Chappell, the central character in Australian cricket during it's most hectic decade. Like every successful athlete's story, it starts with years of practise.

'When I was about five we moved from the eastern suburbs of Adelaide to a new housing development in Glenelg, down near the beach. There weren't many other kids around, so I didn't play cowboys and indians or other kid's games; I used to spend hours and hours at home just throwing a tennis ball

Trevor (left) and Greg Chappell congratulate Ian Chappell (centre) on his selection as vice-captain in 1969. **The Cricketer.**

against a big brick wall we had out the back. Later on I used to play Test matches against that wall for hours on end. I had a score book on the tank stand, and when someone "got out" I'd take my gloves off and go over to write the details in the book.

'Dad started throwing balls to me and I'd block a couple, then I'd go whack and try and hit one over the fence. Dad would say "Now come on, you've got to try and keep the ball on the ground". Then we'd have another go and same thing, I'd block two and then whack, try and hit it over the fence. So Dad started taking me to a coach called Lynn Fuller who lived at Glenelg. Lynn was a good old country cricketer and had played a bit of district cricket—nothing higher than that—but he was an excellent coach and he had a very good turf wicket in his backyard.

'Every Sunday morning of the summer, until I was about 16 or 17, I went to Lynn Fuller for coaching. There were sometimes a couple of other kids there, but usually one other kid and myself, and then Greg came along a bit later. I would bat for an hour and a half minimum and Lynn would bowl these little seamers at me. We started with forward defence. The first things

I can remember were forward defence and back defence. We just got defence, defence, defence until we could actually defend.

'There are a couple of things in particular that I remember Lynn telling me; one was that the whole of your batting is based on your defence; it's no good being a good strokemaker if you can't keep the good balls out of your stumps. And the other thing he told me was that it doesn't matter how good a coach you have, when you're out in the middle you're on your own, so you've got to learn to work things out for yourself.

'When Lynn had finished, and the other bloke had had a bat and I'd done some bowling, Dad would throw catches. He was always throwing balls to us at home too. You'd just be walking along and then suddenly, from five yards, Dad would fire a ball at you, flat out. And it was always a cricket ball, never a tennis ball. He said to me later on that he didn't want us ever to be scared of a cricket ball. That's how we learnt to catch.

'As I got a bit older, once Lynn had finished bowling to me Dad would come on and he'd throw full tosses and long hops. He said, "You're learning how to keep the good balls out, but you've got to realise that the game of cricket is about scoring runs, so you've got to learn how to deal with the loose balls". He would spend half an hour giving me rubbish, so I could learn how to put it away. Lynn's wicket was turf, but it was a half-wicket and because Lynn had been top-dressing it for many years, the wicket was about nine inches higher than the rest of the grass. There was a nice smooth mound where the roller came up onto the wicket. Dad had played baseball for South Australia, so he had a pretty good arm and he said, "Now you're going to have to learn how to protect yourself. Blokes are going to bowl bouncers at you and you'll have to learn how to deal with them". So he would fire the ball off the mound at me and it was "Do the best you can". I don't ever recall thinking that I had to duck or get out of the way. I had to deal with them. That was how I learnt to hook.

'Unfortunately, later on when I got out hooking once or twice people used to say to me: "You've got to give up hooking". In fact Bob Simpson told me at one stage that he had given it up and he said I should too, so I went through a period when I didn't know whether to hook or duck or what to do. It was bad advice and it was sillier of me to take notice of it; what I really needed to do was to go away and practise the hook shot. I was talking to Bradman one day and he said, "You used to have a

Bob Simpson was Australian captain from 1964 to 1967 and returned to first-class cricket, and the captaincy, 10 years later when the players who had signed with World Series Cricket were banned.

good hook shot. What's happened to it?" So I told him and he said, "Go back to it. If you're a natural hooker, you've got to hook". He was right of course. I guess also it's something to do with your nature; I could never just stand there and duck to fast bowlers because it just wasn't in my nature. I didn't like to have them dictating the terms and I always felt you had to show your superiority by putting them back in their places.

'I'll never forget during my first full Shield season, in 1962–63, I came up against Wes Hall when he was playing for Queensland. I had faced some pretty quick bowlers in club cricket and I knew how to deal with bouncers, but I'd heard that even the top players had a problem hooking Wes and I remember wondering how much quicker would he be than the blokes that I'd faced. Will I be able to hook, and if I can't hook him, what the hell do I do? Wes let a couple go and I realised I was going to get about halfway round on them, so I sat down very quickly; I found out it's not so difficult to duck if you have to. But after about half a dozen overs I figured I'd seen something: every time he bowled me a bouncer he went wide on the crease but bowled his normal deliveries in close to the stumps. I reckoned I'd sorted that out and I thought to myself: "Well as soon as I see him go wide I've got the advantage on him and I'll go back looking for the bouncer". He let me have another one, sure enough it was from out wide on the crease, so I was sure I had Wes figured out. Next ball he came in close to the stumps so I wasn't looking for the bouncer — it just caught the peak of my cap as it went past.

'When Greg was old enough we used to play Test matches in the backyard. I was five years older but I never remember feeling that I had to go easy on him because he was younger. It was always flat out. There was a little shed at the back; that was the wicket-keeper and three slips and we had all these other bits of wire netting set up to protect the fruit trees. They were the fieldsmen, if you hit them on the full you were out. When you were out, you'd walk off and fill in the score book and if there was an argument about whether someone was out or not, Mum would come down and she'd say, "Oh look, he's the younger, give him a break". That's why I never took it easy with Greg. I had absolutely no hesitation in bowling bouncers at him. It was just "Do the best you can". They were tremendously competitive matches.

'At primary school we used to play every lunchtime and if you got the wicket — bowled the guy or took the catch — you got the bat. The object was to try to stay in the whole lunch hour if you could. The three of us, Greg, Trevor and I, all went to Prince Alfred College. Greg and I were lucky, in that when we were there Prince Alfred College played in the second grade competition, so we were playing against men a lot of the time. Some of them were good players at the end of their career, others were young blokes on the way up and it was bloody tough cricket. I remember facing Alan Hitchcock in B grade. He'd been playing Sheffield Shield the previous season, so we soon learnt how to look after ourselves.

'Because of my experience playing against the men and because of the coaching I had from Lynn Fuller and my father, by the time I was 17 my technique was sound and ready for district cricket and a year later it was ready for Sheffield Shield cricket. I had my first full season of A grade cricket in 1961—62 with Glenelg and I was picked in the South Australian Sheffield Shield side at the end of that season. I played the next full season of Shield cricket, then I went to the Lancashire League. I was 19. It was a waste of time for me; I learnt how to drink and a fair bit about swearing, but that's all. In fact it set me back a bit; I was 12½ stone when I went there and nearly 14 stone by the time I came back.

'As you go up a step in the game it gets harder because you are playing against better cricketers who are more attuned to looking for your weaknesses and once they find a weakness, they just bang away at it. Obviously the higher you go up the standard, the more accurate the bowlers are. They are also supported by better fieldsmen. If they find a weakness and start hammering away at it, then you've got to overcome that problem. You've got to think about and sort it out at practise in the nets. Because I was used to sorting things out for myself, if I was struggling during an innings, I could take a deep breath at the end of an over and say to myself, "It's not working out at the moment. What am I doing wrong?" You need to be able to do that as you're going along, to work out what bowlers are trying to do and what the wicket is doing. When I first played in India on those flat wickets against Prasanna and Bedi, it was like an entirely different game. I was lucky because right from the start I had been taught I had to work things out for myself.

'I think I would have a problem now if I was in the Australian team. I don't like being regimented. They have all this organised training now; everyone has to do all the loosening up exercises. I know it's important for the fast bowlers to stretch and get properly loosened up, but when I see opening batsmen stretching their fingers and doing all the other things they do for 20 minutes or so before a game, I think to myself, "That's procrastination. It's just putting off the decision". I was always very conscious of the fact that cricket is a team game and that the team spirit is very important — it played a big part in our success in the 1970s — but you've also got to realise that a team is a bunch of individuals. It's no good treating Doug Walters the same as you treat Bill Lawry because they are two entirely different characters. I think the present Australian side would have a problem with Bill Lawry too, because all Bill ever wanted to do was strap the pads on and get into the nets and bat for half an hour, or an hour, or however long the bowlers would bowl to him. By the time he'd been in the nets for 10 minutes he'd be nicely warmed up. If someone had said to Bill Lawry, "You've got to go out there and do 20 minutes of stretching exercises",

I'm sure Bill would have said, "No thanks, I'm going to the nets".'

Chappell played in the last two Tests of the tied series against England in 1965–66 and then became a regular member of the Australian team. Under Bob Simpson, they lost 1–3 to South Africa in 1966–67 then defeated India 4–0 in Australia in 1967–68. Bill Lawry took over the captaincy half way through the Indian series and led the side in another tied series in England in 1968 and consecutive 3–1 wins over West Indies in Australia in 1968–69 and India in 1969–70. After the Indian tour they went to South Africa, where they were crushed 4–0.

'When you are first selected in the Australian side, you're just delighted to be there and you play because that's what you've been working towards all your life. That was your dream and you've achieved it. But by the time I became vice-captain of the Australian side in 1969, I realised we had a problem,' Chappell said. 'I'm not sure whether many people know it, but that's when Bill Lawry first started to have trouble with the board. When we went to India in 1969, we stayed in second class hotels, and when you talk about second class hotels in India nearly 20 years ago you're talking about accommodation that was a health hazard by our standards. Fred Bennett was the manager and we complained to him a couple of times about the standard of the hotels that we were put up in, especially in some of the more out of the way places where we played. We were told that the board had checked them out through the Australian High Commission and had been told they were alright and that there were political reasons why we had to play in certain places. Well we weren't terribly impressed by that, and we let Fred know. After all, it was our health we were talking about, and our livelihood, such as it was in those days.

'Another thing we found out was that if someone happened to get really sick on the tour—and it had happened before, to people like Gordon Rorke and Ian Craig—the board would help with medical expenses, but that was about all. Now that was a pretty violent tour. I don't want to get it out of perspective, because we got on well with the Indian players and there was some very good cricket, but there was a full scale riot in Bombay and in Calcutta there was a demonstration outside our hotel because they thought Doug Walters had fought in Vietnam, which he hadn't. Then there was another riot, over tickets, and six people were killed before the Test started and after the game our bus was stoned when we were on the way to the airport. So you can understand that we were a bit worried now and again and it didn't help when we found out that if we died on that tour, our wives would have got something like $400 from the Australian Cricket Board. We thought it was ridiculous and we gave Fred a pretty hard time.

'At the end of the tour Bill Lawry called a meeting and said, "Rather than just shooting our mouths off, let's list all the things we thought were wrong, and put them in a letter to the board, so that the next team that goes to India won't get it so bad". We all agreed and Bill got the letter written up, but he made one big mistake; he just signed the letter himself and sent it off. I remember saying to him, "Look Bill, don't do that. We'll all sign it. We all feel this way about it. You shouldn't have to take the whole load on your shoulders". But he said "No, no. I'm the captain. I'll sign it". And from that moment on, from the time the board got the letter, it was all downhill for Bill Lawry so far as the board was concerned. Some members of the board were looking for any opportunity to get rid of him.

'When they finally did get rid of Bill and made me captain, I was probably just as unhappy about it as he was. Don't get me wrong, I'm not saying they shouldn't have sacked him as captain, that was their decision to make and I was proud to take his place. What upset me was the way they went about it. That really opened my eyes to the way the board operated and it wasn't very pleasant and in my opinion it wasn't very professional.

'I was sitting in the Overway Hotel in Hindley Street, Adelaide, having a counter lunch when there was a phone call for me. It was Alan Shiell, who was with the *Adelaide News* in those days, and he said "Congratulations", and I said "What are you talking about, Sheffield?" "You're captain of Australia." "You're joking," I said. I couldn't believe it. "No, no," he said. "They've dropped Bill, and you're captain".

'That's how I found out. Now I suppose I would have appreciated it if someone from the board had called me to tell me I'd got the job, but that wasn't important. What I was upset about though was that no one came to me and said, "Do you want Bill Lawry in your team?" I would have said, "Bloody oath I do," and I'm sure we would have won the Sydney Test in 1971, my first Test as captain, if we'd had Bill Lawry instead of Ken

Bill Lawry, captain in 25 Tests, who learnt of his dismissal from the captaincy, and the side, from a team-mate who had heard it on the radio.

Eastwood. It wasn't as if Bill's form was bad, he had batted right through the innings in the first Sydney Test and he was averaging about 40 for the series, so he was in good enough form as a batsman.

'It was a very strange way to run the game. If you look at the way they treated Bill Lawry, you realise that they just didn't have any thought for the players. Whether you admired Bill Lawry's style of captaincy or not, you had to admire what he did for Australia as an opening batsman. He took the best fast bowling in the world for 67 Tests and he averaged nearly 50. If someone had only played two or three Tests, you wouldn't expect the board to write them a long letter and thank them for their services. But someone who had captained Australia and done what Bill had done—I thought that he at least deserved to be called in and told he was being dropped, and why. But Bill heard it from Keith Stackpole who had heard it on the radio. If they weren't prepared to write Bill a note, or to call him in and say, "Look, this is how it is", you'd think they could have spent a few cents on a phone call.'

Chappell considers himself lucky to have come into the captaincy at that time: 'We had some very good, experienced players in the side—Ashley Mallett, Ian Redpath and Doug

Walters—and Rod Marsh and my brother Greg were picked that season. Then within a couple of years we had blokes like Max Walker and Thommo coming along. I know it's said that I moulded the team we had in the mid-1970s, but I'd be a fool if I tried to take too much credit there. Not only did they have a lot of talent, but they were a team of very determined cricketers, and they all had the one thing in mind—they wanted to win cricket matches.

'As a spectator, if you look at people like Dennis Lillee, Rod Marsh or Jeff Thomson, you can tell they were very competitive guys. But some of the others blokes were just as competitive, even though they didn't show much emotion on the field. Doug Walters and Ian Redpath, for example; I can assure you they were very, very competitive guys in their own quiet way. I think the moulding as far as I was concerned was really a matter of making sure that the team got on well together and there was a terrific spirit in the side. That wasn't hard to do because they were a good bunch of blokes. We were lucky that most of us were drinkers so it was easy for us to get together socially.

'I suppose the main thing I did was to make sure each of them knew what I thought their job was in the team. With Rod or Dennis, their role was obvious, but it was different with someone like Doug Walters. Doug was a terrific natural stroke-maker; he was one of the few guys in my time who could win a Test match off his own bat, or could get you out of strife from number six in the batting order. I thought it was very important that he always played his natural game, whether we were 4 for 40 or 4 for 250. So in the early days I said to Doug, "You're a natural strokemaker. That's the way I want you to play all the time. It doesn't matter if we're in trouble—I still want you to play that way". What I was trying to do was to put him in the situation where he wasn't in two minds, so if he walked to the wicket with 4 for 40 on the scoreboard and the first ball came along asking to be square cut to the fence, I didn't want him getting halfway through the shot and thinking: "If I get out, the captain will kick me in the backside". I wanted him to hit it for four. And if he did that a few times, he might turn things around and get us back on top.

'I remember when Jeff Thomson was first picked, I had read the piece where he said he didn't mind seeing a bit of blood on the wicket and he was just as happy to hit a batsman on the head as get him out. This was just before we came up against the

Englishmen in 1974–75 and I thought to myself, "What have I got here?" Dennis was a pretty fiery customer of course and with Thommo up the other end, and knowing what the English press were like, I reckoned I was going to have a real job on my hands. But I'll say to Thommo's credit that I never had any real problem at all. The only bloke he used to go crook at was himself. Some of the things he used to say about himself, about his bowling, well I wouldn't say them to my worst enemy.

'Thomson and Lillee were opposites, really. Dennis always worked very hard and he took it very seriously. He was a non-drinker when he started; it was only our encouragement, telling him that Lindwall and Miller and the great fast bowlers of the past always used to have a couple of beers at the end of the day's play, to put something back in to sweat out, that got him started. Thommo loved a beer; he was a very relaxed sort of guy and a natural athlete. He was the fastest bloke over 100 yards in our side, he had a fantastic arm, he was a good golfer, he could play tennis pretty well. He could do anything. When he was young, it was sheer natural ability. Against the Englishmen in 1974–75 he just jogged up and then went whack. It was all rhythm and sheer ability and it was the quickest stuff I'd ever seen.

'I know I was lucky to have one of the great fast bowling combinations and they were backed up by a team of very good cricketers and athletes who were pretty fit and could catch very well. We didn't do an exceptional amount of practise as a team. I think it is the hard work you do as a youngster — in my case that was from say age five to 17 — those were the important years, building up the techniques, making sure everything was right.'

Chappell took over the captaincy of the final match of the six-Test series against England in 1970–71. He lost his first Test as captain and Australia lost the series 2–0, but the Ashes series in England in 1972 was one of the most hard-fought and exciting for many years. England won the first Test by 89 runs. Australia levelled the series with an eight-wicket win at Lord's, where Bob Massie took 16 wickets. The third Test was drawn and England had an easy win at Headingley. Although the Ashes were to remain in England, Australia levelled the series with a five-wicket win at the Oval after Ian Chappell (118) and Greg Chappell (113) put on 241 for the third wicket in Australia's first innings. The Australian team under Ian Chappell went on to win consecutive series against Pakistan 3–0, the West Indies 2–0

By the mid-1970s the Australians had regained the Ashes and were the strongest Test side in the world.

and New Zealand 2–0 before a one-all result against New Zealand, in New Zealand, in 1974. Australia regained the Ashes in 1974–75 with a crushing 4–1 win over the English tourists, led by Mike Denness.

Despite the success of the Australian XI, there were serious problems in Australian cricket. 'It was really coming to a head in the 1974–75 season,' Ian Chappell told me. 'A number of things happened. We were all starting to realise we were under-paid and Dennis Lillee, who was writing for the Melbourne *Sun*, kept agitating for more money in his column. Dennis had come back from his back injury. He had taken 12 months off from first-class cricket and he had sold his window cleaning business so he could put the time into getting his back right again. But when he came back I think he felt that it was still a day-to-day proposition—it might go on him again and he might be out of the game for good. We were getting $200 a Test match then, with no superannuation. For a Shield match in South Australia we were getting $8 a day. I was writing a column too and I put in one piece about pay before the board made it clear that I had better not pursue that subject in the press. But I had been to a meeting with the board; I spoke to them about some of the things I thought should be done and one of the things I raised was money.

'The most interesting reaction came from Bradman. While I was talking about other subjects, Bradman was sitting back in his chair, pretty relaxed, but as soon as I got onto the subject of money, Bradman was up on the edge of his chair, taking a lot of interest. Nothing came out of that discussion. I had a chat with Richie Benaud afterwards and told him what I'd done and he said: "Look, if you do it again, make sure everything is in writing. The reason for that is firstly, protection for yourself, secondly, anything in writing will have to go into the minutes of the meeting. If you've asked for something and it doesn't happen, and you're still complaining two years later, you can say: "Look I asked for that at the board meeting on such and such a date". So the second meeting I went to, I put the list in front of everyone's spot. There were a couple of items on the list to do with money. One was asking for more pay, the other was superannuation. Again, Bradman was sitting back, but as soon as I got onto the subject of the players getting more money, he came forward and he just said, "No, there's no way we can do that".

'So it was a pretty strange situation. Most of us were doing what we had always wanted to do—play cricket for Australia and win Test matches—but we weren't getting paid what we thought we were worth, we had no security at all, and on top of that we were not happy about some of the other aspects of the administration of the game. The board did not bother to consult us and when we offered advice they didn't take any notice of it. As captain of the Australian team I reckoned I knew a fair bit about the game and the players, but I had no input into the selection of the team. The selectors picked the team and on the morning of the match they told me who was to be twelfth man. The one time I asked for a player was when we went to New Zealand in 1974. I asked for Alan Hurst, because Glenn Turner had the reputation of being a bit shy when it came to fast bowling, particularly if it was pitched a bit short. I figured that Turner was the one batsman in the New Zealand side who could cause us some problems and Hursty was the only quickie around at that time; Dennis was out with his back and Thommo hadn't been picked for Shield cricket that season. Anyway I asked for Hursty and I didn't get him and the one Test we lost was in Christchurch, when Turner got a hundred in each innings. We had the ridiculous situation of my brother Greg trying to bowl bouncers because we didn't have anyone else to bounce him. He actually looked awkward against Greg, but of course Greg wasn't quick enough to cause him any real problems.

'It finally came home to me after the first Melbourne Test in 1974–75, when I read in the paper that 250,000 people had come to the game over the five days, and it was the first time the gate had topped a quarter of a million dollars. That's when I suddenly realised that we were just being used. I sat down and did the figures. It was pretty simple; $200 by 12 players, that's $2400. We were getting $2400 out of gate takings of $250,000 and I thought to myself, "We're a pack of bloody idiots". Now it might look as if we were a bit slow, but I think that probably is an indication that money wasn't all that important to us. When I joined World Series Cricket a lot of people accused me of being money-hungry, of playing the game purely for money, but I reckon anyone that was really money-hungry would have worked out that we were being robbed a long time before that.

'Then there was the quote from Alan Barnes, the secretary of the board, on the front page of the *Australian*; he was quoted as saying "There are 500,000 cricketers in Australia who would play for nothing". We had gone up to Sydney for the fourth Test and I remember I went out to practise at the SCG before the game and when I walked back into the dressing-room, there was Redders with steam coming out of his ears. Now Ian Redpath was probably the quietest bloke in the side, but you couldn't print what he was saying about Alan Barnes. I asked what all the fuss was about and someone showed me the paper. Then Barnes himself walked in and Redders went for him; he grabbed him by the lapels of his jacket and he was really shouting at him: "The guys who are playing are the best in Australia and they should be paid accordingly", and some other things besides. So I didn't have to do anything. Redders did it all for me.

'Redders had an antique business and he had a real problem because if he played cricket he had to pay someone to look after it for him. In fact he couldn't go to England in 1975 because he couldn't afford the time away from his business. When that came up I asked Ray Steele, who was on the board, "Couldn't the board do something? We need Redders in England. Couldn't the board just get someone to manage his shop for him while he's away?" I think Ray genuinely tried, but again the board wouldn't do anything. So Redders didn't go. I was in the fortunate position of being paid from my job while I played cricket, so it wasn't as great a problem for me as it was for some of the other blokes, but I know a few of the guys really did have problems. Some of them didn't eat too well on that tour. Ashley

Ian Chappell sweeping Underwood during his innings of 192 at the Oval in 1975. **Press Association.**

Mallett was one; some of his meals were pretty thin because he was struggling for money. It's unbelievable really, when I look back on it.

'The stupid thing was that if they hadn't treated us like that, the whole thing would not have blown up as it did. They had alternatives. For example, at that time Greg and I were playing in South Africa on a fairly regular basis, in the Datsun double wicket competitions. Now we got paid about $400 to play in those games. We were over there for a week or 10 days. The money wasn't that good, but we could put everything on the tab and the second or third time we went there, the liaison man between the players and the Datsun people, a bloke called Robin Binckes, came to us and said, "Look I'm terribly sorry, because this thing is going very well and we're absolutely delighted with it and the Datsun people have said to me they'd like to pay you more money, but there's a problem; we put it to the South African Cricket Union that we wanted to pay you more and apparently they put it to the other boards and the answer came back "No, don't pay them more money, because if you do that they'll want more money from Test matches".

'The board said they were stabbed in the back by the players when World Series Cricket started, but that's just not true. Before World Series I had two definite approaches to play cricket professionally. One was from a promoter called Jack Neary, who wanted to get a team of Australian cricketers to play against cricketers from other countries in an Australia versus World XI format. We were going to be paid more money, or a percentage of the gate, and he said: "Are you guys interested? Are you available?" And we said, "Yes, sure we are". So I sat down with Jack Neary to talk about it and at the end of the discussion I said to him, "Now look, there's one thing you've got to do; you've got to go to the Australian Cricket Board because they have control of the grounds and if you can't play on the major grounds the thing is not going to work. So go to the board, explain to them what you want to do, explain to them that you don't want to conflict with the cricket they're playing, that you'll put it on at a time when it doesn't conflict, and get their permission". He did that, but they wouldn't give permission.

'Again, when we were in England in 1975 for the first World Cup, an Indian promotor rang me up. He said he'd spoken to Clive Lloyd and he wanted to do something on a professional basis and could we get together and have a chat. I said, "Sure, but I'm not going to last much longer as Australian captain and I think Greg should come along to the meeting". So Greg and I went along, and some others were there; Bishen Bedi and Lloydy, from memory. He wanted to start in India and if it was successful he wanted to expand to other places. He had a financial background and he'd worked out all the money side of it; we discussed the whole thing with him and told him we agreed with it and were very keen to do it. Then, at the end of the discussion I said to him, "Right, having agreed to all that, you'll have to go to the boards and get permission, because if you haven't got the grounds it won't work". The same thing happened; he asked permission and got knocked back.

'Now, rightly or wrongly, it seemed to us that they didn't want us to get any more money, because if the dunces had had any brains, what they would have realised was that it would have taken the pressure off them; we would have been getting some extra income from professional cricket, but obviously we would have needed to keep playing for Australia to keep our reputations so that we'd get invited to play in the professional troupe. They could have kept on paying us peanuts, but we would have picked up this nice little nest egg at the end of the season from the professional series. That would have kept us happy.'

Ian Chappell retired from the captaincy after retaining the Ashes 1–0 in England in 1975. He played under his brother in 1976–77 when the Australia team confirmed its reputation as the best team in the world with a 5–1 win over the West Indies led by Clive Lloyd. 'I retired because I'd had enough and because I could make more money if I wasn't playing cricket for Australia. World Series came along late in the 1976–77 season. I agreed with the principle and obviously the money and the security of having a contract was attractive. That was something we never had when we were playing for Australia. I was offered a contract, so I signed up.'

CHAPTER 34

The breakdown

Like F. R. Spofforth, Dennis Lillee started his working life as a bank clerk. Lillee came into international cricket in a blaze of glory; in his second game for Australia, against a Rest of the World team led by Gary Sobers at Perth in 1971–72, he took 8 for 29. Later in the same season he hurt his back for the first time, but took 31 wickets in Tests in England in 1972. In *Back to the Mark*, he sets out his Sheffield Shield program for Western Australia, leading up to the 1972–73 Test series again Pakistan:

November 4–7	v NSW in Perth	34.7 overs
November 18–21	v Pakistan in Perth	23.7 overs
November 24–27	v Queensland in Brisbane	26 overs
December 1–5	v NSW in Sydney	41.4 overs
December 8–11	v Victoria in Melbourne	41 overs
December 15–18	v South Australia in Adelaide	40 overs

And those were the days of eight-ball overs! The first Test started on 22 December. Lillee bowled another 35 overs and took five wickets. In the Melbourne Test he took three wickets from 27.3 overs. Australia won both Tests comfortably. During the third Test, in Sydney, he came on for a second spell and was just starting to build up some pace: 'Suddenly my back just collapsed. I felt an enormous pain shoot right up my back. I couldn't fathom out what was wrong, so I went straight off the field and was examined by Dr Corrigan immediately. Brian looked me in the eye and said: "You've just had too much cricket. What you need is a long rest".' When it looked as if Pakistan might win the Test, Lillee bowled medium pace while Max Walker won the game for Australia with 6 for 15.

Dennis Lillee. **ABC.**

A couple of weeks later the Australian team left for the West Indies, where Lillee finally broke down. The problem was eventually diagnosed as stress fractures in his vertabrae. He spent six weeks in plaster from his hips to his chest and some months in a restrictive brace. The following summer he played grade cricket as a batsman-captain in Perth while he went about the job of re-building his back. With the help of the Physical Education Department of the University of Western Australia he worked on a series of exercises to strengthen his torso. Late in the 1973–74 season he did some bowling for his club and as he could not stretch out to full pace, learnt to make more use of line, length, swing and cut. He returned for the six-Test series against Mike Denness's England side a different man; broad-shouldered, stronger, fitter and a better bowler than he had been before. Lillee played Test cricket until the 1983–84 season when, along with Greg Chappell and Rod Marsh, he retired, having the then record number of 355 Test wickets at an average of 23.92.

With his lean figure, black hair, craggy features and drooping moustache, Lillee would have looked at home in the Rum Corps in 1800, or in the team which played the first Test in 1877. He bears a striking resemblance to F. R. Spofforth, whose career he emulated 100 years later. Lillee was a showman who played to the crowd and preyed on his opponents. This sometimes got him into trouble but he usually had the Australian crowds on his side. Even at his alleged worst, as he shaped up to the equally fiery Pakistani, Javed Miandad, with only the umpire, Tony Crafter, standing between them, the smile on Dennis Lillee's face shows that he was enjoying himself. He was aggressive, he said what he thought, his capacity for work was enormous and it was equalled by his will to succeed.

The Breakdown: Chappell and a distressed Dennis Lillee: 'I felt an enormous pain shoot right up my back. I couldn't fathom out what was wrong.'

Like Ian Chappell, Dennis Lillee is a pivotal figure in Australian cricket. Lillee was dissatisfied with the way he was treated and paid. He met John Cornell through the sports writer Austin Robertson; Robertson suggested that Cornell, who was managing Paul Hogan, should also manage Lillee. Cornell was amazed at the financial conditions imposed on the players in view of the crowds which came to the games and the takings at the gate. Kerry Packer, at the time, was trying to buy exclusive television rights to Test matches from the Australian Cricket Board. The board was prepared to offer commercial rights but insisted that the ABC should be able to continue its non-commercial broadcasts. John Cornell knew Kerry Packer through his involvement with the *Paul Hogan Show*.

Dennis Lillee. **Patrick Eagar.**

Ian Chappell first heard about their plans at a meeting with Austin Robertson and John Cornell: 'It was at the Gazebo Hotel in Sydney; they told me what they were going to do and then they said: "Are you in, or are you out?" I said, 'I agree with the principle of it. I think it's a good thing. I'm in". You'd think I would have learnt by then, but again I said to them, "If you want my advice, you have to go to the board and get the grounds, because if you haven't got the grounds, it won't work". They told me they had other plans which did not include talking to the board.

'Once I knew that they had spoken to Greg, I rang him up. At that time we really thought that it was just another one of those things, that it wouldn't get off the ground, like the other ideas that had been knocked back by the board. But we kept having meetings and they kept signing more people, and it started to look a bit more solid. Then, one Friday—I was working for Channel 10 in Melbourne, covering a Shield match—I got a message to get on a plane and come up to Sydney immediately for a meeting with Kerry Packer.

'I was wearing a pair of jeans and a denim jacket and I walked into his office and he said: "What are you, a bloody cowboy or something?" Next thing he said was: "Who do you want in this bloody team?" So we went through the list and we pretty much agreed on the players. Then he said: "Righto, I want you to be captain." "Hang on a minute," I said. "Greg's captain of the present Australian side. I think you should check with the players to see whether they want me as captain." "Son," he said, "this isn't a bloody democracy. I'm paying the bills. You're the captain."

'Anyway he agreed to let me have a chat with Greg to sort it out, so I rang Greg, and he was delighted with the idea. He'd had two years of the captaincy and I think he was as fed up with it as I had been. So from that time I was part of the organisation. I think we knew it was going to go ahead once we heard that Kerry was involved. He was the right person, almost the only person who could have done it. Apart from the fact that he loved cricket, it needed money and it needed the media backing. I said to a lot of the young guys, "Look, this is our opportunity, and if we don't take this one I'm not sure that we'll ever get another. You can be pushed around by the board for the rest of your life, or you can stand up now and let yourself be counted". One of my principles was that we had to leave the game a better game for the players who were going to take over from us. I think that everyone involved was conscious of that, because it meant that you would be able to make a living out of cricket, although of course a lot of people said we were just trying to tear the game down and get money for ourselves. I think that if the board's policy of paying the absolute minimum had been followed, it would have got harder and harder to get people to give up their lives just to play Test cricket. You would have had the best people dropping out of the game earlier in their careers and the game would have suffered as a result.'

The story broke in the press in the middle of 1977, while the Australians were losing the Ashes 3–0 to an England side led by Mike Brearley. Then the world of cricket split in two: World Series had signed 66 of the world's best players and set up in opposition to established cricket. When the International Cricket Conference announced that all those who had signed would be banned from Tests, Kerry Packer took the ICC to court. After a hearing which last 31 days the High Court in England found against the ICC on the grounds that their ban represented an unreasonable restraint of trade.

Bob Simpson came back to lead Australia against India in 1977–78 and in the West Indies in 1978. Graham Yallop took over the captaincy of what was in effect Australia's second eleven against England in 1978–79. Meanwhile, World Series, denied the use of the major grounds, staged a series of 'Super-tests'—Australia v West Indies and Australia v World XI, followed by a triangular one-day series between Australia, West Indies and the World XI. The matches were played on grounds including VFL Park, in Melbourne, and the Sydney Showground. They also played a series of one-day games in country centres, known as the Country Cup.

The results were mixed; 25,000 came to an Australia v West Indies match at VFL Park on 24 January but only about 6000 came to the Sydney games. Adelaide's best crowd was 2236. Average attendance was 20,000 at the Supertests and 8000 at the one-day games. Attendance at the country games averaged 2033 per day. Total attendance at 73 days of World Series matches was 319,000. The 'traditional' five-Test series against India drew 257,000 people to 25 days' play. Kerry Packer's losses were estimated at $3 to $4 million.

The breakthrough for World Series Cricket came on 28 November 1978 at the Sydney Cricket Ground. Since its development in the 1870s, the SCG had been administered by a trust responsible to the New South Wales government. The New South

Wales Cricket Association had priority over the ground's use, but not control. In May 1977 World Series had applied to the trust for use of the Sydney Cricket Ground on a number of days during the following season, at a fee of $20,000 per day. When the application was refused in July, the New South Wales government immediately reconstituted the trust and in September the decision not to approve the World Series application was reversed. The association challenged the new decision in court and won its case, but the government immediately introduced legislation which stripped the association of its right to priority over the ground. The government also agreed to the construction of light towers for night cricket.

The first World Series match of the 1978–79 season was played on the Sydney Cricket Ground between Australia and the West Indies on 28 November 1978. By 7 o'clock the ground was packed and the gates were thrown open to let those waiting come in free. The crowd was more than 50,000. Average attendance for the one-day series in 1978–79 doubled to 16,000. The Supertests drew an average of 31,000. Total attendance at the 71 days of World Series games was 585,000. 'Traditional' cricket drew 430,000 to 39 days' play in the five-Test series against England and the two-Test series against Pakistan.

The following season the ban on the players was lifted and the board resumed official control of cricket, but they gave Kerry Packer's Nine Network exclusive television rights.

CHAPTER 35

The sideways game

One-day cricket first became popular in England in the early 1960s. Like World Series Cricket, its origins were commercial: it started with Rothmans sponsoring the Cavaliers—Test and former Test players—in 40-over matches against county sides on Sunday afternoons. Crowds were good and it was ideal for television; it was not long before the cricket establishment took it over as a means of bringing in more money. The MCC introduced the Gillette Cup, a 60-over competition between county sides, in 1963. Australian teams in England played a number of limited overs matches and competitions—most notably the Prudential Cup in 1975—but the one-day game had little encouragement in Australia. A sponsored knockout competition between the States was started in 1969–70, but only four games had been played at an international level to the end of the 1975–76 season; one in 1970–71 against England, two more in 1974–75, and one against the West Indies in 1975–76.

It was obvious that one-day matches would play a significant role in the World Series format, but no one really saw how the game would change as a result of the split. Night cricket came about because they had hired VFL Park which happened to have lights. The white ball came about because of night cricket. The one-day format brought restrictions on field placings and limits on the number of overs per bowler. It has developed its own conventions based on defensive bowling, brilliant fielding and innovative and sometimes crude batting towards the end of each innings. But the really good innings in one-day games are often based on pushing into the gaps, consistently picking up ones and twos without hitting boundaries. Has one-day cricket

Dean Jones. New techniques will keep evolving, but the principles remain the same. **Ken Piesse.**

changed the basics of the game? Ian Chappell does not think so.

'People talk about the changes because of one-day cricket, but the best innings you see in one-day games are still technically correct.' Chappell says. 'Look at Botham's straight hit for six; that's a perfect cricket shot. He comes through the ball with a straight bat, and he has a full, high follow through. Even the bloke who backs away to leg to make some room, like Viv Richards or Dean Jones, is still playing a cover drive with the full face of the bat and his left foot near the pitch of the ball. It's still a proper cricket shot. That technique has evolved because of the one-day game, and things like that will keep evolving, but they will still be based on the same principles. Cricket is mostly a sideways game: the only way to bowl accurately is to get into a side-on position and look at the spot where you are going to land the ball. Those things are basic and you can't ever change them, because you won't be able to bowl accurately any other way and you won't be able to play consistently good cover drives if you don't get your left foot near the ball.

'I'm sure that in a hundred years you'll still be able to recognise the game of cricket by the shots and techniques we know today, because they have evolved as the best techniques. Technically, I don't think the game will change much in the forseeable future. I hope it doesn't, because if it changes that will probably be because of new rules, and like most cricketers, I believe that the fewer rules there are the better. The techniques we use have been worked out over the years as the best way to do things on a cricket field; they've been refined over a couple of hundred years and that's why they are the best, because you've had so many brains trying to come up with something better all the time. Maybe there is still some fine tuning to be done, because people will still think about how we can do things better, but there won't be radical changes like the change from under-arm to round-arm bowling.

'The more you can keep the rules as they are, and keep that fine balance between bat and ball, by making sure the bowlers bowl plenty of overs, and making sure the wickets don't get too much in favour of batsmen like they were in the 1920s, the better. I believe that unless the administrators get out of control, unless we get too many administrators who don't understand the game, and particularly the history of the game, then you will recognise cricket very easily in a hundred years.'

Many people say there is too much cricket now, especially too much one-day cricket. 'There are two things to look at,' Ian Chappell says. 'From the spectators' point of view, it just doesn't seem to be true. The crowds and the viewers don't think there is too much cricket; it doesn't show up in the ratings. Some of the players say they get tired of it, and it can be pretty tiring, but they get well paid for it now, and of course they can always choose not to play.'

Here too, Chappell says, the solution lies with the administration: 'We will have to strike a balance between traditional cricket and the new, more commercial cricket, which is based on the one-day game. We have to keep looking at the balance very closely, and I think one of the important things that we're going to need is a very strong administration. We have always needed it, but it will become even more important because he game is getting more input from television and marketing people, who are experts in their field but who sometimes don't understand the game, and the history of the game of cricket.

'Cricket and television need each other, but when the television people start saying things like, "There would be no major sport without television", as they do, then that worries me, because anyone who says that doesn't understand the history of sport. There were record crowds in the 1932–33 season, and again in 1936–37, and there was no television around then. Now what is important, and what will always get people through the gates, are competitive series and good players. Most people make their own judgements. They might go along once because of the promotion, but they won't go again unless the game delivers the goods. So it's going to be very important that the administrators actually know the game. We must have input from the television and marketing people, and they must have input from the players. It's like anything else, you use the expertise around you to make sure that you've got a good product.

'If you read Jack Fingleton's book, *Cricket Crisis*, written in 1946, he was saying then that there were not enough former players on the Australian Cricket Board, and I'm still saying it today. That worries me, too, especially when people who do not really understand the game start playing around with the rules.

What sort of people do we need as administrators? 'In my opinion, Richie Benaud knows more about cricket than anyone on this earth,' Chappell said. 'His style of captaincy had a great influence on the game. Most of the guys who played under Richie still idolise him as a captain. I'd certainly put Bill Lawry in that category—even now I think Bill still looks upon Richie as the leader. He has also had an influence on the game as a journalist and television commentator, and during his period with World Series Cricket he virtually acted as a cricket admin-

'Richie Benaud knows more about cricket than anyone on this earth.' Benaud and Frank Worrell at the end of the 1960–61 series. **Melbourne Herald.**

istrator. He probably wouldn't want to be on the board—apart from anything else he's probably too busy—but I think if the circumstances were right you might be able to talk him into it. I think that one of the things that's wrong with the present system of cricket administration is that there is not an avenue for someone with Richie Benaud's talents to go straight onto the board, preferably soon after he finishes as a player. The board has had serious problems in recent years, and I think it's because they have no playing knowledge at the top level. For example, Greg Chappell made it quite clear that he was interested in being more than just a selector, but I know that he didn't get much encouragement from the board for many years. I suppose it's pretty obvious, naming two people like Richie Benaud and my brother Greg, but they are the sort of people that the game needs as administrators—they know cricket thoroughly and they know the outside world—and there are not too many people like that around.'

CHAPTER 36

The green baggy cap

In January 1979, following the Sydney Test which Mike Brearley's team won on the last afternoon—after looking likely to lose it for four and a half days—I wrote in the *National Times* that the crowd was poor because 'the 22 players who took part in the game were not, by past and present international standards, particularly good at it'. I also said, 'Traditional cricket of this type has a doubtful economic future ... unless it receives the support of the world's best cricketers', and, of the Australian team, 'only Border looked a complete batsman.'

Traditional cricket survived because administrators around the world had to accept the inevitability of the new commercialism. In Australia, we were lucky that it was taken over by Kerry Packer, who knew what to do with it and was prepared to give it back once he had got what he wanted from it.

Packer wanted television rights. He wanted them because the game was so popular. The game was popular because Australia had gone through a period when, with the Chappell brothers, Doug Walters, Rod Marsh keeping wicket and, perhaps most importantly, the fast bowling combinations of Dennis Lillee and Jeff Thomson, we had the best team in the world and one of the greatest teams of all time.

After the 1970–71 series, when Ian Chappell took over the captaincy from Bill Lawry, Australia went through to 1976–77, playing 10 Test series, without a series loss. But when the first edition of this book was published in 1987, the greats of the 1970s had retired and the wheel had turned again; Australian Test cricket was at its lowest point for 20 years. In eight series played over the previous four seasons, six had been lost and two drawn. Only four Tests had been won from 33 played.

	Won	Lost	Drawn	
1983–84 v West Indies	–	3	2	
1984–85 v West Indies	1	2	2	
1985 v England	1	3	2	
1985–86 v New Zealand	1	2	–	
1985–86 v India	–	–	3	
1985–86 v New Zealand	–	1	2	
1986–87 v India	–	–	2	(1 tied)
1986–87 v England	1	2	2	

Allan Border, who made his debut in the summer of 1978–79, when England won 5–1 while the WSC players were ineligible for selection, went on to become Test cricket's highest run-maker and one of the great figures of the game's history. Border was a great bat, a brilliant field and a useful bowler but his phenomenal success was due to his innate understanding of the need to attend to the basics; to play straight, to keep it simple, to concentrate, to wait, wait, wait until the opportunity occurs.

Border, with coach Bob Simpson, gradually built the team that could not win a Test series into a winning combination which disputed the crown of world champions with the West Indies in the early 1990s. Australia, under Mark Taylor's captaincy, finally won a Test series against a declining West Indies side in 1995. That victory was followed by a series win against Pakistan, which left Australia in a strong position to argue that it was the best Test team in the world.

In cricket, you can't take anything for granted; Australia's performance at the highest level of the one-day game has been the reverse of its record in Tests. In 1987, after a dismal run of Test results and in the difficult conditions of India and Pakistan, we won the World Cup against all the odds. But in 1992, when the World Cup was played in Australia and New Zealand and our Test team was gathering strength, we did not reach the semi-finals. In 1996, having defeated Sri Lanka in the WSC finals in Australia, we were trounced by the same side in the World Cup final in Lahore.

The 1996 World Cup was perhaps the most exciting yet, not least because of Sri Lanka's surprising dominance, not just in

Allan Border, one of the great figures of the game's history.
Sydney Morning Herald.

the final, but throughout the tournament. Perhaps we should not have been surprised; Arjuna Ranatunga, Aravinda de Silva and Asanka Gurusinha were three of the most experienced players in the tournament and Sri Lanka, as an emerging force in cricket, has reflected the times by putting the skills of the one-day game ahead of those of Test cricket. Their win was well-deserved, but Australia, too, made a contribution to new standards; before he faltered at the end of the tournament, Mark Waugh demonstrated a perfection of timing rarely seen even at the highest level and Shane Warne in two important games played a role that was unthinkable five years ago—the economical, match-winning leg spinner. Warne was seriously hampered by a soft, wet ball in the final when Sri Lanka defied the fact that every other World Cup final had been won by the team batting first and chose to bat under lights, knowing that a heavy dew would come with the night.

During the 1980s and 1990s, names like Veletta, Zoehrer, Scuderi, Chee Quee and Kasprowicz have emerged in first class cricket in Australia. Sadly, none of them has established a per-

Shane Warne, one of the game's greatest drawcards.
Trent Parke

Mark Waugh, demonstrated a perfection of timing.
Patrick Eagar

manent place in the Australian team but it is only a matter of time before the wearers of the green baggy cap more fully represent the increasing diversity of Australian ethnic backgrounds; the game will be the richer for it.

But names from outside the Anglo-Saxon circle are well-established in Sheffield Shield cricket, which has maintained its status as an ideal breeding ground for Test players and is referred to by many people who know and love the game as the most watchable cricket in the world.

The Australian Institute of Sport's Academy of Cricket is credited with much of our recent success. Shane Warne, who vies with Brian Lara and India's Sachin Tendulkar for the title of the greatest drawcard in modern cricket, is a product of the Academy and our opponents on the world's cricket fields have been known to blame their defeats on its influence.

Meanwhile, our opponents continue to suffer the same swings and roundabouts as have characterised Australian cricket for the past 150 years, reflecting each country's history in the same way as cricket in Australia has progressed in step with our social and economic development.

England's cricketing fortune continues to reflect its diminishing status in the world. There has been much comment about the fact that England has yet to produce a great cricketer of West Indian, Indian or Pakistani background. I suspect this has something to do with the fact that opportunities for the constant play and practice as a child that produce a Brian Lara or a Sachin Tendulkar are limited in the English climate. Peter Roebuck, one of the best cricketers never to play for England and now a part-time resident of Australia, once said to me that he finds life in England frustrating because 'It's so hard to get anything done'. Despite the obvious need, England has not been able to create an Academy of Cricket.

Television, which has kept the game alive in Australia, is having the opposite effect in the West Indies, who have contributed so much to the game over the past 30 years. Cricket is on the decline there because, it is said, their young athletes are more attracted to American basketball, which is more lucrative and is constantly shown on television in the Caribbean. The growth of basketball culture is regarded as a threat to cricket throughout the world.

The game, already strong in India and Pakistan, is getting stronger. Its strength on the sub-continent, where the population of players and watchers is steadily increasing, may underpin the game's future elsewhere.

Sri Lanka has arrived as a new force and with the re-entry of South Africa onto the world sporting stage, the introduction of black South Africans to cricket may bring a new dimension to the game, as the emergence of the West Indies as a major force in world cricket has done over the past 30 years.

CHAPTER 37

Old times are good times

'A game is exactly what is made of it by the character of the people playing it.' I started with a quote from Neville Cardus and set out to tell the story of cricket in Australia through the people who have played the game. I wanted to show how our cricket and cricketers have reflected the changing times and character of the place. I'm left now with 100 scraps of paper; cuttings from the *Herald* and the *Age*, quotes from books, photocopies of scoresheets, questions to answer; even some ideas of my own, as random and whimsical as the game itself.

My father played most of his cricket on cement wickets on the claypans of western New South Wales. Our team was made up mainly of McAlarys, Beaches, Cosgroves and Egans—on a trip to Ireland a few years ago I saw people just like us on the streets in Limerick, Nenagh and Athlone. A fine team we were, as often as not winners of the local competition against opposition as diverse as Nevertire One, Nevertire Two, the Royal Hotel, the Rugby Union Club and Marthaguy. Marthaguy consisted of 'the Hall' (a large tin shed), four tennis courts and a clearing with a rather irregular cement wicket somewhere near the centre. Even with the matting in place the wicket at Marthaguy was a fearsome, erratic thing. My father called it 'two-faced'; if you played forward the ball hit you in the face, if you played back it hit you in the face too. Dad told me always to play back. That way, he said, you sometimes had the opportunity to choose whereabouts in the face it hit you.

Old times are good times. History repeats itself and power corrupts; there is no way the meek are going to inherit the earth.

The world seems at times to be on the brink of a holocaust which only a madman could want. But Australian soldiers will not die in tens of thousands in hand-to-hand combat or from bullets fired at short range again. That took what F. Scott Fitzgerald described as 'religion and years of plenty and tremendous sureties and the exact relation that existed between the classes'; that relationship simply does not exist in the 1980s. Many people still live in relative poverty, but they will not be manacled in irons and banished to the other side of the earth for petty theft.

History seems to me to be rather haphazard and cricket, it is said, is only a game. I don't want to make too much of it, but there are some parallels between Australian history and the broad sweep of the story of cricket in Australia. It was born in chaos, developed by the energy of the extroverts and entrepreneurs in the middle of the nineteenth century and fired by the seeds of nationalism in the 1870s and 1880s. Cricket's so called 'Golden Age' at the turn of the century reflected the national mood of optimism after Federation. Then the game was hijacked by administrators who soon made it clear that cricket was not just a game for players. We were subjugated by the British, in a final fling of Empire, during the 1930s. The conservatism of the 1950s and 1960s led to an explosion of self-expression in the 1970s and a return to the commercial roots of 100 years before.

In the mid-1980s, the series of defeats inflicted on the Australian cricket team shared top billing on televison and radio and in the newspapers with the decline in Australia's economic outlook. The cricket team, at least, has recovered its status. Bob Simpson, Allan Border, Mark Taylor and their teams have shown that success comes from working hard and concentrating on the basics.

First class cricket in the 1990s is a business, of course. The current Australian team is probably as businesslike and professional as any in the game's history.

More than 100 years ago Anthony Trollope wrote of the feeling, common in England, 'that everything that is being done is bad ... it was bad to interfere with Charles, bad to endure Cromwell, bad to banish James, bad to put up with William ... The meddling with the universities has been grievous. The treatment of the Irish Church has been Satanic. The overhauling of schools is most injurious to English education. Every step taken has been bad. And yet to them old England is of all the countries of the world the best to live in, and is not at all the less comfortable because of the changes that have been made'.

I played cricket for 25 years with a club in Sydney; 35-overs games on Saturday afternoon, with the occasional 50-overs match on a Sunday. The result was nearly always a mad scramble in the last five or 10 overs to get the run rate up, or to overhaul our opponents' total; technique was abandoned, tempers became frayed, the nerve and patience of umpires were tested. We loved it. But to a man we deplored the takeover of traditional cricket by commercial interests in 1977 and the adoption by the Australian cricket team of the techniques which we used every weekend. Although at first we boycotted 'the pyjama game' at the Sydney Cricket Ground, we meet at the day-night fixtures fairly regularly now. If the game isn't worth watching, we enjoy complaining about it over a few beers.

Having started with a quote from an Englishman, I will close with two quotes from Australians. Jack Fingleton, who opened the batting for Australia in the 1930s and later became a distinguished journalist, wrote: 'The cricket world, surely, is just as crazy and inconsistent as the outside one.' And Arthur Mailey, the leg-spin bowler of the 1920s, who believed that, 'if cricket remains static it must atrophy and die'.

Index